·A·
CASA

ALSO BY ANNA DEL CONTE

Portrait of Pasta
Italian Cookery
Pasta Perfect
Gastronomy of Italy
The Italian Pantry

A
CASA

Seasonal Italian Home Cooking

Anna Del Conte

HarperCollins*Publishers*

*I would like to thank Susan Friedland, my editor at HarperCollins,
for her constant support and her total confidence in my work.*

HarperCollins books may be purchased for educational, business,
or sales promotional use. For information, please write:
Special Markets Department, HarperCollins Publishers, Inc.,
10 East 53rd Street, New York, NY 10022.

FIRST EDITION

DESIGNED BY JOEL AVIROM

Library of Congress Cataloging-in-Publication Data

Del Conte, Anna.
A casa : seasonal Italian home cooking / Anna Del Conte. — 1st ed.
p.   cm.
Includes index.
ISBN 0-06-016524-3
1. Cookery, Italian.   I. Title.
TX723.D429   1992
641.5945—dc20   92-52583

92 93 94 95 96 DX/RRD 10 9 8 7 6 5 4 3 2 1

A MIA MADRE

at whose table I learned the basic principles that guided me
while writing this book

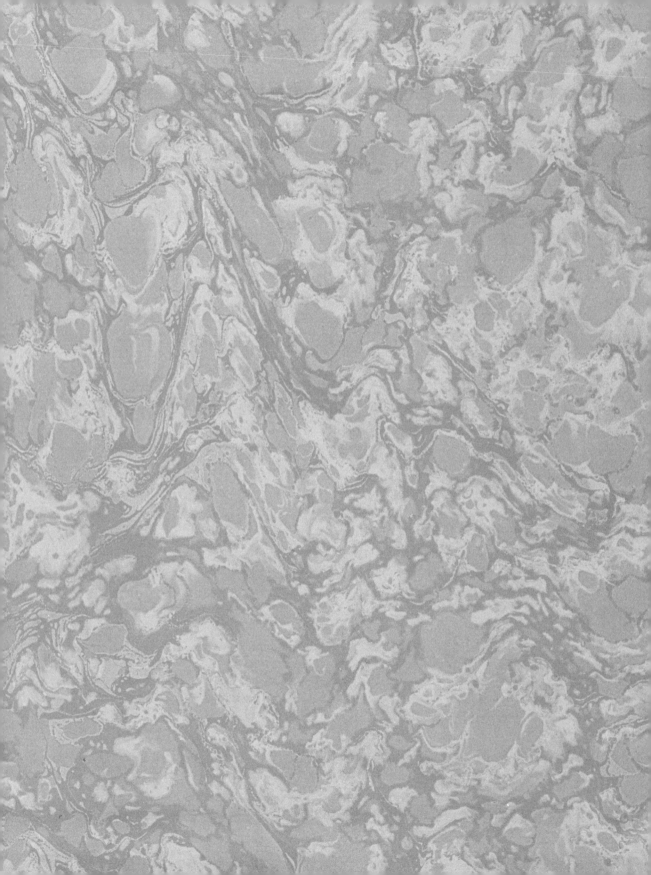

CONTENTS

Introduction
1

Notes on Equipment
5

SPRING

7

SUMMER

6 5

AUTUMN

1 4 1

WINTER

1 9 9

MY FAVORITE MENUS

2 6 5

BASIC RECIPES

3 2 3

Index
3 4 5

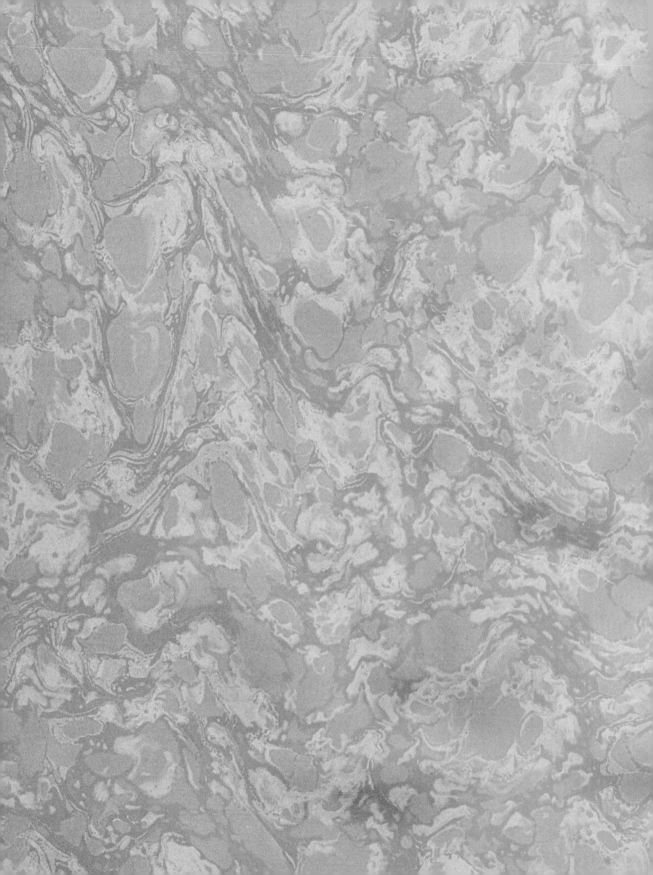

"*D*omenica sera siamo a casa. Perché non vieni a mangiare un boccone?" (We'll be home Sunday night. Why not come and have a bite?) Often, in Italy you will be asked out to dinner in just such a seemingly casual fashion. The dinner may be a family affair or a more formal occasion, but it will hardly ever be just a *boccone*. It is more likely to be a meal on which time, care, and love have been lavished. The menu will be well balanced and carefully constructed.

I first became aware of how important this is as a child, when I overheard a friend of my mother's declare, "La cosa più importante quando si dà un pranzo è avere un menù equilibrato" (The most important thing when giving a dinner party is to have a well-balanced menu). This woman was very chic and beautiful, and anything she said made a great impression on me. Her words have echoed in my mind over the years. Now, when *I* give a dinner party I spend a lot of time planning my *menù equilibrato*. By the same token, when I come home from a dinner party with the impression that something was wrong, the something in question is usually not the food, which was good, but the menu.

When you plan a dinner you should think of it as a whole and not as a succession of dishes. This is considered very important in Italy. You want, above all, to avoid a series of jarring contrasts. Not that all the courses should have a similar taste, rather that their flavors should be in harmony.

It is also very important to plan your menu so that you are totally at ease and ready to enjoy yourself. To this end, choose dishes that you know you can do well. Your friends would prefer to eat time after time the baked fish steaks you make to perfection than a new, esoteric dish that caused a visible strain on your nerves.

Most of my dishes come from Italian home cooks rather than restaurateurs. Restaurant food is usually complicated, last-minute food that the chef assembles or cooks to order. The easiest and most traditional Italian home cooking, and often the best, is based on slow cooking, generally involving large pieces of meat, vegetable stews, large fish, or other dishes that may have to be prepared well in advance and are best made in reasonably large quantities. In Italy the food is usually brought to the table on a large serving dish rather than on individual plates. It is not portioned; on the contrary, you would like your friends to have second helpings, a sure sign of appreciation. To make serving easier, you may want to place portions of meat or fish on individual plates, but after that you should hand around the vegetables and salads in dishes and bowls. Frills and bows have never been a characteristic of the Italian scene. The only dishes that might at times be served on individual plates are some kinds of antipasto and some desserts.

You may feel that the quantities in my recipes are too large for the number of people specified. It is very difficult to judge people's appetites, but more important you want to have enough food for people to have a second helping. Perhaps only a few of your guests will have that second helping—and you will finish up today's dinner tomorrow. But you cannot be sure in advance. So, enjoy the rest from cooking and planning a meal.

How many people make the perfect number at a dinner party? Brillat-Savarin said they should be no fewer than the Graces nor more than the Muses. Between three and nine stands six, and this is a very good number. There is usually a single conversation round the table, mainly carried on by the two most articulate diners, to whom everyone else is quite happy to listen. The only danger with six people is that two of them might take an instant dislike to each other or might disagree violently about some important topic.

From this point of view, a dinner for eight or ten is safer, but it demands considerably more effort. For these numbers I have tried to choose dishes that need a minimum of last-minute attention. Fish, for instance, appears more often in the menus for six, because it usually needs to be cooked just before serving, while large braised cuts of meat or casseroles are planned for larger parties.

The menus are divided into sections, one for each season plus an extra section for some of my favorite menus. Then there are some basic recipes, including instructions on how to make pasta and prepare polenta, as well as standard methods for preparing certain vegetables.

Seasons . . . I begin to wonder if they still exist. As far as food and produce are concerned, they hardly do, and in the last few years even the seasons themselves seem to have changed! Here I am, writing this at the beginning of November on an amazingly warm and sunny day, and that is in London, not Rome. My *mentuccia,* special mint from Tuscany, has survived the past two winters in the garden, and the new arugula is already large enough to be picked. Even if I did not have it growing in my garden, I could easily go to a good supermarket and buy it. Less tasty, for sure, but still arugula in November. In the same way, I could buy zucchini, tomatoes, and other "out of season" vegetables too numerous to mention.

Some might say how lucky we are, yet I miss the time when the months were marked by the different produce that appeared in the shops and markets. And just as there were seasonal vegetables, so there were seasonal dishes. In Italy there still are. In April, *brasati* and *umidi* (braised meats) are forgotten in favor of roasts and sautéed meat. Polenta slowly gives way to pasta, and by the summer it has disappeared altogether along with risotto and pasta with heavy meaty sauces. I remember the joy of seeing the first peas in April, and at Easter *soncino* (mâche). These were followed by all the glories of summer fruits and vegetables. As much as the food itself, the expectation was a keen pleasure. But although there is little of that left, we can still prepare a dinner suitable for the season.

Here and there in the book you will find some vegetarian menus. Italian cuisine has a marvelous range of meatless dishes, thanks partly to the superb quality of the sun-ripened vegetables, including artichokes, bell peppers, zucchini, eggplant, fennel, and, of course, the marvelous range of salads and fresh herbs. Another reason for the wealth of meatless dishes is that vegetables combine so well with both pasta and rice, two staples of Italian cuisine. Italian cooking is also very rich in ways of cooking beans, which are widely cultivated and whose quality is outstanding. Particularly good are the buttery borlotti beans of northern Italy, the tiny lentils of Castelluccio in Umbria, and the sweet fava beans of Tuscany. The only snag is that many vegetarian dishes take time and some require a bit of expertise once the vegetables are no longer an accompaniment but the centerpiece of the meal.

By and large all the menus are designed on the traditional pattern of a three-course dinner consisting of a *primo* (first course), a *secondo* (main course), and a *dolce* (dessert). Some lunches or informal dinners have only a *primo* and a *secondo,* plus cheese and fruit, very *all'italiana.* It is also very Italian to have four courses at formal parties or on special occasions, as I have done in my menus for Christmas, New Year's Day, and Easter. A four-course meal does not necessarily mean that more food is eaten: the food is prepared in smaller quantities and is more varied.

The antipasto usually consists of something bought, be it a lovely platter of prosciutto or a light and colorful *insalata di pesce* (fish salad). These days, with the renaissance of *cucina povera* (peasant cooking), the antipasto might well be a garlicky bruschetta (page 71) or a platter of crostini (page 214), something appetizing and informal. My first courses are mainly Italian *primi*: pasta, risotto, and soup. There are other dishes for times when a dish of pasta or a risotto would be too heavy for a first course. The *secondi* are mostly meat or fish, as tradition demands, although a few menus are constructed in an unorthodox way. The dessert is usually elaborate for more formal occasions, but if you are too busy, tired, or just fed up with being in the kitchen, do not hesitate to offer cheese and fruit. Cheese is rarely served at dinner in Italy, being considered too heavy for the evening meal, but at lunch it is very often on the table. Cheese and fruit can also be served together, as in the recipe for walnuts, grapes, and parmesan (page 153). Another ideal match is aged pecorino served with pears, a traditional ending to many Tuscan feasts. A bowl of velvety peaches accompanied by a bottle of good wine, red or white, or some raspberries served with mascarpone cream (page 15) are other fine and easy endings. My job is to write the recipes, yours to make the choices.

*T*o cook Italian food you will need a large heavy saucepan, preferably round-bottomed pan for risotto and polenta. You will also need a heavy sauté pan, about 10 inches in diameter, with a close-fitting lid. If you want to cook pasta for more than six people you will need a very large saucepan, about five quarts, preferably tall. The pan need not be heavy-bottomed, because it is used only for boiling water. A heavy pasta saucepan, on the other hand, can double as a stockpot.

In addition, you would do well to have a large earthenware pot for beans and soups and a small round earthenware pot for slow-cooking sauces, both of the type that can be put directly on the heat. Earthenware is the perfect material for dishes that need long slow cooking, since it retains heat and moisture well. Earthenware dishes also convey a sense of homey food and abundance, and they can be brought directly to the table.

Over my many cooking years I have learned the wisdom of buying only the minimum equipment and tools. Many of them, acquired years ago on impulse, sit there simply cluttering up my cupboards. But there are a few kitchen tools I could not do without. The first is my food mill. Many cooks have a food processor but not a food mill, yet the mill can do more than the processor, without the noise. It also helps make mashed potatoes, tomato sauces, and bean puree. Be sure to get one with changeable disks.

Another tool I could not live without is a large footed colander for draining pasta, potatoes, and boiled vegetables. A colander has the advantage over a large strainer in that the water drains more slowly, so that the cooked pasta does not become a sticky mass and vegetables are less likely to break. You need only a shake or two at the end for the little water left among the holes to run out.

Together with the large saucepan and the colander a cheese grater makes the requisite trio for a perfect pasta dish.

A set of measuring spoons is a great help to any cook. Where I give measurements in teaspoons and tablespoons, they refer to a level measure.

There are, of course, a few other tools I am attached to. My mortar and pestle are invaluable for crushing herbs and spices and for making pastes of any sort, allowing the deeper flavor of the ingredients to come through. An inexpensive, hand-cranked pasta machine that clamps onto the table is a great boost. The other tool I like, although it is not vital, is the ice-cream machine. I find it solves the "which dessert" problem.

SPRING

A VEGETARIAN LUNCH FOR FOUR

10

Cappelletti alle erbe
Cappelletti Filled with Ricotta and Herbs

~~~

Asparagi alla milanese
Asparagus Milanese

~~~

Lamponi con crema di mascarpone
Raspberries with Mascarpone Cream

DINNER FOR SIX

25

Risotto con le verdure in forma
Risotto Molded with Vegetables

~~~

Arrosto morto
Italian Roast Veal

~~~

Funghi al funghetto
Sautéed Mushrooms (page 328)

~~~

Zabaione con la purè di fragole
Zabaglione with Strawberry Puree

EASTER LUNCH FOR EIGHT

16

Salame e uova sode
Salami and Hard-boiled Eggs

~~~

La torta pasqualina
Easter Torta

~~~

Cosciotto di agnello arrosto con le cipolline
Roast Leg of Lamb with Small Onions

~~~

Insalata bianca e verde
Mâche, Arugula, and Fennel Salad

~~~

Colomba pasquale
Easter Cake

A GREEN AND WHITE DINNER FOR SIX

31

Pecorino con le fave
Pecorino and Raw Fava Beans

~~~

Quaglie nel nido di paglia e fieno
Braised Quail in a Nest of Straw and Hay

~~~

Insalata verde
Green Salad (page 325)

~~~

Panna cotta
Molded Cream Dessert

A VEGETARIAN DINNER FOR EIGHT

3 7

Pasta e fagioli alla contadina
Bean and Pasta Soup with Radicchio

~

Scarpazzone lombardo
Spinach Torta

~

Torta di ricotta e mandorle con la salsina di arancia
Ricotta and Almond Cake with Orange Sauce (page 188)

DINNER FOR EIGHT

5 1

Zuppa alla santé
Vegetable Soup

~

Pollastri al riso
Braised Chicken with Rice

~

Funghi al funghetto
Sautéed Mushrooms (page 328)

~

Bavarese lombarda
Lombardy Marquise

DINNER FOR EIGHT

4 3

Bresaola con la rucola
Bresaola with Arugula

~

Rotolo di spinaci al burro e formaggio
Spinach and Pasta Roll with Butter and Parmesan

~

Torta di patate e mandorle
Potato and Almond Cake

~

Rabarbaro all'arancia
Baked Rhubarb with Orange

DINNER FOR EIGHT

5 8

Tagliatelle coi carciofi
Tagliatelle with Artichokes

~

Agnello arrosto alla moda rinascimentale
Leg of Lamb Renaissance Style

~

Sformato di patate e carote
Potato and Carrot Mold (page 227)

~

Arancie e kiwi
Oranges and Kiwis

A VEGETARIAN LUNCH FOR FOUR

Cappelletti alle erbe
Cappelletti Filled with Ricotta and Herbs

Asparagi alla milanese
Asparagus Milanese

Lamponi con crema di mascarpone
Raspberries with Mascarpone Cream

Vegetarian meals are often thought of as being ethnic and peasant (none the worse for that!). Not this one. It is quite elegant.

As with all stuffed pasta, the cappelletti is the sort of dish you should make a few times before you serve it to your friends. Making pasta is a job that needs practice, and stuffing the pasta is an extra task to learn. But the result is so much nicer than commercial ravioli, whose stuffing always seems to taste the same.

The asparagus is served in the Milanese way, with fried eggs: you dip the spears into the yolks. I have no qualms about including the recipe here, even though it has already appeared in my previous book, *The Italian Pantry,* since it is the perfect dish for this vegetarian menu.

A note about cooking asparagus. Not too long ago, at a Guild of Food Writers lunch, I had to leave the asparagus because it was what I call raw. The inner part was still hard and the asparagus had had no time to develop its full flavor. This was no doubt due to the al dente mania that has infected Britain and the United States in the last few years. I am certainly not campaigning for the return of the kind of overcooked, mushy vegetables that were often served before the al dente craze. I am only saying that cooked vegetables should be cooked long enough for them to develop their full flavor, even at the expense of appearance. The American food scientist Harold McGee writes in his book *The Curious Cook* that flavor and color evolve from two different chemical reactions. Chlorophyll breaks down quickly, but flavor compounds take time to develop. When the asparagus—and the green bean—releases its aroma, it is beginning to be properly cooked. The green tip of the asparagus should bend gracefully so that you have to lift your head up and open your mouth wide to receive it. It should not be like a stiff green stick. The exact cooking time depends on age and quality. I have had asparagus that was cooked in 5 minutes and other that took 20 minutes. Just lift a spear out of the pan when you can smell the asparagus aroma; if it bends, taste it. It is probably ready.

The dinner closes with a bowl of seasonal raspberries, served with a mascarpone cream. This cream is lighter in texture than plain mascarpone and tastier than plain cream.

Cappelletti alle erbe
Cappelletti Filled with Ricotta and Herbs

⅓ cup flat-leaf parsley leaves

⅓ cup mixed fresh herb leaves, including rosemary, sage, thyme, marjoram, basil, and 2 leaves borage, if available

1 tablespoon unsalted butter

1 garlic clove, peeled and bruised

1 scant cup fresh ricotta

3 tablespoons freshly grated parmesan

3 tablespoons freshly grated pecorino or 3 tablespoons additional parmesan

¼ teaspoon grated nutmeg

salt and freshly ground black pepper

1 egg yolk

1 tablespoon olive oil

pasta made with 2 eggs and 1⅓ cups unbleached flour

CREAM SAUCE

1 cup heavy cream

4 teaspoons unsalted butter

salt and freshly ground black pepper

¼ cup freshly grated parmesan

freshly grated parmesan for serving

1. Chop all the herbs by hand or in a food processor.

2. Heat the butter with the garlic in a small frying pan, add the herbs, and sauté for a minute. Remove and discard the garlic. Transfer the herbs to a bowl, scraping up all the bits stuck to the bottom of the pan. Add the ricotta, the grated cheeses, and the nutmeg to the bowl. Add salt, if necessary, and a good grinding of pepper. Mix very thoroughly and then blend in the egg yolk. Mix again so that everything is thoroughly mixed. Cover the bowl with plastic wrap and refrigerate while you make the pasta.

3. Prepare the basic dough as directed on page 333. If you are rolling out by hand, roll out about a third of the dough as thin as you can, keeping the rest of the dough covered by a bowl to use later. If you are using a hand-cranked machine, stop at next to the last notch. Cut and stuff each strip of pasta as soon as you have thinned it out.

4. Cut into strips about 1½ inches wide, then cut the strips across to form 1½-inch squares. Put about ½ teaspoon of filling in the center of each square, then fold the square over to form a triangle. Press the edges down firmly to seal, moistening them with a little cold water if necessary. If you are making cappelletti in a very dry atmosphere, moisten a narrow strip all around the

edges with a wet pastry brush before you fold the dough to form the triangle. Pick the triangle up by one corner, with the point of the triangle pointing up, and wrap it around your index finger. Press the 2 ends firmly together. The peaked part of each of the cappelletti should stand upright. As you make them, place them in rows on a clean dish towel.

5. Cook the cappelletti in plenty of salted boiling water with 1 tablespoon oil added to keep them from sticking to each other. Fresh cappelletti take about 5 minutes to cook, but if you have made them beforehand and they have dried out, they will take longer.

6. While the cappelletti are cooking, heat half the cream with the butter in a large heavy sauté pan. Simmer gently for 1 minute to thicken the sauce. Season with a little salt and plenty of black pepper. Remove from the heat while you drain the cappelletti.

7. Lift the cappelletti out of the water with a large slotted spoon or a large metal strainer and transfer to the pan containing the cream. Put the pan back on the heat, add the remaining cream and half the cheese and cook for a couple of minutes, turning the cappelletti over and over to coat them evenly with sauce. Transfer to a heated bowl and serve, passing the extra cheese separately in a small bowl. You can keep the dish warm, covered with foil, in a low oven, about 15 to 20 minutes.

PREPARATION

Fresh cappelletti must be eaten within 24 hours. These cappelletti can be frozen if absolutely necessary. Freeze in single layers interleaved with plastic wrap. Cook while still frozen. Do not keep in the freezer for longer than 1 week.

SERVES 4

Asparagi alla milanese
Asparagus Milanese

3 pounds asparagus | *4 tablespoons freshly grated parmesan*
salt | *8 eggs*
4 tablespoons unsalted butter | *freshly ground black pepper*

1. First scrape the ends of the asparagus stems and snap off or cut off the hard part. Wash thoroughly. Tie the asparagus in small bundles in two places, at the top near the tips and at the bottom above the butts.

2. If you haven't got an asparagus boiler, use a tall narrow saucepan, half full of boiling salted water. Stand the bundles of asparagus, tips up, in the water. If necessary, put some potatoes in the saucepan to keep the bundles upright. If the saucepan is not tall enough to put the lid on without damaging the tallest spears, make a domed lid from a sheet of foil and tie it under the rim of the saucepan.

3. When the asparagus is cooked, lift the bundles out and place them on paper towels to drain properly before you divide them and place them on individual plates. Keep warm.

4. Melt 3 tablespoons butter in a nonstick frying pan and pour it over the asparagus spears. Sprinkle with the cheese.

5. Melt the remaining butter in the same pan and break the eggs into the pan. When fried, slide 2 eggs onto each plate next to the asparagus tips. Grind some pepper over them and serve immediately with plenty of crusty bread.

PREPARATION

You can cook the asparagus up to 1 hour in advance and reheat them in a double boiler. They can also be kept warm, on a heated serving dish, tightly covered with buttered foil, for up to 30 minutes.

SERVES 4

Lamponi con crema di mascarpone
Raspberries with Mascarpone Cream

	FOR THE CREAM
1 pound raspberries	*²/₃ cup heavy cream*
2 tablespoons lemon juice	*²/₃ cup mascarpone*
6 tablespoons orange juice	*confectioners' sugar*
4 tablespoons sugar	
1 tablespoon kirsch	

1. Rinse, dry, and hull the raspberries. Place them in a serving bowl.

2. Put the lemon juice and orange juice in a small saucepan, add the sugar, and bring gently to the boil to dissolve the sugar. Allow to cool and then stir in the liqueur. Pour the mixture over the raspberries. Cover with plastic wrap and place in the refrigerator for 1 hour.

3. Lightly whip the cream. Fold in the mascarpone and whip again until well blended.

4. Add enough confectioners' sugar to sweeten the cream. I add 2 tablespoons. Transfer the cream to a bowl, cover with plastic wrap, and chill.

PREPARATION

The raspberries can be prepared a few hours in advance, but the citrus syrup must be added no longer than 1 hour in advance. The cream can be prepared up to 2 hours in advance.

SERVES 4

EASTER LUNCH FOR EIGHT

Salame e uova sode

Salami and Hard-boiled Eggs

La torta pasqualina

Easter Torta

Cosciotto di agnello arrosto con le cipolline

Roast Leg of Lamb with Small Onions

Insalata bianca e verde

Mâche, Arugula, and Fennel Salad

Colomba pasquale

Easter Cake

y Easter lunch borrows recipes from many different regions. The antipasto, however, is the traditional Easter antipasto served in most regions, matching the new-season salami with the ancient tradition of eating eggs on Easter Sunday. For eight people you need one pound of different kinds of salami and eight hard-boiled eggs, shelled and cut in half lengthwise.

In the past eggs were eaten in large quantities on Easter, not only as a symbol of new life but also because, as a result of abstinence during Lent, everyone had a surplus of eggs. There were plenty to eat, and plenty more to give to friends who did not keep hens. Chocolate, porcelain, wooden, or even Fabergé Easter eggs are all an embellishment of that custom.

Torta pasqualina is the Genoese Easter dish, just as lamb is that of Romans. The traditional cooking of Liguria is largely based on vegetables. Meat used to be very scarce and appeared only in the shape of a hen or, more often, a rabbit, neither of them considered festive food in Italy. Ligurian cooks created superb dishes from easily available ingredients, in this case Swiss chard, which by Easter time was just ready to pick, and a curd cheese called *quagliata*. A more modern—and mundane—version is filled with artichokes.

The pastry is made with flour, oil, and water, a mixture similar to that used for phyllo pastry. This kind of stretched eggless pastry is a specialty of Liguria. It makes you wonder whether the Genoese sailors brought back the know-how from their journeys to the eastern Mediterranean.

Years ago in Santa Margherita, in Liguria, I was shown how to make an authentic *torta pasqualina*. Albina, my friend's cook, stretched the dough by rolling it with a long Italian rolling pin, then stretching it first with one hand and then with the other. The whole operation was performed with such grace and dexterity that it reminded me of a ritual Arab dance. In Savona, on the western Riviera, they make 33 layers of pastry, one for each year of Christ's life, but Albina made only 20 layers, as they do in Genoa. My recipe here is based on the one in the classic book of Ligurian cooking, *La cuciniera genovese,* by Giobatta and Giovanni Ratto, which has been in print since the last century. I have taken the easy way out and used phyllo pastry, however.

Just as eggs are traditionally associated with Easter, so is lamb. Originally part of Jewish rituals, lamb later became symbolic of Christ. Lamb in Italy is very young at Easter time and is often cooked whole on the spit and served with an olive sprig stuck in the middle.

I have chosen this recipe from a lovely old book that I found in my mother's bookcase. The book, published in 1863, is called *Il cuoco milanese* (The Milanese Cook) and subtitled An Indispensable Cooking Manual for Families of Every Class. Perhaps indispensable is an overstatement, but the book is full of good recipes. The lamb should be cooked for three hours according to the original recipe, but we are now so used to meat that seems to be on the undercooked side, I cut the time to two hours. This will give you a cooked roast, not a pink one, which is better for this kind of slow roasting with wine and onions. You can always shorten the time if you like your lamb pink. The meat juices are sharpened by the lemon and orange juice. Use oranges that are not too sweet.

With the lamb I would serve a bowl of buttery new potatoes. Mâche, also called lamb's lettuce, is the traditional Easter salad in Italy, but it is so expensive that I thought you might like to mix it with something else, as I do in my mâche, arugula, and fennel salad, and serve it after the meat.

Colomba is a traditional cake from Lombardy, made in the shape of a dove, *colomba* in Italian. It has a light dough, similar to that of panettone but without any raisins or candied fruit. It is covered with sugar crystals and almonds. *Colomba* is a soft, sweet bread, or cake, which for me has a most nostalgic aroma. When we used to spend Easter at our apartment in Venice, we would go to buy our *colomba* after Mass on Easter Sunday from a bakery near the Campo San Barnaba. The whole of the Dorsoduro was pervaded by its vanilla scent.

Italians do not make this type of traditional cake at home because buying it is part of the tradition. On Easter Sunday everybody goes to Mass in their best clothes, and then to the *pasticceria* to buy a delicious *colomba* and have an *aperitivo* with their friends. If you feel you should slave in the kitchen to redeem your soul, I suggest you make the irresistible but easy to prepare cassata on page 170, which is the Easter sweet in Sicily, and leave the *colomba* to the experts.

The origins of *colomba,* variously claimed by Milan and Pavia, are legendary. The Milanese legend is based on the appearance of two doves over the war chariot of the Lombard League in 1176 during the battle of Legnano against the German Emperor Frederick Barbarossa. The Lombards won, and since then the dove has been a memento of their victory.

The Pavia legend concerns a maiden who baked such a delicious cake in the shape of a dove for the Longobard Alboin that he spared her—and only her—from the abduction of twelve virgins he demanded when he conquered Pavia in 572. Alboin was a very cruel king, as all Italian children know from a poem by Carducci. He ordered his wife, Rosamunda, to drink wine from her dead father's skull.

Bevi Rosamunda
Tu lo baciasti prima ch'ei mora,
Bacialo ancora.

Drink, Rosamund,
You kissed him before he died,
Kiss him once more.

La torta pasqualina
Easter Torta

<hr>

4 pounds Swiss chard
½ cup olive oil
2 garlic cloves, peeled and bruised
3 tablespoons chopped fresh marjoram
freshly ground black pepper
2½ cups fresh ricotta

12 to 14 ounces frozen phyllo pastry, thawed
½ cup freshly grated parmesan
4 tablespoons unsalted butter
6 eggs

1. Strip off the green part of the leaves of the chard. Cut the stalks into thin strips. Wash and put them in a pan half full of boiling salted water.

2. Cut the green part of the leaves into thin strips and wash them. Add to the pan 5 minutes after the stalks. Cook until both the stalks and the leaves are tender. Drain thoroughly and once cool enough to handle, squeeze out all the liquid with your hands.

3. Combine 2 tablespoons of the oil, the garlic, and the marjoram in a frying pan. When the aroma of the garlic rises, remove and discard it. Add the chard and sauté for 5 minutes, stirring frequently. Season with lots of pepper and leave to cool.

4. Preheat the oven to 350° F.

5. Put the ricotta in a bowl and break it up with a fork into thick crumbs.

6. Grease a 10-inch springform pan with a little of the oil. Fit 10 sheets of phyllo pastry into the pan, one on top of the other, so that the edges drape over the sides of the tin. Brush each sheet with some of the oil. Keep the rest of the pastry covered while you put the sheets in place, because phyllo pastry dries out and cracks very quickly. Spread with the chard, the crumbled ricotta, half the parmesan, and a generous amount of pepper.

7. Form 5 hollows around the edge and 1 in the center of the filling. Place a knob of butter in each hollow and then slip an egg into the hollow, being careful not to break the yolk. Sprinkle with the remaining parmesan and cover with 10 sheets of phyllo, cutting them so that they fit neatly into the pan and brushing each sheet with oil. Turn the overhanging phyllo over the top and roll it over to form a ridge round the edge. Brush generously with oil and place the pan in the oven.

8. Bake for 30 minutes, then turn the heat up to 400° F. and bake for 20 minutes more to crisp the top. Let the torta cool in the pan. Remove the band and transfer the torta on the bottom of the pan to a serving platter. The torta is eaten warm or at room temperature.

PREPARATION

The torta can be baked up to 1 day in advance and reheated in a low oven for long enough to make the pastry crisp.

SERVES 8

Cosciotto di agnello arrosto con le cipolline
Roast Leg of Lamb with Small Onions

---

1 ounce pancetta or unsmoked streaky bacon

3 garlic cloves

1 small leg of lamb (5 to 6 pounds)

MARINADE

1½ teaspoons coarse salt

4 tablespoons olive oil

6 peppercorns, bruised

fresh herbs, such as 1 sprig parsley, some celery leaves, 1 sprig rosemary, 2 or 3 sage leaves, 2 sprigs thyme, 1 sprig marjoram

1½ cups light Italian red wine

1 pound small white onions

1 teaspoon sugar

4 tablespoons lemon juice

½ cup orange juice

2 tablespoons unsalted butter

1. Chop the pancetta and the garlic. Make a few deep slits in the lamb along the grain of the meat and push little pellets of the mixture into the slits.

2. Rub the leg with salt, place it in a roasting pan, and pour over the olive oil. Add the peppercorns and the herbs and leave to marinate for 24 hours in a cold place, preferably not in the refrigerator. Unless the weather is hot and sultry, you can keep the pan, covered, in the kitchen.

3. Preheat the oven to 350° F.

4. Pour the wine over the lamb and place in the oven. Baste the meat every 30 minutes or so.

5. Put the onions in a pan, cover with cold water, bring to a boil, then drain. This makes them easier to peel. Remove the outside skin and any dangling roots, but do not remove any layer of onion or cut into the root: this is what keeps them whole during the cooking.

6. About 1 hour after you put the lamb in the oven, add the onions. Put the pan back in the oven and continue cooking until the meat is to your liking, basting every 30 minutes or so. A roast this size needs about 2 hours; the lamb will be well cooked, not pink.

7. Remove the leg of lamb from the pan and set aside to cool while you prepare the sauce. Any large roast should be left to rest for at least 10 minutes before carving, for the juices to penetrate the meat. Lift out the onions with a slotted spoon and put them in a heated dish or bowl.

8. Strain the cooking juices into a clean saucepan. Skim off as much fat as you possibly can. Heat the cooking juices, and add the sugar and the lemon and orange juices. Taste and adjust seasonings. When the sauce is simmering, add the butter in little pieces and let it dissolve, while swirling the pan. Transfer to a heated sauceboat.

9. Carve the roast at the table and pass around the onions, sauce, and other vegetables.

PREPARATION

Roasts cannot be cooked in advance and reheated.

SERVES 8

Insalata bianca e verde
Mâche, Arugula, and Fennel Salad

¾ pound mâche	5 tablespoons sour cream
⅓ pound arugula	3 tablespoons extra-virgin olive oil
2 fennel bulbs, preferably round	4 tablespoons lemon juice
6 scallions, white part only	1 teaspoon sugar
1 cup green olives	salt and freshly ground white pepper

1. Clean and wash the mâche and arugula. Dry well and arrange on a dish.

2. Remove and discard any brown patches on the outside of the fennel. If the fennel has some feathery green attached, cut it off, wash and dry it, and add it to the green salads.

   Quarter the fennel lengthwise, then cut across into very thin strips, no more than ¼ inch thick. Wash and dry them and scatter over the salad.

3. Trim and wash the scallions. Cut the white part into thin rings and scatter them over the salad. Put the olives here and there on the dish.

4. Beat the sour cream, oil, lemon juice, sugar, and salt and pepper to taste until well blended. Pour over the salad. Do this just before you bring it to the table or the green leaves will wilt.

PREPARATION

You can trim and wash all the different vegetables up to 1 day in advance. Keep them wrapped in a clean cloth or in a closed container in the refrigerator. The dressing can be made up to 3 days in advance.

SERVES 8

DINNER FOR SIX

Risotto con le verdure in forma
Risotto Molded with Vegetables

~

Arrosto morto
Italian Roast Veal

~

Funghi al funghetto
Sautéed Mushrooms (page 328)

~

Zabaione con la purè di fragole
Zabaglione with Strawberry Puree

*S*ix is a good number of people to fit around the table, and the host or hostess can take part in the conversation without having to jump up every two minutes to attend to something or another. Besides, most of the time there will be one general conversation, which is usually much more interesting than the small talk you tend to have with your neighbor to the left or right at a larger dinner party.

The risotto in this menu is made entirely with seasonal vegetables. If you want to make this dish later in the year, decorate it with some green beans or other seasonal vegetables. Choose vegetables with the same type of flavor to avoid a clash. I make the risotto in a mold because I can cook it beforehand, put it in the mold, and reheat it in the oven for 20 minutes. It tastes good and it looks great.

The *secondo* is a veal roast. Cooked in this way—covered, on top of the stove—the meat dries less and absorbs more of the flavorings than when roasted in the oven. The meat used in Italy is usually *vitellone*, the meat of a calf that is already grazing but is no more than three years old. *Arrosto* is usually accompanied by roast potatoes. Try mine on page 326, and serve a green salad as well.

Zabaglione is wonderful, but I prefer cold zabaglione, which is less rich, especially when mixed with the tanginess of fresh fruit. You can leave the strawberries whole and mix them in just before serving, but I'd rather puree them beforehand. The flavor of the fruit is better distributed, and the zabaglione looks stunning. Try not to blend the puree in too thoroughly—it looks much prettier, like Verona marble, pink and yellow.

Risotto con le verdure in forma
Risotto Molded with Vegetables

---

²/₃ cup fresh or frozen peas

salt

2 zucchini, about 5 ounces

3 canned plum tomatoes, seeded

6 cups vegetable broth or Italian Broth (page 338)

5 tablespoons extra-virgin olive oil

½ cup chopped flat-leaf parsley

2 garlic cloves, peeled and bruised

5 tablespoons unsalted butter

3 shallots, chopped

1½ cups Arborio rice

²/₃ cup dry white wine

6 basil leaves, torn

½ cup freshly grated parmesan

freshly ground black pepper

1 pound asparagus

1 tablespoon unsalted butter for the mold

4 tablespoons dried breadcrumbs for the mold

1. Cook the fresh peas in lightly salted water until just tender. If you are using frozen peas, blanch for about 2 minutes. Blanch the zucchini, drain, and cut into small cubes. Cut the tomatoes into short strips.

2. Heat the broth until just simmering. Keep it simmering.

3. Meanwhile, put half the oil, the parsley, and garlic in a sauté pan, sauté for 1 minute, then stir in the already prepared vegetables. Season lightly with salt and sauté over low heat for 2 minutes. Remove and discard the garlic.

4. Put the rest of the oil and about a third of the butter in a heavy saucepan. Add the shallots and sauté until tender. Add the rice, cook for 2 minutes, then splash with the wine. Boil rapidly, stirring constantly, until the rice has absorbed the wine. Add 1 ladleful (about ½ cup) of broth and let the rice absorb it while you stir constantly. Continue to add the broth gradually, while you stir, until the rice is nearly, but not quite, cooked, about 15 minutes from the moment you begin to add the broth.

5. Remove the rice from the heat and add the vegetables, the basil, half the remaining butter, cut into small pieces, and the parmesan. Stir thoroughly but gently, then taste and check seasonings. Spread the risotto on a cold surface to cool.

continued

6. Snap off the tough ends of the asparagus. For this dish you want only the tips with about 2 inches of stalk. Remove any tiny leaves sprouting below the tips. Wash the asparagus and place in a large sauté pan. Cover with boiling water, season with a little salt, and add the remaining butter. Cook until tender but firm. Drain and transfer to a dish. Cover with foil and keep warm. Do not throw away the cooking water; you can use it to make a soup with the rest of the stalks.

7. Preheat the oven to 400° F.

8. Generously butter a 4-cup ring mold and sprinkle with breadcrumbs. Shake out the excess crumbs. Spoon the cold risotto into the mold and place in the oven. Bake for 20 minutes until the risotto is heated through.

9. To unmold, run a metal spatula around the sides of the mold, place a round dish on top, and turn it upside down. The mold should lift off quite easily.

10. Place the asparagus tips in the center hole and around the risotto. Serve at once.

PREPARATION

Both the risotto and the asparagus can be cooked a few hours in advance. Reheat the risotto in the oven as directed and the asparagus in a bain-marie or double boiler.

SERVES 6

Arrosto morto
Italian Roast Veal

2 tablespoons unsalted butter

3 tablespoons olive oil

1 fresh rosemary sprig, about 4 inches long, or 1 teaspoon dried rosemary

3 garlic cloves, peeled and bruised

3½ pounds boneless leg of veal roast, neatly tied in several places

⅔ cup dry white wine

salt

freshly ground black pepper

1. Heat the butter, oil, rosemary, and garlic in a heavy-based casserole in which the meat will fit snugly. When the butter foam begins to subside, remove the garlic, add the meat, and brown well on all sides over medium heat. This browning will take about 15 minutes; it is essential to do it thoroughly.

2. Heat the wine in a small saucepan and pour it over the meat. Bring the wine to a lively bubble. Season with salt to taste and cover the casserole with a piece of wax paper and the lid, leaving a small opening for the steam to escape. Turn the heat down to low and cook for about 2 hours, turning the meat over and basting every now and then. If the meat gets too dry, add 2 or 3 tablespoons of hot water during the cooking. The meat is ready when it can be easily pierced with a fork. Add the pepper to taste, taste the juices, and check the salt.

3. Remove the meat from the pan and place on a carving board to cool a little; this will make it much easier to carve.

4. Add a few tablespoons of warm water to the pan and while scraping the cooking residue at the bottom of the pan, reduce over high heat until the juices are rich and syrupy. Strain and keep warm.

5. Carve the veal into ¼-inch slices and arrange them, slightly overlapping, on a warm dish. Spoon the juices over the meat and serve at once.

PREPARATION

The roast should be made as short a time as possible before serving, though you can cook it and prepare the juices before your guests arrive, and keep it warm in the oven in the covered casserole. Carve at the last minute.

SERVES 6

Zabaione con la purè di fragole
Zabaglione with Strawberry Puree

—◠—

4 egg yolks	*1 pound (1 pint) strawberries*
¾ cup superfine sugar	*4 tablespoons orange juice*
⅔ cup moscato or sweet white wine	*3 tablespoons confectioners' sugar*
⅔ cup heavy cream	

1. In the top of a double boiler, beat the yolks with ½ cup of the superfine sugar. Add ½ cup of the moscato and cook, whisking constantly over boiling water until thick and frothy. Do not let the water boil or the yolks will curdle. Set aside to cool.

2. Whip the cream and fold into the egg-yolk mixture.

3. Blend two-thirds of the strawberries with the confectioners' sugar in a food processor and then pass through a sieve to remove the seeds. Marinate the rest of the strawberries with the remaining superfine sugar, the orange juice, and the remaining wine.

4. Fold the strawberry puree into the zabaglione and mix a little so that the mixture is marbled. Transfer to 6 chilled glasses and decorate with the marinated strawberries.

PREPARATION

The fruit puree can be made up to 2 days in advance and refrigerated. It also freezes well. Make the zabaglione and fold in the puree up to 1 day in advance and keep in the refrigerator. Do not marinate the strawberries for longer than 2 hours or they will become mushy.

SERVES 6

A GREEN AND WHITE DINNER FOR SIX

Pecorino con le fave
Pecorino and Raw Fava Beans

~

Quaglie nel nido di paglia e fieno
Braised Quail in a Nest of Straw and Hay

~

Insalata verde
Green Salad (page 325)

~

Panna cotta
Molded Cream Dessert

*I*n Italy pasta is almost always served as a first course, rather than a main course. I am particularly happy to follow this custom because once I sit down at the table I want to stay put rather than dash into the kitchen to cook the pasta halfway through the meal. So, when serving this menu recently, I offered pecorino and fava beans as a snack with drinks, reversing the Tuscan habit of eating them at the end of the meal. The pecorino was a particularly good one, which a friend had brought from Tuscany. The first fava beans had just arrived in the shops, so they were small and young, which is what they must be when you eat them raw. If they are not, serve the pecorino with some green olives.

The *secondo* is my adaptation of a dish I had some years ago at the Ristorante Peck in Milan. The joy of quail is that you can pick it up in your hands and eat it just like that, especially when it is cooked slowly, in the Italian manner, so that the meat comes away easily from the tiny bones. The long cooking time, 45 minutes, might amaze you, but I assure you it is not a mistake!

The quail look attractive in their nest of green and white tagliolini. You can use a large round dish and put all the quail in the middle with the pasta around, or you can put two birds surrounded by the tagliolini on each individual plate.

The green salad is served afterward, and I suggest a change of plates rather than serving it on a side plate. The salad has a slightly tart flavor that fits perfectly between the courses that come before and after.

The *dolce* is one of my favorites. It is a traditional dessert from Piedmont with a light, subtle flavor, traditionally served on its own. In modern times I have seen *panna cotta* served with a coulis of raspberries, or with an apricot sauce, or with some fresh strawberries. Purists would cry out at the sacrilege. I am more open-minded, and I have dared to serve *panna cotta* with crème anglaise. It was heavenly.

Pecorino con le fave
Pecorino and Raw Fava Beans

This is hardly a recipe. All you have to do is to buy 1 pound of pecorino, preferably seasoned and Tuscan, and 3½ pounds of young fava beans—in the pod. Cut the pecorino into wedges and place on a dish. The pecorino to serve with favas should be a young cheese, available in gourmet markets. Put the unshelled fava beans in a bowl and let everybody get on with it. The drink must be red wine; a good Chianti Classico would be perfect.

SERVES 6

Quaglie nel nido di paglia e fieno
Braised Quail in a Nest of Straw and Hay

<hr>

12 quail	6 juniper berries, bruised
MARINADE	1/2 tablespoon peppercorns, bruised
2/3 cup red wine vinegar	some celery leaves
5 tablespoons olive oil	
4 bay leaves	1/4 pound prosciutto, chopped
2 strips lemon peel	1 tablespoon tomato paste
sprig fresh rosemary	2/3 cup heavy cream
6 sprigs parsley with stems	1 pound dried green and white tagliolini or 1 1/2 pounds fresh green and white cappellini
sprig fresh sage	
1 onion, cut into pieces	1 tablespoon vegetable oil
3 garlic cloves	5 tablespoons unsalted butter
2 teaspoons salt, preferably coarse salt	4 tablespoons freshly grated parmesan

1. Clean, wash, and trim the quail. Put them in a pot, preferably earthenware, or in a casserole.

2. Heat all the marinade ingredients (up to and including the celery) and then refrigerate to cool. When the marinade is cool, pour over the birds and leave for at least 6 hours. Turn the birds over as often as you can remember.

3. Preheat the oven to 325° F.

4. Put the casserole with the quail and the marinade on the heat and add the prosciutto and the tomato paste. Turn the birds over and over until the marinade is boiling. Lay the birds breast down. Cover the pot with a sheet of foil and put the lid on tight. Place the pot in the oven and cook for 45 minutes.

5. Remove the quail from the pot and keep warm, loosely covered with the foil.

6. Remove the bay leaves and any tough sprigs from the cooking juices and puree in a food processor. Put the pureed sauce in a clean saucepan and add the cream. Taste and check the seasoning and keep warm on a flame tamer placed over very low heat or in a bain-marie or double boiler.

7. Cook the pasta in plenty of salted boiling water with vegetable oil added. Drain very quickly, reserving 1 cup of the pasta water. Return the pasta to the pan and toss with the butter and the cheese. Add some of the pasta water to achieve the right fluidity.

8. Shape the pasta into a ring on a large round heated dish, or divide into 6 portions and place on individual heated plates. Put all the quail in the large common nest or 2 birds into each little nest. Spoon all the sauce over the birds and serve at once.

PREPARATION

The quail can be prepared up to 2 days in advance. Reheat in the oven. The sauce can be made up to 30 minutes in advance, while the quail are kept warm, covered with foil, in a low oven. The pasta must be cooked at the last minute.

SERVES 6

Panna cotta
Molded Cream Dessert

~~~~~~~

¾ cup plus 2 tablespoons sugar	*4 tablespoons peach eau de vie or white rum*
1 teaspoon lemon juice	
2 cups heavy cream	*2 teaspoons gelatin*
⅔ cup whole milk	*24 rose geranium leaves, if available*

1. Heat the oven to 325° F. Heat six ½-cup ramekins in it for 5 minutes.

2. Put ⅓ cup of the sugar, 3 tablespoons of water, and the lemon juice into a small saucepan and bring slowly to a boil. The syrup will heat up very slowly at fist and then it will begin to turn very pale gold. It will turn dark brown quite quickly. At that moment remove the pan from the heat and pour the caramel into the heated ramekins. Tip the ramekins in all directions for the caramel to slide and coat the surface evenly. Set aside and prepare the pudding.

3. Heat the cream, milk, and eau de vie or rum in a heavy saucepan. Add the remaining sugar and bring slowly to a boil, stirring constantly. Boil for 1 minute. Set aside to infuse for 1 hour or so, then strain the mixture.

4. Sprinkle the gelatin into 4 tablespoons warm water in a saucepan and let stand for a few minutes. Heat the gelatin while beating with a metal whisk until it has dissolved. Spoon 2 or 3 tablespoons of the cream mixture into the gelatin, stirring rapidly. Now add this mixture to the cream mixture, stirring very thoroughly to incorporate.

5. Pour the cream mixture into the ramekins. Allow to cool, then cover with plastic wrap and chill for at least 2 hours.

6. Run a spatula around the side of the ramekins and then unmold onto individual plates. Place the rose geranium leaves around each mold as if they were petals of a flower.

PREPARATION

The cream mixture can be prepared up to 1 day in advance. Keep in the ramekins and unmold just before serving.

SERVES 6

A VEGETARIAN DINNER FOR EIGHT

Pasta e fagioli alla contadina

Bean and Pasta Soup with Radicchio

‿

Scarpazzone lombardo

Spinach Torta

‿

Torta di ricotta e mandorle con la salsina di arancia

Ricotta and Almond Cake
with Orange Sauce (page 188)

*A*fter years of eating various versions of *pasta e fagioli,* I recently came across an excellent dish of it in the Trattoria Veneta in Milan, where peasant dishes from Veneto are served to the sophisticated Milanese. It was decorated with leaves of red radicchio and half a hard-boiled egg. I was surprised by both. The owner told me that the *soffritto* (fried mixture) in the soup was based on radicchio, hence the decoration, while the egg was "for nourishment." As a peasant soup, it would have been the only course. He told me to mash the egg into the soup and mix it up. So I tasted, and once again I was pleasantly surprised, this time by a slightly tart flavor. "Aceto," the owner said. "Aceto?" I queried. "Eh si, signora." Vinegar used to be added to counteract the lard with which the *soffritto* was traditionally made. Now the lard has been replaced by olive oil for health and diet reasons, but vinegar is still used for the sharp lift it gives to the beans.

My suggestion for the second course is a spinach torta, an ancient recipe from Lombardy that incorporates some sweet flavorings, something often done in the past. Recipes for similar spinach tortas can also be found in old English recipe books. A recipe by Patrick Lamb, a royal chef active in the early eighteenth century, is very similar to this Italian one, as my friend the food historian Michelle Berriedale-Johnson pointed out to me. Lamb spread a similar spinach mixture on toasted bread, then brushed it with egg white, and baked it in the oven. These spinach toasts were flavored at the end with orange juice. I sometimes pass around a warm tomato sauce (pages 336, 337), which gives a good combination of taste and color, but it is not essential.

For dessert I suggest a ricotta and almond cake; the recipe is on page 188.

Pasta e fagioli alla contadina
Bean and Pasta Soup with Radicchio

1 pound dried borlotti (or navy, northern, or pinto) beans (about 2¼ cups)

2 Russet potatoes, cut into large chunks

10 cups vegetable broth or water

salt

1 medium head radicchio (about ½ pound)

⅔ cup extra-virgin olive oil

1 celery stalk, with leaves, finely chopped

1 small onion, finely chopped

3 tablespoons chopped flat-leaf parsley

4 tablespoons red wine vinegar

freshly ground black pepper

8 ounces small tubular pasta, such as ditalini

⅓ cup freshly grated parmesan

4 hard-boiled eggs, shelled and cut in half

freshly grated parmesan for serving

1. Soak the beans overnight in cold water to cover.

2. Rinse and drain the beans and put them in a large pot, preferably earthen-ware, with the potatoes. Cover with the broth or water and bring very slowly to a boil with the lid on tight. Turn the heat down and skim. Simmer until the beans are soft, 1 to 2 hours, depending on quality and length in storage.

3. When the beans are soft, puree about two-thirds of them and the potato using a food mill or food processor, and return the puree to the pot. Taste, add salt, and bring the soup back to a boil.

4. Remove 8 of the larger outside leaves from the radicchio head and wash them. Set aside. Cut the rest of the radicchio into small strips, wash, and dry it.

5. Put about two-thirds of the oil, the celery, onion, parsley, and shredded radicchio in a frying pan, add a pinch of salt, and sauté over low heat until the vegetables are soft, about 10 minutes. Add to the soup together with the vinegar and cook for 15 minutes. Season with a good grinding of pepper.

6. Add the pasta to the soup. If the soup seems too thick, add a little hot water before adding the pasta, but remember that this type of soup should be quite thick and very creamy.   *continued*

7. When the pasta is done, remove from the heat. Pasta in this kind of soup does not need to be al dente. Mix in the cheese and allow the soup to stand for 5 minutes. Ladle the soup into soup plates and drizzle with the remaining oil. Float the radicchio leaves on the soup and lay half a hard-boiled egg on top of each leaf. Serve with the extra parmesan separately in a bowl.

PREPARATION

The soup, without the pasta, can be prepared 1 or 2 days in advance and refrigerated. In fact, it is better that way. It also freezes very well. The pasta, however, must be added just before serving.

SERVES 8

Scarpazzone lombardo
Spinach Torta

4 ounces stale white bread, crust removed

2 cups whole milk

3¼ pounds spinach or 2 packages (10 ounces each) frozen leaf spinach, thawed

salt

¼ cup yellow raisins

3 tablespoons freshly squeezed orange juice

10 tablespoons unsalted butter

5 eggs

2 ounces plain cookies, crushed (½ cup, scant measure). I use Digestive, which are not very sweet and are made with whole wheat flour.

4 tablespoons pine nuts

4 tablespoons almonds, blanched, peeled, and chopped

2 teaspoons sugar

1 teaspoon fennel seeds, crushed

½ teaspoon ground cinnamon

½ teaspoon ground nutmeg

¾ cup freshly grated parmesan

freshly ground black pepper

1. Put the bread in a bowl, cover with the milk, and leave for 30 minutes or so. Then break it up with a fork and beat it to a paste.

2. Meanwhile, pick over the spinach, removing any roots or thick stems. Wash in several changes of cold water until no more soil settles on the bottom of the sink or basin.

3. Put the spinach in a saucepan with the water that clings to the leaves. Add 1 teaspoon salt and cook, covered, until tender. Drain and set aside. If you are using frozen spinach, you do not need to blanch it; just allow to thaw.

4. Preheat the oven to 400° F.

5. Put the raisins in a bowl, cover with the orange juice, and set aside.

6. Melt the butter in a saucepan, add the bread and milk mixture, and cook over very low heat for 5 minutes, stirring constantly.

continued

7. Squeeze all the water out of the spinach with your hands. Chop coarsely by hand (a food processor would liquefy it) and add to the bread mixture. Cook for a couple of minutes, stirring constantly, then transfer to a bowl and allow to cool slightly.

8. Beat the eggs lightly and mix thoroughly into spinach mixture. Add the raisins and all the remaining ingredients. Taste and adjust seasonings.

9. Butter a 10-inch springform pan. Line the bottom with parchment paper and butter the paper. Sprinkle with a little flour and shake off the excess. Spoon the mixture into the pan and cover with foil.

10. Bake for 20 minutes, remove the foil, and bake for about 25 minutes more, turning down the heat to 350° F. The torta is ready when a toothpick inserted in the middle comes out dry. Allow to cool. Remove from the pan and serve at room temperature, set in a round dish.

PREPARATION

The torta can be made up to 2 days in advance and refrigerated. I have never tried freezing it (I'm not keen on freezing dishes, because they lose their freshness). Do not serve chilled.

SERVES 8

DINNER FOR EIGHT

Bresaola con la rucola
Bresaola with Arugula

~

Rotolo di spinaci al burro e formaggio
Spinach and Pasta Roll with Butter and Parmesan

~

Torta di patate e mandorle
Potato and Almond Cake

~

Rabarbaro all'arancia
Baked Rhubarb with Orange

*B*resaola, a specialty of Valtellina, an Alpine valley in Lombardy, is raw fillet of beef that has been cured in salt and air-dried for two to four months. It is like the Swiss Bündenerfleisch. The flavor is similar to prosciutto though a little sharper. Bresaola is served thinly sliced and lightly dressed with olive oil and lemon juice. Or at least this is the modern way to serve it. The old-fashioned way, still observed by the purists, is to eat bresaola as it is. Last year the food historian Massimo Alberini and his wife took me to the Ristorante Peck in Milan. He ordered bresaola and the maître d' asked, "Così, al naturale?" Alberini was shocked and replied, "E me lo domanda? Ma certamente." (You ask me that? Of course.)

My mother is another purist as far as bresaola goes, and at home in Milan I still have bresaola as it used to be served, by itself with fresh bread. But the perfect bresaola one can buy in Milan is hard to come by anywhere else. Non-Italian bresaola benefits from a drizzling of good olive oil. I sometimes add some arugula dressed with olive oil and lemon juice. Buy bresaola—thinly sliced—the day you want to eat it, or it will become dark and leathery. If you cannot find bresaola, use a good prosciutto.

After the meat in an easy first course, my *secondo* is an elegant vegetarian dish, a homemade pasta roll stuffed with spinach and ricotta, the most traditional of all vegetarian pasta fillings. The pasta must be rolled out by hand, but it is not too difficult to handle. Once cooked, allow the rotolo to cool; it is then easier to slice. I use an electric carving knife which I find one of the most useful tools. It is as invaluable for carving roast meat as it is for slicing a roulade like this, or a lovely stuffed fish, or a piece of braised meat that would otherwise tend to crumble.

After experimenting with different sauces, I came to the conclusion that the best is the simplest: melted butter and parmesan. Should you prefer something stronger, I have included a recipe for a fontina and cream sauce.

There's nothing Italian about the potato and almond cake. It comes from the Hotel Mar y Vent in Bañalbufar, Majorca. The way it was served there, lavishly covered with confectioners' sugar, seemed very Italian indeed. It reminded me of all the different tortas covered with confectioners' sugar that are on display at most bakeries and pastry shops in central Italy. In keeping with the American belief that sweets at the end of a meal should not be eaten dry—something I totally agree with—I have served the cake with various ice creams or stewed fruit. In the spring I use rhubarb—not an Italian fruit, but one I have taken to since coming to England.

Bresaola con la rucola
Bresaola with Arugula

¹/₂ pound arugula

5 tablespoons extra-virgin olive oil

2 tablespoons lemon juice

salt and freshly ground black pepper

1 pound bresaola

1. Wash the arugula. Dry very thoroughly and put it in a bowl. Dress with the oil, lemon juice, and salt and pepper to taste. Toss well. Taste and add a little more lemon juice, if necessary.

2. Place the bresaola in the middle of a dish and surround it with the arugula. Serve immediately.

PREPARATION

The arugula can be prepared up to 1 day in advance and kept in the refrigerator, loosely wrapped in a dish towel.

SERVES 8

Rotolo di spinaci al burro e formaggio

Spinach and Pasta Roll with Butter and Parmesan

1 pound frozen spinach, thawed, or 2 pounds fresh spinach or Swiss chard

salt

2 tablespoons finely chopped shallot

10 tablespoons unsalted butter

2 ounces prosciutto or mortadella, chopped

1 cup ricotta

1 cup freshly grated parmesan

¼ teaspoon grated nutmeg

1 egg yolk

1 large sheet homemade pasta dough, made with 1⅓ cups unbleached flour, 2 eggs, and 1 teaspoon olive oil

2 garlic cloves, peeled and bruised

small sprig fresh sage

1. If you are using frozen spinach, cook the thawed spinach in a covered pan with salt for 3 minutes. Drain and squeeze to remove all the liquid. If you are using fresh spinach, discard any wilted or discolored leaves, roots, and long stems. Wash in a basin in several changes of cold water until the water shows no trace of grit. Cook with just the water that clings to the leaves in a covered pan with salt until tender. Drain and squeeze the spinach to remove most of its moisture. Set aside.

2. In a frying pan, sauté the shallot in 3 tablespoons of the butter over medium heat. Chop the spinach coarsely by hand (a food processor would liquefy it) and when the shallot turns pale gold in color, add the spinach to the pan with the chopped prosciutto. Sauté for 5 minutes, turning the spinach over and over.

3. Transfer the contents of the frying pan to a mixing bowl and add the ricotta, half the grated parmesan, the nutmeg, and the egg yolk. Mix all the ingredients with a fork until they are well combined. Check seasoning.

4. Make the dough following the directions on page 33. Remember to let the dough rest for at least 1 hour before rolling it out. Roll out a sheet of dough about 14 inches in diameter. Spread the filling over the dough, starting about 2 inches in from the edge near you. The filling should cover all but a ¼-inch border all around the sheet except for the wider border near you. Fold this border over the filling, and continue to fold until you have rolled it all up. Wrap the roll tightly in cheesecloth and tie the ends securely with string.

5. Use a fish poacher or other long, deep pan that can hold the roll and 3 to 4 quarts of water. Bring the water to a boil, add 1 tablespoon of salt, then put in the pasta roll and cook at a gentle but steady boil for 25 minutes after the water has come back to a boil. Lift out the roll, using the fish rack in the poacher or 2 pancake turners (slotted spatulas) and place on a wooden board. Unwrap the roll as soon as you can handle it and set aside to cool.

6. Preheat the oven to 400° F.

7. Cut the roll into ½-inch slices. Generously grease a large baking dish with some of the remaining butter and lay the slices in it, overlapping them a little.

8. Heat the rest of the butter in a heavy frying pan with the garlic and sage. When the garlic begins to turn golden, remove from the heat. Remove and discard the garlic and sage and spoon the butter evenly over the roll.

9. Cover the dish with foil and place in the oven until the slices are hot, about 20 to 30 minutes, depending on how hot they were when they went in the oven. Remove the dish from the oven, uncover it, and serve, passing around the remaining parmesan separately.

PREPARATION

The roll can be made up to 2 days in advance and refrigerated, wrapped in foil.

SERVES 8

Salsa alla fontina e panna
Fontina and Cream Sauce

~~~~~~

2½ cups heavy cream | *salt and freshly ground white pepper*
½ pound fontina or raclette cheese |

1. Bring the cream slowly to a simmer in a heavy-bottomed saucepan and simmer over low heat for 2 minutes. A few bubbles should occasionally break the surface. Do not boil.

2. Meanwhile slice the cheese into very thin slices. Add the cheese to the cream and stir constantly until it is dissolved. Stir in 4 tablespoons boiling water to dilute the sauce to the right consistency. Taste and add seasonings. The sauce should be very creamy and glossy.

3. Preheat the oven to 400° F.

4. Spread 2 or 3 tablespoons of the sauce over the bottom of a large buttered baking dish. Cover with the rotolo slices and coat with a few tablespoons of sauce. Cover the dish with foil and heat for 20 to 30 minutes. Pour the remaining sauce into a heated sauceboat and serve with the rest of the parmesan in a separate bowl.

PREPARATION

The sauce can be prepared up to 30 to 45 minutes in advance and kept hot in a bain-marie or double boiler.

Torta di patate e mandorle
Potato and Almond Cake

1½ pounds potatoes | *1¾ cups chopped almonds*
1 soft white bread roll | *2 teaspoons grated lemon peel*
6 eggs, separated | *salt*
1 cup sugar | *confectioners' sugar for decoration*

1. Boil the potatoes in their skin. Peel and puree them through the small disk of a food mill.

2. Remove the soft inside of the roll and crumble it by hand or in the food processor.

3. Preheat the oven to 475° F.

4. Put the egg yolks in a bowl. Add the sugar, almonds, lemon peel, a pinch of salt, the breadcrumbs, and the potatoes. Mix thoroughly. Beat the egg whites until stiff but not dry and fold them gently into the mixture.

5. Butter a 10-inch springform pan. Sprinkle a generous tablespoon of flour into the pan, shake to cover the surface, and discard the excess flour. Fill the pan with the batter and place in the oven. Turn the heat down to 325° F. and bake for 50 minutes to 1 hour, until a toothpick inserted in the middle of the cake comes out dry. Loosen the band around the pan and turn the cake onto a wire rack to cool. Serve lavishly sprinkled with sifted confectioners' sugar.

PREPARATION

The cake is best eaten the day it is baked, but it can be made up to 2 days in advance.

SERVES 8

Rabarbaro all'arancia
Baked Rhubarb with Orange

2 oranges | *1¾ cups sugar*
2 pounds rhubarb |

1. Wash one of the oranges and grate the peel. Squeeze the juice from both oranges.

2. Trim and wash the rhubarb. Cut into 1-inch pieces and place in an oven dish. Sprinkle with the sugar and add the grated orange peel and the orange juice. Cover the dish and let stand for 2 hours for the sugar to draw the juices from the rhubarb.

3. Preheat the oven to 300° F.

4. Place the rhubarb in the oven and bake for 45 minutes or until the rhubarb is tender but still holds its shape.

5. Remove the rhubarb from the dish with a slotted spoon and place in a bowl. Transfer the juices to a pan and boil briskly to reduce until very syrupy and tasty. Pour over the rhubarb. Cover the bowl with plastic wrap and chill.

6. Serve warm or chilled.

PREPARATION

The rhubarb can be baked up to 3 days in advance and refrigerated. It also freezes very well.

SERVES 6 TO 8

DINNER FOR EIGHT

Zuppa alla santé
Vegetable Soup

~~~

Pollastri al riso
Braised Chicken with Rice

~~~

Funghi al funghetto
Sautéed Mushrooms (page 328)

~~~

Bavarese lombarda
Lombardy Marquise

*I*n honor of my native city and its cooking, I have composed this menu with recipes adapted from nineteenth-century northern Italian cookery books. As I was browsing through them, I could taste in my imagination many of the dishes of my childhood in Milan. Plenty of soups, warming casseroles, braised roasts, vegetables, and rich puddings. Not much Mediterranean flavor in this cooking, but rather one looking north toward Austria and France. Fundamentally, this is still the cuisine of northern Italy, which has been infiltrated by the lighter and fresher approach of the south over the past thirty years.

At home, no dinner was considered a proper dinner by my father if it did not start with a soup. And a proper soup, at that, rich and nutritious and *non quel consommé che si beve in tazze, e sembra una specie di tè* (not that consommé that you drink from a cup, like some kind of tea).

The soup in this menu is very representative of the kind of soup served at Milanese dinner parties of the period: lighter than a minestrone yet similar in flavor and reinforced with bread so that it becomes thick. It is a soup traditionally served in the spring with an assortment of new-season and old-season vegetables. If you want to make it more elegant, serve small croutons instead of the large.

The main course is my adaptation of a recipe that appears in *Trattato di cucina* by the Piedmontese Giovanni Vialardi, published in 1854. It is a large tome, illustrated by the author and divided into nineteen chapters embracing all culinary subjects. One of the chapters, for example, is dedicated to cooking suitable for children and contains a recipe for a "pappa"—pappy food—for a child of three or four hours, "lacking his or her mother's milk or because of the late arrival of his or her wet nurse." The recipe is too long, I'm afraid, to find room here. Vialardi's style is rather dull, but his recipes are good, and his drawings for the presentation of the dishes are extremely interesting and very artistic. He was, in fact, a *chef pâtissier* of the first king of Italy and was greatly influenced by Carême and other French masters.

The dish in this menu, however, does not need a master for its preparation nor for its presentation. Vialardi suggests serving the chicken with a garnish of asparagus or mushrooms. Try my sautéed mushrooms on page 328.

The dessert is one of my favorite recipes by Pellegrino Artusi, possibly the greatest Italian cookery writer, who although a northerner was the first to see, late in the nineteenth century, some movement toward the unification of the cooking of Italy following its political unification. This dessert was often made at home in Milan, and it still is today. Considering the amount of butter it contains and the longevity of many members of past generations of my family, I begin to wonder about the harm butter is supposed to do! This is a rich sweet that I find irresistible, with its subtle eggy flavor enhanced by virtue of the eggs being hard-boiled. At home we children called it simply *il dolce squisito.*

Zuppa alla santé
Vegetable Soup

6 tablespoons unsalted butter

8 slices country-style white bread

1 pound vegetables, including potato, turnip, onion, carrot, and celery

½ cup fresh peas

2 leeks, white part only

salt and freshly ground black pepper

6 cups Italian broth (page 338)

freshly grated parmesan

1. Preheat the oven to 400° F.

2. Melt the butter in a stockpot. Place the bread slices on a baking tray and, using a pastry brush, moisten one side with a little melted butter. Place the tray in the oven for 8 minutes. Turn the heat off and leave the bread in the oven.

3. Peel and wash the potato, turnip, onion, and carrot, keeping them separate. Cut into short matchsticks and dry with paper towels. Wash the celery, remove the threads from the stalks, and cut into matchsticks. Thoroughly wash and trim the leeks. Cut them into matchsticks.

4. Add the potato, turnip, onion, and peas to the stockpot and sauté for 5 minutes over low heat. Season with a pinch of salt, which will prevent the vegetables from browning. They should soften just a little. Add the carrot and celery and cook for 3 minutes, stirring frequently. Finally add the leek and gently sauté it for 1 or 2 minutes, turning it over and over.

5. While the vegetables are cooking, bring the broth to a boil. Pour the broth over the vegetables, add pepper, and cook for 10 minutes or until the vegetables are cooked. Taste and check the seasonings.

6. Put the toasted bread in individual soup bowls and ladle the soup over the bread. Serve at once, passing the parmesan around separately.

PREPARATION

The soup can be prepared up to 3 days in advance and refrigerated in a covered container. Reheat the soup and simmer gently until it is hot.

SERVES 8

Pollastri al riso
Braised Chicken with Rice

8 tablespoons unsalted butter

1 tablespoon olive oil

2 small carrots, peeled and diced

2 onions, sliced

2 celery stalks, cut into strips

6 sprigs flat-leaf parsley

2 small chickens (3 to 3½ pounds each)

salt and freshly ground black pepper

2 teaspoons, all together, fresh rosemary needles and fresh sage leaves, chopped

1½ to 2 cups meat or chicken broth

1¼ cups long-grain rice

6 tablespoons freshly grated parmesan

1. Preheat the oven to 400° F.

2. Put half the butter, the oil, vegetables, and parsley in a heavy casserole into which the chickens will fit snugly. Cook for 10 to 15 minutes over low heat, turning the vegetables over quite frequently.

3. Meanwhile wash the chickens under cold water and pat dry with paper towels. Season each cavity with salt and pepper and with the chopped herbs. Place the chickens over the bed of vegetables, pour over 1 cup of broth, and season, if necessary, with salt and pepper. Cover with a piece of foil and with the lid. Place the casserole in the oven and cook until the chickens are done, about 1½ hours. Test by piercing a thigh with a skewer. The liquid that runs out should be clear. Remove from the oven and let stand for 10 minutes.

4. Meanwhile, put a large saucepan of water on the heat for the rice.

5. Carve the chickens into neat pieces and place on a dish. Cover loosely with foil and keep warm in the oven with the heat turned off.

6. Skim off as much of the fat from the surface of the cooking juices as you can. Turn the cooking juices with all the vegetables into a food processor or blender and blend to a smooth puree. It should have the consistency of heavy cream; if it is too thick, add a little of the reserved broth. Taste and check the seasonings. Transfer the sauce to a bowl and place the bowl in a saucepan half full of boiling water or use a double boiler. Cover with a lid.

continued

7. Cook the rice with 1½ tablespoons of salt in the boiling water. When the rice is al dente, drain well and return immediately to the pan. Toss with the remaining butter, season with the parmesan and a few grindings of pepper, then add a few tablespoons of the sauce to coat the rice thoroughly.

8. Transfer the rice to a large heated serving dish, making a well in the middle. Place the chicken pieces in the well and spoon over the rest of the sauce. Serve at once.

PREPARATION

The chicken can be cooked up to 2 days in advance. Leave whole and refrigerate in a covered container. Cut the chicken into pieces and reheat in the oven, then make the sauce.

SERVES 8

Bavarese lombarda
Lombardy Marquise

———

6 large eggs
5½ tablespoons unsalted butter
1½ cups confectioners' sugar, sifted
12 drops pure vanilla extract

6 ounces sponge cake, storebought or homemade (page 343)
6 tablespoons white rum

1. Gently lower the eggs into a saucepan of boiling water and cook them for 7 minutes exactly. The timing is important because the yolks must be just soft in the middle. Put the saucepan under cold running water and leave for 2 minutes, then peel the eggs. Cut them in half and scoop out the yolk (you can use the whites, chopped up, in a salad).

2. Cream together the butter and the yolks, then add the sugar, reserving about 3 tablespoons for the decoration, and the vanilla. Blend very thoroughly using a wooden spoon or a food processor.

3. Cut the cake into ¼-inch-thick slices and lay half of the slices on a serving dish or use a loaf tin for a better shape. Pour the rum into a small bowl. Moisten the cake with rum, using a pastry brush. Cover with the buttercream, spreading it evenly all over. Place the rest of the cake over the cream and moisten it well with rum. Cover with plastic wrap and chill for at least 3 hours.

4. Just before serving, remove the plastic wrap and sprinkle the reserved sugar all over the top using a sugar sifter or pressing it through a fine sieve with a metal spoon.

PREPARATION

Artusi recommends leaving the marquise "on ice" for 3 hours. I prefer to make it the day before. You can make it even 2 or 3 days in advance. It keeps very well in the refrigerator.

SERVES 8

DINNER FOR EIGHT

Tagliatelle coi carciofi
Tagliatelle with Artichokes

—

Agnello arrosto alla moda rinascimentale
Leg of Lamb Renaissance Style

—

Sformato di patate e carote
Potato and Carrot Mold (page 227)

—

Arancie e kiwi
Oranges and Kiwis

*T*his is a dinner that needs the touch of an experienced cook. It is well worth the time and effort. On the other hand, the first and last courses, and much of the second course, too, can be prepared in advance.

The roast lamb is an interesting and excellent dish that I have adapted from a recipe in Maestro Martino's *Libro de arte coquinaria,* published in 1450. Maestro Martino was the chef of the Patriarch of Aquileia, a town near Venice. Little is known about the man, but fortunately his manuscript was incorporated in full in the book *De honesta voluptate et valetudine* by Platina, first published in Latin in 1475, which became well known throughout continental Europe.

In those days, spices were liberally used; they came from the Middle East via one of Italy's maritime republics. Since they were sold at very high prices, their use was a sign of wealth. Saffron was especially popular, because of its golden color. In this dish the color does not come through the rich brown of the gravy, but the highly aromatic taste certainly does.

If you have a butcher who knows his job, ask him to saw off the bone at the end of the shank just above the knuckle. The "aitch" bone can then be removed, making the carving much easier. Also ask your butcher to remove any excess surface fat. The cooking time is a question of personal taste, but my strong recommendation is not to overcook lamb. Fifteen minutes per pound is enough. I serve this roast with the potatoes and carrot mold on page 227.

After these two very filling dishes, the only fitting way to end the meal is with a light dessert based on fruit. I chose the salad of oranges and kiwis because of its beautiful appearance. Slightly unripe kiwis have a tingling acidity that goes well with oranges. I like the fruit salad au naturel, but if you wish you can add half a glass or so of dry white wine or champagne if you are opening a bottle before dinner.

Tagliatelle coi carciofi
Tagliatelle with Artichokes

———

tagliatelle made with 3½ cups unbleached flour and 5 eggs or 2½ pounds storebought fresh tagliatelle or 1¼ pounds dried egg tagliatelle

6 or 7 artichokes (3 to 3½ pounds)

4 garlic cloves, peeled

5 tablespoons olive oil

salt and freshly ground black pepper

2 cups heavy cream

4 tablespoons unsalted butter

4 tablespoons freshly grated parmesan

1 cup whole milk

1. If you are making your own tagliatelle follow the directions on pages 333–335.

2. Trim and prepare the artichokes as directed on page 272. Cut the artichokes into quarters lengthwise and remove the choke and the prickly purplish leaves at the base. Slice the artichokes into very thin wedges, about ⅛ inch thick, so that the cut-up leaves remain attached to the bottom. Remove all the tough outside skin of the stems, keeping only the tender inner part. Cut the stems into rounds. Put in a bowl of acidulated water.

3. Thread a wooden toothpick through the garlic cloves. (This makes it easier to fish them out when the artichokes are cooked.) Put them in a large sauté pan with the oil and add the artichokes. Sauté gently for about 5 minutes, turning them over to *insaporire* (make them tasty) and then add enough water to come one-third of the way up the side of the pan. Season with salt and pepper.

4. Put the lid tightly on the pan and cook, over very low heat, for 35 to 45 minutes, until the artichokes are very tender. Add a little water as necessary, whenever all the liquid has evaporated.

5. Set aside while you cook the tagliatelle in plenty of boiling salted water. Remember that if the tagliatelle is fresh it will take no longer than 2 minutes to cook.

6. Preheat the oven to 375° F.

7. While the pasta is cooking, heat the cream. Drain the tagliatelle and immediately put it back into the pan. Toss with the butter and the hot cream. Add the artichokes and the parmesan and mix thoroughly.

8. Butter the oven dish and pour the tagliatelle into it. Before baking, heat the milk and pour it over the tagliatelle. You may not need to add it all, but remember that the dish will dry while baking.

9. Put the dish in the oven and bake for about 20 minutes. Let it rest a few minutes before you bring it to the table. The flavors will settle and combine, and your guests will be able to appreciate the delicacy of the dish without burning their tongues.

PREPARATION

The tagliatelle can be made up to 2 days in advance. Leave the pasta on trays to dry and cover it with a cloth as soon as it is thoroughly dry. The artichokes can also be cooked 1 or 2 days in advance and refrigerated, covered with plastic wrap. The whole dish can be prepared up to 1 day in advance, covered with plastic wrap and refrigerated. Bring back to room temperature before adding the hot milk and baking.

SERVES 8

Agnello arrosto alla moda rinascimentale
Leg of Lamb Renaissance Style

4 or 5 garlic cloves

2 tablespoons mixed fresh herb leaves, such as rosemary, sage, thyme, marjoram, parsley, lovage, or celery

salt and freshly ground black pepper

2½ ounces pancetta or unsmoked streaky bacon, in a single slice

1 small leg of lamb (4½ to 5 pounds)

2 tablespoons olive oil

2 cups beef stock

¼ teaspoon saffron powder or saffron strands

4 tablespoons balsamic vinegar

1 egg yolk

2 tablespoons unsalted butter

1. Preheat the oven to 425° F.

2. Chop the garlic and herbs and add salt and pepper. Cut the pancetta into strips, coat with the herb mixture, and lard the lamb with the coated strips. Rub with the oil and any leftover mixture of garlic and herbs and place the leg on a rack in a roasting pan.

3. Heat the stock. If you are using saffron strands, pound them in a mortar. This is easier to do if you sprinkle a pinch of sugar in with the saffron. Dissolve the saffron into half the stock, then beat in half the balsamic vinegar and the egg yolk. Add a little salt and pepper and pour the mixture into the roasting pan. Place in the oven.

4. Cook for 15 minutes and then turn down the heat to 375° F. and cook until the meat is done. (If you like the meat pink, allow about 1½ hours from the time you put it into the oven.) Baste the lamb every 20 minutes or so. Remove the meat from the oven and leave it in a warm place for 15 to 30 minutes.

5. Meanwhile make the sauce. Strain the contents of the roasting pan into a saucepan and add the remaining stock. Bring to a boil and add the rest of the balsamic vinegar and the butter, little by little, swirling the pan until completely incorporated. Taste and check the seasoning. Pour into a heated sauceboat. Carve the meat into fairly thick slices and pass the sauce separately.

PREPARATION

The lamb can be larded a few hours beforehand, but like any other roast it cannot be cooked long in advance. Both the meat and the sauce can be kept warm for up to 30 minutes. I keep the meat warm by wrapping it loosely and placing in a turned-off oven; I keep the sauce warm, with the sauceboat set in a bowl or pan of very hot water.

SERVES 8

Arancie e kiwi

Oranges and Kiwis

— — — —

12 large navel oranges } *sugar (optional)*
8 kiwi fruits }

1. Peel and slice the oranges on a plate to collect the juice. Remove the skin and the white pith underneath. Slice the oranges crosswise. Reserve the smaller slices for another occasion. Allowing 3 to 4 slices per person, lay the large central slices on a large round dish.

2. Peel the kiwi fruits and slice them crosswise. Lay a slice of kiwi fruit on each orange slice.

3. Pour the juice that has collected from the oranges over the fruit and sprinkle with a little sugar, if you wish. Cover the dish with plastic wrap and refrigerate.

PREPARATION

I like to make this dessert no more than 8 hours before serving it, keeping it covered in the refrigerator.

SERVES 8

SUMMER

LUNCH FOR EIGHT

6 9

Bruschetta toscana
Grilled Bread with Olive Oil, Garlic, and Tomato

⌇

Riso all'insalata
Rice Salad with Anchovies and Mozzarella

⌇

Peperoni all'aceto
Bell Peppers with Vinegar

⌇

Crema di frutti della passione
Passion Fruit Fool

AN ALFRESCO LUNCH FOR TEN

7 5

Schegge di pecorino e parmigiano con le olive verdi
Pecorino and Parmesan Wedges with Green Olives

⌇

Spaghettini eccitanti
Spaghettini with Sundried Tomatoes, Hot Peppers, and Olives

⌇

Frittata di cipolle
Onion Frittata

⌇

Frittata di peperoni e tonno
Pepper and Tuna Fish Frittata

⌇

Frittata di zucchine
Zucchini Frittata

⌇

Verdure alla griglia
Grilled Vegetables

⌇

Frutta di stagione
Fruit of the Season

A GARDEN LUNCH FOR TEN

8 4

Prosciutto e melone
Prosciutto with Melon

⌇

Linguine aglio, olio, e peperoncino
Linguine with Garlic, Oil, and Hot Peppers

⌇

Il polpettone di tonno della Mamma
Tuna Roll

⌇

Salsina all'uovo
Egg and Lemon Sauce

⌇

Pomodori al basilico
Tomatoes with Basil

⌇

Gelato di fragola all'aceto balsamico
Strawberry Ice Cream Flavored with Balsamic Vinegar (page 287)

⌇

Sorbetto di limone al sapor di basilico
Basil-Lemon Sorbet (page 109)

DINNER FOR SIX

91

Soffiato di Capelli d'angelo
Angel Hair Soufflé

~

Filetti di pesce con scaglie di patate
Fish Fillets with Potato Scales

~

Budino alla pesca
Peach Mousse

DINNER FOR SIX

104

*Pasticcio di pasta e melanzane
in bianco*
Baked Ziti with Eggplant

~

Filetti di San Pietro in salsa di broccoli
Fillet of Flounder with Broccoli Sauce

~

Sorbetto di limone al basilico
Basil–Lemon Sorbet

DINNER
FOR SIX

98

I ricchi e i poveri
Shrimp and Bean Salad

~

Cannelloni di melanzane in salsa
Eggplant Cannelloni with Tomato Sauce

~

Formaggio
Cheese

~

Granita al caffè
Coffee Granita

DINNER
FOR SIX

110

Ravioli di pesce
Fish Ravioli

~

Gamberi in salsa all'abruzzese
Shrimp in a Piquant Tomato Sauce

~

*Insalata di pomodori, cetrioli,
e peperoni*
Tomato, Cucumber, and Pepper Salad

~

Gelato di albicocca
Apricot Ice Cream

DINNER FOR EIGHT

1 1 7

Insalata di zucchine e pomodori all'aceto balsamico e alla menta

Zucchini and Tomato Salad with Balsamic Vinegar and Mint

~~~~~

Bocconcini di coda di rospo alla purè di lenticchie

Monkfish Morsels with Lentil Puree

~~~~~

Spinaci all'agro

Lemon Spinach (page 331)

~~~~~

Macedonia di frutta con la neve al limone

Fruit Salad with Lemon Granita

DINNER FOR TWELVE

1 2 3

Passato di pomodoro

Tomato Soup

~~~~~

Petti di cappone alla Stefani

Chicken Breasts Seventeenth-Century Style

~~~~~

Prugne al vino

Plums Stewed in Wine

~~~~~

Gelato di mascarpone

Mascarpone Ice Cream

A BUFFET PARTY FOR TWENTY-FIVE

1 2 9

Vitello tonnato alla milanese

Veal in Tuna Sauce

~~~~~

Mousse di prosciutto cotto

Truffle-flavored Ham Mousse

~~~~~

I ricchi e i poveri

Shrimp and Bean Salad (page 100)

~~~~~

Petti di cappone alla Stefani

Chicken Breasts Seventeenth-Century Style (page 126)

~~~~~

Insalata di pasta, fontina, noci, e sedano

Pasta Salad with Fontina, Walnuts, and Celery

~~~~~

Conchiglie rosse ripiene di spaghettini in insalata

Radicchio Leaves Filled with Spaghettini

~~~~~

Insalate varie

Assorted Salads

~~~~~

Torta di patate e mandorle

Potato and Almond Cake (page 49)

~~~~~

Gelato di ricotta

Ricotta Ice Cream

~~~~~

Pere alla crema del Lario

Poached Pears with Pear Liqueur Cream

~~~~~

Macedonia di frutta con la neve al limone

Fruit Salad with Lemon Granita (page 122)

LUNCH FOR EIGHT

Bruschetta toscana
Grilled Bread with Olive Oil, Garlic, and Tomato

Riso all'insalata
Rice Salad with Anchovies and Mozzarella

Peperoni all'aceto
Bell Peppers with Vinegar

Crema di frutti della passione
Passion Fruit Fool

*B*ruschetta originated in Rome and the word comes from *bruscare,* which means to burn slightly in the local dialect. The Roman *bruschetta* is usually made without tomatoes; the Tuscan version has a few ripe tomatoes sprinkled on top. If you can't find good tomatoes, forget about the bruschetta and settle for a frittata (pages 79–81), which you can serve cold.

There are countless versions of rice salad, and this is mine. I like it because it has a clean taste that emphasizes the flavor of the rice. Sometimes I add a handful of dried tomatoes soaked in oil or two or three fresh ripe tomatoes, peeled and cut into small pieces, but here I have left the tomatoes out, since they already are in the bruschetta. If you want to make this a vegetarian meal, do not add the anchovy fillets.

The dessert is as easy as it is irresistible, with the elusive orange-blossom flavor of passion fruit. Passion fruit is at its best when it begins to shrivel. Keep them on the windowsill until ready, but don't forget them.

Bruschetta toscana

Grilled Bread with Olive Oil, Garlic, and Tomato

6 firm ripe tomatoes, preferably plum tomatoes

a handful of fresh basil leaves

8 slices good crusty bread, about ½ inch thick

3 large garlic cloves, peeled and crushed

salt and freshly ground black pepper

4 tablespoons extra-virgin olive oil

1. Blanch and peel the tomatoes, cut them in half lengthwise and remove as many seeds as you can. Cut the tomatoes into ½-inch cubes.

2. Wash and dry the basil. Tear the leaves into small pieces.

3. Grill the bread slices on both sides and then rub them on each side with the garlic. Cut the slices in half, to make them easier to eat.

4. Spoon some tomato cubes and some basil leaves over each slice and sprinkle with salt and a generous grinding of pepper. Drizzle the olive oil over the bread and serve at once.

PREPARATION

The tomatoes can be cut up and refrigerated, in a covered bowl, up to a few hours in advance.

SERVES 8

Riso all'insalata
Rice Salad with Anchovies and Mozzarella

<hr>

2 cups long-grain rice

salt

½ cup extra-virgin olive oil

2 eggs

12 anchovy fillets

½ pound fresh mozzarella, cut into small cubes

8 tablespoons chopped flat-leaf parsley

2 garlic cloves, peeled and very finely chopped

20 drops Tabasco

24 black olives, pitted and cut into strips

2 tablespoons capers, rinsed and dried

freshly ground black pepper

1. Cook the rice in plenty of salted boiling water until just al dente. Remember that when served cold, rice (like pasta) is better a touch undercooked. Drain the rice, rinse under cold water and drain again. Pat dry with paper towels and place in a bowl. Immediately add 2 tablespoons of the oil. Leave to cool.

2. While the rice is cooking, cook the eggs in simmering water for 3½ minutes. Run the eggs under cold water and then very gently crack the shells all around and peel them. Place the eggs on a plate and chop them. the yolk should still be runny. Scoop the eggs, whites, and runny yolks into the rice and mix well.

3. Chop the anchovy fillets and place in a bowl. Mix in the mozzarella, parsley, garlic, Tabasco, olives, and capers. Beat in the remaining oil with a fork and season to taste with salt and pepper.

4. Spoon this dressing into the rice and mix very thoroughly with 2 forks so as to separate all the grains. Taste and adjust seasoning to your liking. Serve cold but not chilled.

PREPARATION

Ideally the rice should be dressed 2 to 3 hours before serving.

SERVES 8

Peperoni all'aceto
Bell Peppers with Vinegar

2 large sweet onions

5 tablespoons extra-virgin olive oil

salt

8 bell peppers, red, yellow, and green

4 tablespoons sugar

4 tablespoons red wine vinegar

freshly ground black pepper

1. Coarsely chop the onions and sauté slowly in the oil. Add 1 teaspoon of salt to release the moisture in the onion and prevent it from browning too quickly. Cover the pan and cook gently for 45 minutes, until the onion is very soft. Add 1 or 2 tablespoons hot water if the onion begins to stick to the bottom of the pan.

2. Wash and dry the peppers, cut them in quarters, and remove the seeds, cores, and ribs. Cut them into ½-inch pieces.

3. Add the peppers to the onion and sauté for 5 minutes, stirring frequently. Turn the heat up a little, add the sugar, and leave it to caramelize for 10 minutes or so, stirring frequently. Stir in the vinegar, add salt and pepper, and cover the pan tightly. Cook over very low heat for 1 hour more, checking every now and then that the peppers do not burn. Add hot water by the tablespoonful whenever necessary. If, on the other hand, there is too much liquid at the end of the cooking, uncover the pan and boil to reduce the juices until they are syrupy.

4. Serve warm or at room temperature.

PREPARATION

The dish can be prepared up to 8 days in advance, covered and refrigerated. It also freezes well.

SERVES 8

Crema di frutti della passione
Passion Fruit Fool

20 passion fruits
3 tablespoons sherry
2 cups heavy cream

9 tablespoons confectioners' sugar, sifted
3 egg whites

1. Cut the passion fruits in half and scoop out the insides into a bowl. Add the sherry and let stand for at least 1 hour.

2. Whip the cream until stiff and fold in the sugar. Beat the egg whites until stiff; mix 3 tablespoons into the whipped cream and fold in the remaining whites. Combine the passion fruits with the cream mixture, cover with plastic wrap, and refrigerate for at least 1 hour.

3. Place 8 long-stemmed glasses in the refrigerator. Before serving, whip the cream mixture briefly and spoon into the chilled glasses.

PREPARATION

The passion fruits can be prepared up to 1 day in advance and refrigerated in a covered bowl. The whole dessert can be made up to 2 hours in advance.

SERVES 8

AN ALFRESCO LUNCH FOR TEN

Schegge di pecorino e parmigiano con le olive verdi
Pecorino and Parmesan Wedges with Green Olives

Spaghettini eccitanti
Spaghettini with Sundried Tomatoes, Hot Peppers, and Olives

Frittata di cipolle
Onion Frittata

Frittata di peperoni e tonno
Pepper and Tuna Fish Frittata

Frittata di zucchine
Zucchini Frittata

Verdure alla griglia
Grilled Vegetables

Frutta di stagione
Fruit of the Season

*T*his menu was designed for a warm, sunny summer's day in England, a rare enough occasion. I imagine that my American readers will have the chance of trying these dishes more often, given the near certainty of hot summer weather. It is a very simple and rustic lunch, very Italian.

I thought the occasion called for cheese and green olives to be served with wine before lunch, something that is often done in Italy. Then to the table for the *spaghettini eccitanti,* literally titillating spaghetti. My friend Grazia prepared this dish for us when we arrived at her house in Lerici, near Genoa. The view is breathtaking—a cozy little harbor littered with small boats to the west, the great expanse of the sea to the east. In that balmy Mediterranean setting, the spaghettini was superb, but afterwards I was afraid that perhaps was the secret of its success. After a year I decided to give it a try and found to my delight that it was excellent, served hot or cold, anywhere. It must, however, be made with good olive oil and plain olives kept in brine, with no other flavoring.

Sundried tomatoes have been used in southern Italy for centuries. What is new is that they have been taken up by fashionable people and restaurants in northern Italy, and then in England and America, and launched as a discovery. Sundried tomatoes are plum tomatoes, cut in half and dried on wooden slats in the sun. You see them outside every house in the south, under nets to keep off the flies. The liquid evaporates slowly in the heat, leaving a dried fruit with a concentrated, sweet flavor. They are used here in a sauce, but they most commonly appear as a dish in an antipasto, dressed with olive oil and a little garlic. Sadly enough, what are called sundried tomatoes nowadays are often in fact dried in the oven, a process that does not allow the acidity in the fruit to evaporate, so the tomato is tougher in texture and darker in color than one dried in the sun.

For a *secondo* I suggest cold frittatas. A frittata is an Italian omelet, more like a Spanish tortilla or a Middle Eastern eggah than a French omelet. It can be plain, dressed with parmesan, or mixed with a variety of ingredients; I have an example of each in this menu. I find the frittata with tuna and peppers most appealing visually and gastronomically, provided it is made with the very best tuna packed in olive oil.

Other good frittatas are made with sautéed fennel, mushrooms, and even cooked spaghetti.

The grilled vegetables are particularly delicious when grilled outdoors. Another suitable accompaniment is the tomato, cucumber, and pepper salad on page 115.

Informality being the theme of the day, a bowl of seasonal fruit is perfect for the finale.

Schegge di pecorino e parmigiano con le olive verdi

Pecorino and Parmesan Wedges with Green Olives

For 10 people, allow 1 pound young pecorino, 1 pound parmesan, and 1 pound green olives. Buy the cheeses at a reliable shop with good turnover and ask to taste the cheese to make sure it is good. For eating, as opposed to cooking, I prefer pecorino and parmesan that are young and less strong. I would choose a young Tuscan or Sardinian pecorino and a grana padano. It is similar to Parmigiano-Reggiano, which is better for grating and cooking. Cut the cheese into chunks and serve them with the green olives. (If you cannot find good pecorino, use a good grana or a fresh Parmigiano-Reggiano.)

SERVES 10

Spaghettini eccitanti
Spaghettini with Sundried Tomatoes, Hot Peppers, and Olives

½ pound sundried tomatoes

1 cup red wine vinegar

1 cup extra-virgin olive oil

4 or 5 dried chilies, seeded and crumbled

10 garlic cloves, bruised

12 basil leaves

1 cup (5 ounces) black olives in brine, such as kalamatas

1¾ pounds spaghettini

salt

1. Put the sundried tomatoes in a bowl. Heat the vinegar with 1 cup water to a boil. Pour it over the tomatoes. Leave to soak for 2 to 3 hours.

2. Drain the tomatoes and dry thoroughly. Cut into thin strips and put in a bowl large enough to hold the pasta later. (Or use 2 bowls and divide all the ingredients between them.) Add the oil, chilies, garlic, and basil. Pit the olives, cut into strips, and add to the bowl.

3. Cook the spaghettini in plenty of salted water. If you are serving it cold, drain it when it is chewier than you would like for eating it hot. Turn the pasta into the bowl or bowls and toss very thoroughly, lifting the strands high to separate them. To serve cold, let stand for 2 hours or so, then remove and discard the garlic. To serve hot, prepare the sauce 2 hours in advance for the flavors to blend and cook and add the pasta just before serving.

PREPARATION

The tomatoes can be soaked and sliced up to 2 weeks in advance; they should be kept in a jar covered with olive oil. The olives, too, can be prepared in advance and kept covered with olive oil. You can use the oil for the sauce in Step 2.

SERVES 10

Frittata di cipolle
Onion Frittata

½ to ¾ pound white onions, thinly sliced	5 eggs
2 tablespoons olive oil	4 tablespoons freshly grated parmesan
salt	freshly ground black pepper
	2 tablespoons unsalted butter

1. Put the onions and the oil in an 8-inch nonstick frying pan. Add 1 teaspoon salt to help the onion release its moisture and cook very slowly until the onion has wilted. Stir frequently and add hot water by the tablespoonful if necessary. The onion should turn a golden color but not get brown. Set aside to cool.

2. Break the eggs into a bowl and beat them lightly until well blended. Scoop the onions out of the pan, leaving behind the oil, and mix gently but thoroughly into the eggs. Stir in the parmesan, pepper, and salt.

3. Wipe the frying pan clean with paper towels, add the butter, and heat it until foaming. Pour the egg mixture into the pan, stirring it with a fork while pouring so that the onion doesn't sink to the bottom. Do not stir the mixture further. Turn the heat down to very low and cook for 15 minutes, until the eggs have set and only the top is runny.

4. There are two ways to cook the top. The better method is to turn the frittata over. Loosen the sides with a spatula, then turn the frittata over onto a round dish or lid. Slide the frittata back into the pan and brown for no longer than 1 minute. The second method, which is easier but tends to harden the surface too much, is to put the pan under the broiler for 1 minute, just long enough to set the top. Transfer the frittata to a dish or wooden board lined with paper towels to absorb the extra fat.

5. Leave the frittata to cool. Cut it across in strips about 1½ inches wide and then cut across the other way.

PREPARATION

Frittata should not be cooked more than 1 day in advance.

SERVES 4 TO 6

Frittata di peperoni e tonno
Pepper and Tuna Fish Frittata

———

2 bell peppers, preferably of different colors

4 tablespoons olive oil

1 large white onion, very thinly sliced

salt

5 eggs

1 can (6½ ounces) albacore tuna, packed in olive oil, drained and finely shredded

12 to 15 green olives, pitted and cut into narrow strips

freshly ground black pepper

1. Wash and dry the peppers. Cut in half, remove the core, seeds, and ribs, and cut into thin short strips.

2. Put 3 tablespoons of the oil in a pan, add the onion and pepper and sprinkle with salt to help release the liquid and keep the onion and pepper from burning. Cover with a piece of buttered wax paper and with a tight-fitting lid. Leave to sweat until very soft, about 40 minutes. Keep an eye on the pan and add hot water by the tablespoonful whenever the vegetables are cooking dry.

3. Lightly beat the eggs and add the tuna, the olives, and pepper to taste.

4. When the vegetable mixture is ready, let it cool a little, then add it to the egg mixture, scooping it out of the pan with a slotted spoon. Leave the cooking juices in the pan. Mix everything together very thoroughly.

5. Put the remaining tablespoon of the oil in an 8-inch nonstick pan. When the oil is hot, add the egg mixture. Turn the heat to very low and cook until the bottom is set but the top still runny, about 15 minutes.

6. To finish the frittata, follow the directions for onion frittata, Steps 4 and 5, on page 79.

SERVES 6

Frittata di zucchine
Zucchini Frittata

———

2 zucchini (³⁄₄ pound)	*5 eggs*
salt	*freshly ground black pepper*
2 tablespoons olive oil	*1 tablespoon dried oregano*
2 garlic cloves, peeled and finely sliced	*6 tablespoons freshly grated parmesan*
2 tablespoons chopped flat-leaf parsley	*2 tablespoons unsalted butter*

1. Wash the zucchini thoroughly, dry with paper towels, and cut into ½-inch cubes. If you have time, put the cubes in a colander, sprinkle with salt, and let stand for 30 minutes to release some liquid. Dry the zucchini and set aside.

2. Put the oil, garlic, and parsley in an 8-inch nonstick frying pan. When the aroma of the garlic rises, remove it and add the zucchini. Cook until lightly browned, about 10 to 15 minutes, stirring frequently.

3. Meanwhile lightly beat the eggs in a bowl until blended. Season with salt and pepper and stir in the oregano and parmesan.

4. When the zucchini is done, remove from the pan with a slotted spoon and transfer to the bowl with the eggs. Follow the directions for onion frittata, Step 3 to the end, on page 79.

SERVES 4 TO 5

Verdure alla griglia
Grilled Vegetables

~~~~~~

	BASIL SAUCE
2 eggplants	2 tablespoons pine nuts
salt	3/4 cup basil leaves
2/3 cup extra-virgin olive oil	4 garlic cloves
freshly ground black pepper	1/2 cup flat-leaf parsley leaves
4 zucchini	2/3 cup extra-virgin olive oil
10 large mushrooms (3/4 pound)	salt and freshly ground black pepper
4 bell peppers	

1. Wash and dry the eggplants. Cut them across into slices about ⅓ inch thick and put them in a colander. Sprinkle liberally with salt and set aside while you prepare the other vegetables.

2. Heat the broiler and oil a broiling pan or baking tray. To save time, fill the pan or tray with as many vegetables as fit, so that they cook together. Broil them in the following order to allow for the difference in cooking times.

3. Wash and dry the zucchini, cut off the ends, and cut them lengthwise into ½-inch-thick slices. If the slices are too long cut them across in half. Put them in the broiling pan, drizzle with olive oil, sprinkle with salt and pepper and broil on both sides.

4. Rinse the eggplants and pat them dry. Put them in the pan as soon as there is room. Pour some olive oil over them and season only with pepper, since they have already been salted. The eggplants will take 4 to 5 minutes on each side. They should be tender when pricked with a fork.

5. Wipe the mushrooms and detach the stems, which you can use for another dish. Broil the mushroom caps, moistened with olive oil and seasoned with salt and pepper. The mushrooms are the quickest to cook.

6. Grill the peppers directly over a flame, turning them over and over so that all the skin is charred. As soon as they are cool enough to handle, peel them by wiping them with paper towels. Do not rinse them under running water, which would wash away the juice. Cut the peppers in half, remove the core, seeds, and ribs, and cut them into wide strips.

7. Arrange all the vegetables on a very large dish or, preferably, 2 dishes so that you can place one at each end of the table.

8. For the basil sauce, toast the pine nuts in a nonstick frying pan until just golden, shaking the pan very frequently. Put them in the food processor with the basil, garlic, and parsley and process, pulsing until very coarsely chopped. Slowly add the oil through the beaker with the machine running. Add salt and pepper to taste. Spoon over the vegetables about 1 hour before serving. (If you do not have a food processor, pound the pine nuts, basil, garlic, and parsley in a mortar moistened with 2 or 3 tablespoons of the oil. Add the oil while beating with a small wire whisk or fork.)

PREPARATION

All the vegetables can be broiled or grilled up to 1 day in advance. Keep them, separated and covered, in the refrigerator. The sauce can be made up to 2 days in advance and chilled.

SERVES 10

Prosciutto e melone
Prosciutto with Melon

—◆—

Linguine aglio, olio, e peperoncino
Linguine with Garlic, Oil, and Hot Peppers

—◆—

Il polpettone di tonno della Mamma
Tuna Roll

—◆—

Salsina all'uovo
Egg and Lemon Sauce

—◆—

Pomodori al basilico
Tomatoes with Basil

—◆—

Gelato di fragola all'aceto balsamico
Strawberry Ice Cream Flavored with Balsamic Vinegar (page 287)

—◆—

Sorbetto di limone al sapor di basilico
Basil-Lemon Sorbet (page 109)

I am not, in general, too fond of luncheon parties; they break the day in two, leaving a second half that seems to lack focus, except in summer, when there is the prospect of sitting in the garden. The menu should be simple, with a cold *secondo* and no dessert, except for one or two ice creams made one or two days before.

A lovely platter of prosciutto and melon or prosciutto and figs is the ideal summer antipasto. You will need 1½ pounds of prosciutto and two canteloupe melons or a dozen ripe figs.

The first course of any of my lunches is definitely pasta, because I love it and because it requires a minimum of work. Linguine makes the simplest of all pasta dishes, one that is most popular with southern Italians. No grated cheese is needed for this typically Neapolitan quick pasta.

My mother's tuna roll is different from the usual kind. She uses tuna fish, eggs, and parmesan and seasons it with nutmeg, an extremely successful combination of flavors. It is important to buy good tuna packed in olive oil. Italian and Spanish brands are available in gourmet shops and many supermarkets. The roll can be covered with a thin mayonnaise or with the egg and lemon sauce in this menu.

Ripe and juicy tomatoes, cut in half, drizzled with the best olive oil, and sprinkled with a few torn basil leaves, have always been a firm favorite of mine. Other salads to serve would be a green salad such as that on page 325, and/or the tomato, cucumber, and pepper salad on page 115.

I would end with two ice creams, one the exquisite strawberry ice cream flavored with balsamic vinegar on page 287, the other the lemon sorbet flavored with basil (page 109).

Linguine aglio, olio, e peperoncino
Linguine with Garlic, Oil, and Hot Peppers

2 pounds linguine	*6 garlic cloves, peeled and sliced*
salt	*2 or 3 dried chilies, according to taste,*
⅔ cup extra-virgin olive oil	*seeded and crumbled*

1. Cook the pasta in plenty of salted boiling water. You might prefer to cook it following the Agnesi method on page 335, which requires less careful attention.

2. Meanwhile, put the oil, garlic, and chilies in a frying pan large enough to hold all the pasta. Cook for 1 minute over low heat. As soon as the garlic aroma rises, the sauce is ready. Take off the heat immediately or the garlic might burn, and this would ruin the taste of the oil.

3. When the pasta is ready, drain, reserving 1 cup of water. Transfer the pasta immediately to the frying pan. Stir-fry for a minute or so, lifting the pasta high into the air so that every strand is coated with oil. Add a couple of tablespoons of the reserved pasta water if the dish seems too dry. Serve at once, preferably straight from the pan.

PREPARATION

This dish, like every pasta dish, must be made at the last minute.

SERVES 10

Il polpettone di tonno della Mamma
Tuna Roll

⸻

2 cans (6½ ounces each) tuna,
preferably albacore tuna packed in
olive oil, drained

3 eggs

1 egg yolk

2 hard-boiled eggs, shelled and
coarsely chopped

¾ cup freshly grated parmesan

2 pinches grated nutmeg

freshly ground black pepper

salt

1 cup wine vinegar

1 cup dry white wine

10 to 12 sprigs flat-leaf parsley

2 small onions, sliced

3 tablespoons olive oil

1 teaspoon lemon juice

egg and lemon sauce (recipe follows)

black olives, lemon slices, and capers,
for garnish

1. Flake and mash the tuna in a bowl. Add the eggs, egg yolk, hard-boiled eggs, parmesan, nutmeg, and plenty of pepper. Taste and check salt. Mix thoroughly.

2. Rinse a piece of cheesecloth under cold water, wring it out until just damp, and lay it out double on the work surface. Place the tuna mixture on the cloth and roll it into a log about 3 inches in diameter. Pat it all over to eliminate air pockets. Wrap the cheesecloth around the tuna log and tie both ends with string.

3. Place the roll with the vinegar, wine, parsley, onions, and a little salt in an oval casserole that just fits. Add enough water to cover the roll by about ½ inch. Cover the casserole and bring to a boil. Cook over very low heat for 45 minutes.

4. Remove the tuna roll, place it between 2 plates, and put a weight on top. Leave to cool for at least 2 hours.

5. When the roll is cold, unwrap it carefully and cut into ½-inch slices. Arrange the slices, very slightly overlapping, on a dish. Mix together the olive oil and the lemon juice and spoon over the slices 2 hours before serving. Coat lightly

continued

with egg and lemon sauce (recipe follows) and garnish with black olives, lemon slices, and capers. If you prefer, pass the sauce around separately in two small bowls and let people help themselves.

PREPARATION

The tuna roll can be made and cooked up to 2 days in advance and kept wrapped in the refrigerator. Slice it, bring it back to room temperature, and dress it with the oil and lemon.

SERVES 10

Salsina all'uovo

Egg and Lemon Sauce

—〰—

5 egg yolks	*5 tablespoons lemon juice*
1 teaspoon English mustard powder	*6 tablespoons extra-virgin olive oil*
salt and freshly ground black pepper	*½ cup heavy cream*

1. Whisk the egg yolks in a bowl. Add the mustard, salt and pepper, and lemon juice and put the bowl over a saucepan half full of simmering water or use a double boiler.

2. Add the oil slowly while whisking constantly, until the sauce thickens. Be careful not to let it boil, or the egg will curdle. Remove from the heat and beat in the cream. Return to the bain-marie or double boiler and cook for another couple of minutes, beating constantly.

3. Transfer the bowl or top of the double boiler to a large metal bowl of cold water and leave to cool.

PREPARATION

The sauce can be prepared up to 1 day in advance and refrigerated. Remove from the refrigerator at least 2 hours before you want to use it.

MAKES ABOUT 1¼ CUPS

Pomodori al basilico
Tomatoes with Basil

For 10 people you need about 4 pounds ripe but firm tomatoes, preferably plum tomatoes. Blanch them in boiling water for 15 seconds, then plunge them into a bowl of cold water. Peel and cut in half. Squeeze out some of the seeds. Sprinkle with salt and place, cut-side down, on a dish to drain. Place in the refrigerator for at least 1 hour. Dry the tomatoes inside and out and put them on a large platter. Dribble ½ cup of your best olive oil all over them and season with a generous grinding of black pepper. Place 1 small basil leaf or a piece of a large leaf on each tomato. Place a thin slice of garlic on top of the basil, so that people who do not like raw garlic can see it and remove it. Serve chilled.

PREPARATION

You can prepare the tomatoes up to 6 hours in advance and keep them upside down on a dish in the refrigerator. Dress just before serving.

SERVES 10

DINNER FOR SIX

Soffiato di capelli d'angelo
Angel Hair Soufflé

—

Filetti di pesce con scaglie di patate
Fish Fillets with Potato Scales

—

Budino alla pesca
Peach Mousse

*T*his soufflé is one of my oldest recipes, which has been revised—and improved—by one of my good friends who is an excellent cook. It is an elegant dish yet quick and easy to make and there is little danger of it appearing at the table as a fallen soufflé.

The fish dish is one of the few dishes that I serve directly onto my guests' plates. Since it is rather difficult to handle, I prefer to serve it in the kitchen when no one is watching. I have found flounder to be the best fish for this recipe because of its size and the firmness of its flesh. Sole is good too, but it must be large enough for one fish to serve two people. Both fish lend themselves to simple treatment as in this recipe, where the only flavoring is melted butter and dill. If possible, buy whole fish and have the fishmonger fillet them. Bring home the heads, bones, and skin for a fish broth (page 340). Serve a green salad after, not with, the fish.

I love the peach mousse, but then I love peaches. Be that as it may, this is a delicious dessert. It calls for peaches that are full of flavor, so buy white peaches if you can. They are usually more fragrant than yellow ones, but unfortunately they are rarer.

Soffiato di capelli d'angelo
Angel Hair Soufflé

8 tablespoons (1 stick) unsalted butter

2/3 cup freshly grated parmesan

2 1/3 cups whole milk

4 1/2 tablespoons flour

2 ounces gruyère

2 ounces bel paese

1/2 teaspoon grated nutmeg

4 eggs, separated

2 egg whites

salt and freshly ground black pepper

1/2 pound dried angel hair pasta or egg vermicelli

1 tablespoon oil

1. Generously butter a 2-quart soufflé dish and sprinkle the buttered surface with a little grated parmesan.

2. Prepare the soufflé base. Heat the milk to simmering. In a separate saucepan, melt 4 tablespoons of the butter, blend in the flour, and cook for 30 seconds. Remove the pan from the heat and gradually add the milk, beating vigorously with a wooden spoon. When all the milk has been incorporated, transfer the sauce to the top of a double boiler and cook with the lid on for at least 30 minutes, stirring occasionally. If you do not have a double boiler, put the saucepan into another pan half full of simmering water.

3. Meanwhile grate the gruyère and the bel paese through the large holes of a grater. When the sauce is ready, mix in the cheeses and the nutmeg. Allow to cool a little and then add the egg yolks.

4. Mix very thoroughly and add seasonings to taste, with emphasis on the pepper.

5. Preheat the oven to 400° F.

6. Drop all the angel hair pasta or vermicelli nests one at a time into plenty of salted boiling water with 1 tablespoon of oil. Mix quickly with a fork to prevent the pasta strands sticking together. Drain when very al dente, reserving 1 cup of the water. Return the pasta immediately to the pan, add the remaining butter and a couple of tablespoons of the reserved water. Mix thoroughly, then add the cheese sauce. Toss well.

continued

7. Whisk the 6 egg whites until stiff but not dry and fold, by the spoonful, into the pasta mixture. Turn the mixture into the prepared soufflé dish and bake for 25 minutes, until the top is golden brown. Serve at once.

PREPARATION

The dish can be prepared up to 1 day in advance, but do not add the egg whites until ready to bake.

SERVES 6

Filetti di pesce con le scaglie di patate
Fish Fillets with Potato Scales

---

6 medium-size waxy potatoes (about 1¼ pounds)

6 ½-pound fillets of flounder or sole

salt and freshly ground black pepper

6 tablespoons unsalted butter

6 tablespoons chopped dill

1. Wash the potatoes and boil them in their skins for 5 minutes. Peel them as soon as you can handle them and set aside to cool.

2. Skin the fillets if necessary and wash and dry them with paper towels. Sprinkle with salt and pepper and lay them in a baking dish or pan, preferably metal, greased with 1 tablespoon of the butter.

3. Preheat the oven to 400° F.

4. When the potatoes are cold (they slice better when cold), cut them into very thin slices.

5. Sprinkle some dill over each fillet. Cover each fillet with the potatoes, laying them down like the scales of a fish. Sprinkle with salt and pepper. Melt the remaining butter and pour it over the potatoes, using a brush to cover all the gaps and corners.

6. Bake for 15 to 20 minutes, basting 2 or 3 times, until the potatoes are tender.

7. Place the dish under a very hot broiler to brown the surface of the potatoes. Place the fillets on individual heated plates and spoon over the cooking juices. Serve at once.

PREPARATION

The dish can be prepared, but not baked, up to 1 hour in advance but no more.

SERVES 6

Budino alla pesca
Peach Mousse

1½ pounds ripe peaches, preferably white

⅔ cup sweet white wine

¾ cup sugar

1½ tablespoons unflavored gelatin

6 tablespoons freshly squeezed lemon juice

1 cup heavy cream

½ pound strawberries for garnish

1. If the peaches are really ripe they should peel quite easily. If not, put them in a bowl and cover with boiling water. Leave them for about 20 seconds, then refresh them under cold water. Peel them and cut in half.

2. Poach the peaches in the wine with the sugar until tender. Leave to cool. Puree coarsely in a food mill set with a large-hole disk. You can also mash them with a fork.

3. Sprinkle the gelatin over 4 tablespoons of the lemon juice, leave for a minute or so, then cook over very low heat until the liquid is clear.

4. Partly whip the cream and add to the peach puree. Mix a couple of table-spoons of the cream and peach mixture into the dissolved gelatin, then spoon this back into the cream and peach mixture. Fold very thoroughly.

5. Wet a 4½-cup ring mold with cold water. Spoon the peach mixture into the mold and chill for at least 4 hours.

6. Wash, hull, and dry the strawberries. Put them in a bowl and sprinkle with 1 tablespoon of sugar and the remaining lemon juice. Cover the bowl and chill.

7. To unmold, run a spatula down the side of the mold. Put a round dish over the mold and turn it over. If the mousse does not drop, place a cloth soaked with hot water over the mold and give the mold a few sharp jerks. You should now be able to lift the mold off the pudding.

8. Put some strawberries in the center of the ring and the rest around the dish for garnish.

PREPARATION

The pudding can be prepared up to 1 day in advance and refrigerated. The strawberries must be prepared no longer than 2 or 3 hours in advance or they will "cook" in the lemon juice.

SERVES 6

I ricchi e i poveri

Shrimp and Bean Salad

Cannelloni di melanzane in salsa

Eggplant Cannelloni with Tomato Sauce

Formaggio

Cheese

Granita al caffè

Coffee Granita

I often serve meatless dinners, especially on informal occasions like this one. The first course, *I ricchi e i poveri,* literally means the rich and the poor, and it is easy to see why. Inspired by the classic tuna and bean salad, it was created by Tuscan restaurateurs who, though not afraid to alter old recipes, liked to stay within their tradition of simplicity.

The *secondo* I got from Betsy Newell, a friend and superb cook, who runs a cookery school in Kensington, London. She ate the eggplant cannelloni somewhere in Italy, and she later added her special touch, the tomato sauce. Remember to serve plenty of good bread to mop up the tomato sauce, or prepare some mashed potatoes. The eggplant is also good served at room temperature.

This being a cozy informal dinner, a platter of cheeses would be just right. It should include at least three different kinds, ranging from a strong blue cheese to one that is mild and soft.

The dessert I suggest is coffee granita. But if raspberries are still available, you might prefer the dessert on page 15.

I ricchi e i poveri
Shrimp and Bean Salad

¾ pound dried cannellini beans (1¼ cups) or two 16-ounce cans cannellini beans (about 6 cups)

2 onions, cut in half

2 bay leaves

½ cup extra-virgin olive oil

salt

6 tablespoons lemon juice

1 tablespoon wine vinegar

pinch cayenne

1 garlic clove, chopped (optional)

1 pound raw shrimp

8 tablespoons chopped flat-leaf parsley

1. If you are using dried beans, put them in a bowl, cover with cold water, and soak overnight. Drain, rinse, and put them in an earthenware stockpot with the onions and the bay leaves. Do not add salt, as it might make the beans burst. Cover with water by about 2 inches and cook at a slow and steady simmer until done, no longer than 1½ hours. Drain the beans (you can keep the liquid for a soup for another occasion) and remove and discard the onions and bay leaves. (If you are using canned cannellini, empty the cans into a colander and rinse the beans.)

2. In a large bowl, combine the olive oil, lemon juice, wine vinegar, and garlic. Mix well. Add the beans, and, if you are using dried beans, season with 2 teaspoons salt. The canned ones are already salted.

3. Place the shrimp in a saucepan, cover with cold water, and add 1 tablespoon vinegar and 1 tablespoon salt. Bring to a boil and cook until a white foam forms on the surface. Drain immediately, shell the shrimp while they are still warm and cut into small pieces. Half an hour before serving, mix the shrimp gently with the beans. Serve at room temperature, sprinkled with parsley.

PREPARATION

The beans can be cooked up to 2 days in advance and refrigerated, but the shrimp must be cooked and served the day they are bought.

SERVES 6

Cannelloni di melanzane in salsa
Eggplant Cannelloni with Tomato Sauce

———

2 eggplants (12 to 14 ounces each)

4 celery stalks (1½ cups)

2 or 3 leeks (1½ cups), white part only

1 pound zucchini

7 tablespoons olive oil

salt and freshly ground black pepper

½ pound Emmentaler

1½ cups fresh white breadcrumbs

2 tablespoons chopped fresh herbs, including rosemary, thyme, oregano, and parsley

2 garlic cloves, finely chopped

2 cups tomato sauce, canned or homemade (page 336)

1. Wash and dry the eggplants, leaving the skin on. Cut them lengthwise into ¼-inch-thick slices. Salt the slices and place in a colander for at least 30 minutes to drain the bitter juices.

2. Wash and dry the celery, leeks, and zucchini and cut them into 2-inch-long julienne strips. Sauté the vegetables lightly in 3 tablespoons of the oil, beginning with the celery alone, as it takes a little longer to cook, then the zucchini, and finally the leeks. Cook the vegetables until just tender. This takes about 6 minutes in all. Season well with salt and pepper and set aside to cool.

3. Cut the Emmentaler into similar julienne strips and mix into the vegetables. Mix together the breadcrumbs, herbs, and garlic.

4. Rinse the eggplant slices and pat dry. Brush each side lightly with olive oil. Broil quickly until soft but not overcooked. Set aside.

5. Preheat the oven to 400° F.

6. Choose an ovenproof serving dish large enough for the eggplant rolls to fit snugly in a single layer. Spread half of the tomato sauce over the bottom of the serving dish. Season each eggplant slice with salt and pepper. Place a rounded tablespoon of the vegetable/cheese mixture in the middle of each slice and wrap the eggplant around the filling along the length of the slice. Place in the dish and sprinkle with the herbed breadcrumb mixture. Drizzle over the remaining oil. Bake for 10 to 15 minutes, or until the cheese begins to melt and the rolls are thoroughly heated.

continued

7. Remove from the oven and let the dish rest for 5 minutes to allow the flavors to blend. Serve with the remaining tomato sauce.

PREPARATION

The entire dish can be prepared 2 days in advance and refrigerated in the covered baking dish. Heat through just before serving.

SERVES 6

Granita al caffè
Coffee Granita

---

4 cups freshly brewed espresso coffee	*1 cup heavy cream*
7 tablespoons sugar	*2 tablespoons confectioners' sugar*

1. Heat the coffee, add the sugar, and stir to dissolve. Taste and add a little more sugar, to taste. Pour the coffee into freezer trays, let cool, and freeze until solid.

2. Plunge the bottom of the tray in a bowl of hot water for a few seconds, break up the coffee ice into chunks, and process with an electric beater or food processor until small crystals form. Return to the trays and place back in the freezer.

3. Before serving, place 6 long-stemmed wine glasses in the refrigerator to chill.

4. Whip the cream and stir in the confectioners' sugar.

5. Remove the granita from the freezer. If too solid, process again for a few seconds just before serving. Spoon the granita into the chilled glasses and top with whipped cream.

PREPARATION

The coffee granita can be prepared up to 1 week in advance.

SERVES 6

DINNER FOR SIX

Pasticcio di pasta e melanzane in bianco
Baked Ziti with Eggplant

Filetti di San Pietro in salsa di broccoli
Fillet of Flounder with Broccoli Sauce

Sorbetto di limone al basilico
Basil~Lemon Sorbet

*T*he excellent *pasticcio* in this menu proves once again the eggplant's rare ability to blend with other flavors while retaining its own. Here the eggplant, so often treated in a rustic and earthy manner, is combined with a delicate cheese-flavored béchamel, a sauce usually associated with elegant dishes. The pasta shape I like best for this pasticcio is ziti. Since it is thick and hollow it holds the sauce, and it matches the size of the eggplant pieces.

I tasted the second course years ago at the Restaurant Dante in Bologna. I still remember my surprise at being offered such an unlikely combination as fish and broccoli in a restaurant in Bologna, where dishes outside the traditional, yet excellent, range of local cooking are viewed with suspicion.

The fish at the Dante was the fine but rather ugly John Dory, a fish with a very large head, which accounts, with the backbone, for two-thirds of its weight. Unfortunately, John Dory hardly exists outside the Mediterranean, but flounder or sole fillets are perfect substitutes.

Buttered new potatoes would be a welcome though not necessary accompaniment, and afterwards a green salad, for which my favorite recipe is on page 325.

After these two courses, which are quite substantial, you will want a sorbet with a sharp edge to cleanse the palate. Besides being delicious, this one looks very pretty, pale lemon green speckled with dark green basil. While the flavor of the lemon is immediately identifiable, the basil blends in so well as to become a mystery ingredient. It transforms an everyday lemon sorbet into a conversation piece.

Pasticcio di pasta e melanzane in bianco
Baked Ziti with Eggplant

1½ pounds eggplant	*1 small dried chili, seeded*
salt	*2 garlic cloves*
BECHAMEL	*a bunch of flat-leaf parsley (½ cup)*
2½ cups whole milk	*5 tablespoons olive oil*
2 bay leaves	*¾ pound ziti or penne*
4 tablespoons unsalted butter	*½ cup finely grated gruyère*
3 tablespoons flour	*½ cup finely grated parmesan*
salt and freshly ground black pepper	

1. Wash and peel the eggplants. Cut into thick slices and then into strips about 1¾ inches long, the same length as the pasta you are using. Put the eggplant in a colander, layered with salt, and leave to drain for about 1 hour. Rinse and dry the eggplant with paper towels.

2. Meanwhile, make the béchamel. Heat the milk with the bay leaves to the boiling point, turn off and set aside to infuse for about 30 minutes, if you have the time. Melt the butter, add the flour, and cook for 1 minute or so, stirring constantly. Bring the milk back to the simmer and add a little at a time to the roux off the heat. Beat hard to incorporate. When all the milk has been added, return to the heat, add salt and pepper to taste, and bring to a boil. Set the pan on a flame tamer or in a bain-marie or double boiler and continue cooking for 20 minutes or so. Remove and discard the bay leaves.

3. Chop the chili, garlic, and parsley together and put in a frying pan with the oil. Fry gently for 1 minute, then add the eggplant. Sauté over low heat for about 7 to 10 minutes until soft, turning frequently. Taste and adjust seasonings. Turn off the heat and set aside.

4. Preheat the oven to 400° F.

5. Boil the pasta in plenty of salted boiling water. Drain when al dente and transfer to the pan with the eggplant. Sauté the pasta for 2 to 3 minutes, mixing it well with the eggplant.

6. Butter a shallow dish large enough for the pasta and eggplant. Add them.

7. Add the cheeses to the béchamel. Taste and check seasonings. Pour the sauce over the pasta and bake for 20 minutes until a light crust has formed on top. Remove from the oven and let stand 5 minutes before serving.

PREPARATION

The dish can be prepared 1 day in advance and covered with plastic wrap. Reheat in a 300-degree oven until hot all through.

SERVES 6

Filetti di San Pietro in salsa di broccoli
Fillet of Flounder with Broccoli Sauce

4 tablespoons unsalted butter | 1 cup fish broth (page 340)
2 shallots, finely chopped | freshly ground black pepper
salt | 2 pounds flounder fillets
1¼ pounds broccoli | 4 tablespoons heavy cream

1. Preheat the oven to 375° F.

2. Put half the butter in a sauté pan. Add the shallots and a little salt and sauté for 5 to 7 minutes until soft.

3. Remove the tough outer layer of the broccoli stalks. Wash the broccoli thoroughly, cut into small pieces, and add to the shallots with a small ladleful of the broth. Cook until quite tender, adding a small ladleful of the broth whenever needed—there should always be broth in the pan. It will take about 20 minutes. Season with salt and pepper to taste.

4. While the broccoli is cooking, butter a baking dish with the remaining butter and lay the fish fillets in it. Season with salt and pepper, cover the dish with foil, and bake for 10 minutes.

5. When the broccoli is done, put it with all the cooking juices in the food processor and puree. Spoon the puree into a clean saucepan and add the cream. Bring slowly to a boil and cook over very low heat for 5 minutes, stirring frequently. Taste and check seasoning. Keep the sauce warm.

6. Transfer the fish fillets to a heated serving dish and surround them with the broccoli sauce. Pour the cooking juice from the fish over the dish and serve at once. If you find it easier for serving, place the fish on individual heated plates and spoon the sauce around it.

PREPARATION

The sauce can be prepared a few hours in advance and refrigerated, tightly covered with plastic wrap. The fish must be cooked at the last minute.

SERVES 6

Sorbetto di limone al basilico
Basil-Lemon Sorbet

———

8 lemons (to yield 1¼ cups juice)
2 oranges (to yield ⅔ cup juice)
1½ cups sugar

24 large young basil leaves, torn or chopped

1. Scrub, wash, and dry the fruit. Remove the rind, without cutting into the white pith, and put it into a saucepan. Add the sugar and 2½ cups water. Bring slowly to a boil and simmer until the sugar has dissolved. Turn the heat up and boil rapidly for 3 or 4 minutes. Remove from the heat and allow the syrup to cool completely.

2. Meanwhile squeeze the lemons and the oranges. Strain the juice and add to the cold syrup, together with the basil leaves.

3. If you have an ice-cream machine, pour the mixture into it and freeze according to the manufacturer's instructions. If you do not have an ice-cream machine, pour the mixture into a metal bowl and freeze for about 2 hours, until the mixture is half frozen. Remove from the freezer, put the bowl in the sink (because the mixture will splatter), and beat with a hand-held electric mixer or a whisk. This will break down the crystals. You can also do this in a food processor. Freeze again and then beat once more. Return the bowl to the freezer. Transfer to the refrigerator about 30 minutes before serving.

PREPARATION

Sorbets, especially those based on fruit, lose flavor if made more than 24 hours in advance.

SERVES 6

DINNER FOR SIX

Ravioli di pesce
Fish Ravioli

Gamberi in salsa all'abruzzese
Shrimp in a Piquant Tomato Sauce

Insalata di pomodori, cetrioli, e peperoni
Tomato, Cucumber, and Pepper Salad

Gelato di albicocca
Apricot Ice Cream

*T*his is an elegant menu for fish lovers, which opens grandly with white ravioli filled with fish and ricotta.

Until twenty years ago ravioli were either *di grasso* (filled with meat) or *di magro* (filled with ricotta and spinach). With the advent of *nuova cucina, nuovi ravioli* appeared everywhere, some more successful than others. These *ravioli di pesce* are to my mind the best of the newcomers, combining in a very Italian way three basic ingredients in the best tradition: pasta, fish, and ricotta. The only catch is that they are none too quick to make. But ravioli never were everyday cooking. In my home in Milan tortellini and ravioli were made no more than three or four times a year: always at Christmas, for *Sabato Grasso* (the last Saturday before Lent) and in November, when pumpkins were in season. Then we had *ravioli di zucca,* large ravioli filled with pumpkin puree, *mostarda di Cremona,* and crumbled amaretti.

The *ravioli di pesce* are a perfect preamble to the second course. The recipe for large shrimp in a piquant tomato sauce is an old one from Abruzzi. The flavor of the shrimp is emphasized by a touch of anchovy paste, and they are enveloped in the classic Mediterranean ambience of tomato and garlic. Hot peppers, the characteristic spice of Abruzzi cooking, are added. The shrimp and tomatoes cook for a very short time, so that their fresh flavor comes through intact. You can serve some long-grain rice tossed with olive oil to mop up the sauce of the shrimp.

After that you need a salad, and for a change from the usual green salad I suggest a very summery and colorful salad. For best results you must macerate the onion in lemon and sugar for 24 hours. I have made the apricot ice cream with raw apricots and with poached ones, and I prefer the poached. The syrup and orange juice bring out more of the flavor of the fruit. Amaretto is optional, but it does add a deep almondy tone that goes well with the apricots. Pass around a dish of almond crescents (page 341) if you like. They are very good, and they go well with the ice cream.

Ravioli di pesce
Fish Ravioli

FILLING

4 tablespoons unsalted butter

1 shallot, very finely chopped

¾ pound white fish fillet, such as flounder, turbot, sea bass, or sea bream

1 tablespoon anchovy paste

½ cup dry white wine

¾ cup ricotta

4 tablespoons heavy cream

3 tablespoons freshly grated parmesan

2 egg yolks

salt and freshly ground black pepper

homemade pasta made with 1½ cups unbleached flour, 2 large eggs, and 1 tablespoon olive oil

SAUCE

6 tablespoons unsalted butter

3 tablespoons very finely snipped fresh chives

freshly grated Parmigiano-Reggiano

1. Heat the butter and the shallot and cook for 5 minutes, stirring and pressing the shallot against the side of the saucepan to release the flavor. Meanwhile, clean, trim, and cut the fish into very small pieces and add to the pan together with the anchovy paste. Cook until the fish becomes opaque, no longer than 2 minutes. Turn the heat up and splash with the wine, then boil rapidly until it has totally evaporated. Coarsely flake the fish, transfer to a bowl, and let cool for a few minutes. Add the ricotta, cream, parmesan, and egg yolks. Season with salt and pepper to taste and mix very well. Set aside.

2. Make the pasta, following the directions on page 333. Cut off a quarter of the dough, leaving the rest wrapped in plastic wrap. Thin the dough down in the pasta machine notch by notch as far as the next-to-the-last notch, as described on page 334. If you are rolling out by hand, roll the dough out as thin as you possibly can. Cover all but one strip of the dough with a dish towel to keep it from drying.

3. Place small dollops of filling in a straight line along the length of the strip, spacing them about 1½ inches apart and the same distance from the edge. Fold the dough over the filling and using a pastry wheel, trim the edges where they meet. Then cut into squares between each mound of filling. Separate the squares and squeeze out any air. Seal tight with moistened fingers. In dry

climates or hot kitchens, brush all around the edges and in between each dollop of filling with cold water before folding the dough over the filling.

4. Place the ravioli on clean, dry dish towels. Do not let them touch or they will stick together. Cut off another quarter of the dough, knead in any trimmings from the previous batch, and thin the strip down as before. Continue making ravioli until you have used up all the filling and/or all the dough. Leave the ravioli uncovered until they are dry; you can then cover them with a cloth.

5. Bring a large saucepan full of water to a boil. Add 1½ tablespoons salt and the olive oil. Drop the ravioli gently into the pan and bring back to a boil. Adjust the heat so that the water simmers gently; if it boils too hard the ravioli might break. Cook until done, about 2 to 3 minutes, stirring gently every now and then. The best way to tell is to try one: the pasta should be al dente at the edge. Lift the ravioli out with a slotted spoon and pat them dry with paper towels. Transfer immediately to a heated buttered bowl.

6. While the ravioli are cooking, melt the butter for the sauce in a small saucepan. Add the chives and pour over the ravioli. Serve at once, passing around the grated Parmigiano-Reggiano in a separate bowl.

PREPARATION

The ravioli can be prepared up to 1 day in advance and refrigerated. Sprinkle them with semolina and place in plastic containers between sheets of wax paper. Ravioli stored in this way can also be frozen. Cook them when still frozen.

SERVES 6

Gamberi in salsa all'abruzzese
Shrimp in a Piquant Tomato Sauce

2 pounds large shrimp

4 garlic cloves, peeled and finely chopped

1 cup flat-leaf parsley leaves

1 or 2 dried chilies, according to taste, seeded

6 tablespoons extra-virgin olive oil

2 teaspoons anchovy paste

1 pound ripe tomatoes, preferably plum tomatoes, peeled, seeded, and very coarsely chopped

½ cup dry white wine

salt

freshly ground black pepper (optional)

1. Shell and devein the shrimp. Rinse and set aside in a colander.

2. Chop the garlic, parsley, and chilies either by hand or in a food processor.

3. Put the oil in a large sauté pan, preferably a round earthenware pan, and add the parsley mixture. Sauté for 1 minute over low heat, stirring very frequently, then mix in the anchovy paste. Add the shrimp and the tomatoes. Turn them over once or twice in the pan, then splash with the wine. Cook for 5 minutes. If you have a nice-looking sauté pan, serve directly from it.

PREPARATION

You can prepare the shrimp and the parsley mixture in advance. You can even do the *soffritto* (fry the mixture) beforehand, but cook the shrimp just before serving.

SERVES 6

Insalata di pomodori, cetrioli, e peperoni
Tomato, Cucumber, and Pepper Salad

1 large red onion
1/3 cup freshly squeezed lemon juice
2 teaspoons sugar
1 cucumber
salt

4 ripe tomatoes
3 red and yellow bell peppers
1/2 cup extra-virgin olive oil
freshly ground black pepper

1. Peel the onions and slice them very thin. Put them in a bowl and add 6 tablespoons of the lemon juice and the sugar. Mix well, cover the bowl, and leave for 24 hours.

2. The next day, peel the cucumber and slice it thin. Put the slices in a bowl and sprinkle with salt. Leave for 1 hour.

3. Wash and dry the tomatoes, slice them thin, and place in a salad bowl.

4. Wash and dry the peppers, cut them into quarters, remove the cores, ribs, and seeds, and cut the quarters across into 1/3-inch strips. Add to the bowl.

5. Squeeze the liquid out of the cucumber and add the cucumber to the bowl. Do the same with the onion.

6. Just before serving, toss with the olive oil and the remaining lemon juice and season with a generous amount of pepper and some salt. Taste and correct seasonings, adding a little more lemon juice, according to your taste.

PREPARATION

The tomatoes and peppers can be prepared up to 1 hour in advance, after you have sliced and salted the cucumber.

SERVES 6

Gelato di albicocca
Apricot Ice Cream

1 pound apricots
½ cup sugar
6 tablespoons orange juice

⅔ cup heavy cream
1 tablespoon confectioners' sugar
2 tablespoons amaretto

1. Wash the apricots, cut in half, and remove the pits.

2. Put the sugar, orange juice, and 4 tablespoons water in a heavy pan. Bring gently to a boil and simmer for about 3 minutes, stirring very frequently, to dissolve the sugar. Add the apricots, cover, and cook until soft.

3. Pour the contents of the pan into a food processor or blender and process or blend to a coarse puree.

4. Lightly whip the cream with the confectioners' sugar. Mix in the amaretto and the apricot puree. Transfer the mixture to an ice cream machine and freeze following the manufacturer's instructions. If you do not have one, freeze to a slush, whisk thoroughly, and put back in the freezer until set.

5. Remove the ice cream from the freezer and place in the refrigerator about 1 hour before serving.

PREPARATION

Any fruit ice cream or sorbet loses flavor if made too long in advance. Try to make it no more than 2 days before you want to serve it.

SERVES 6

DINNER FOR EIGHT

Insalata di zucchine e pomodori all'aceto balsamico e alla menta

Zucchini and Tomato Salad with Balsamic Vinegar and Mint

~~~~~

Bocconcini di coda di rospo alla purè di lenticchie

Monkfish Morsels with Lentil Puree

~~~~~

Spinaci all'agro

Lemon Spinach (page 331)

~~~~~

Macedonia di frutta con la neve al limone

Fruit Salad with Lemon Granita

I find it reassuring and relaxing for the host or hostess to serve a first course that can be totally prepared in advance, tasted, adjusted, and then forgotten about until it is time to serve it. As a matter of fact, this menu is ideal for the last-minute cook; everything except the fish can be made in advance.

The second course might seem *nuova cucina,* but a similar dish of fish and lentils was made in my home in Milan as far back as I can remember. The fish was *baccalà* (salt cod) and the lentils were not pureed, but the underlying principle was the same. Here I substitute monkfish for the salt cod; it has the necessary firm and chewy texture.

A word about the lentils. I feel the little slate-colored Puy lentils from France are worth the extra cost. The taste is sweeter yet deeper, the skin is softer, and there is much less waste than with ordinary lentils. The other lentils I recommend are the Italian ones from Castelluccio in Umbria, but they are very difficult to find outside Italy. If you use Puy lentils or *lenticchie di Castelluccio* you do not need to soak them or to puree them. Just cook them—30 to 40 minutes is usually enough—drain them, dress them with oil, and spoon them around the fish. The lemon spinach on page 331 is an ideal accompaniment. You might also like to serve a bowl of small new potatoes.

The last course, like the first, is an embellishment of a classic dish. It is rather like eating a sorbet of mixed summer fruit dressed with lemon juice.

If you want some cookies with the fruit salad, I recommend the almond crescents on page 341.

Insalata di zucchine e pomodori all'aceto balsamico e alla menta

Zucchini and Tomato Salad with Balsamic Vinegar and Mint

———

2 pounds small zucchini

salt

7 tablespoons extra-virgin olive oil

3 tablespoons balsamic vinegar

freshly ground black pepper

1 garlic clove, very thinly sliced

4 tomatoes, preferably plum tomatoes

3 tablespoons chopped fresh mint for garnish

1. Wash and scrub the zucchini thoroughly, but leave the ends on to prevent water getting inside. Cook them in boiling salted water until tender but not soft. Take them out of the saucepan and refresh under cold water. Leave them to cool a little, then dry them and cut off the ends. Cut each zucchini in half lengthwise and lay the halves neatly on a serving dish.

2. Mix together the oil, vinegar, pepper, and salt to taste and spoon over the zucchini, reserving 2 tablespoons of the dressing. Sprinkle the garlic slivers on top. Cover with plastic wrap and set aside for about 1 hour.

3. Blanch and peel the tomatoes. Cut them in half and squeeze out the seeds and some of the liquid. Cut each half into ½-inch cubes. Before serving, place the tomatoes on top of the zucchini, sprinkle lightly with salt and pepper, and spoon the remaining dressing over the vegetables.

PREPARATION

Zucchini are best eaten the day they are cooked. The tomatoes can be peeled, seeded, and cubed and kept in a covered container in the refrigerator up to 1 day in advance. Remember to take both vegetables out of the refrigerator at least 2 hours before serving so that they are at room temperature when served.

SERVES 8

Bocconcini di coda di rospo alla purè di lenticchie

Monkfish Morsels with Lentil Puree

LENTIL PUREE

2 cups lentils (about 1 pound)

8 garlic cloves, washed but unpeeled

½ onion, stuck with 1 clove

2 bay leaves

2 tablespoons wine vinegar

5 tablespoons extra-virgin olive oil

salt and freshly ground black pepper

3 pounds monkfish

6 sage leaves

2 sprigs rosemary, about 4 inches long

1 garlic clove

3 tablespoons olive oil

½ cup dry white wine

4 tomatoes, preferably plum, peeled, seeded, and cut into very small cubes

salt and freshly ground black pepper

4 tablespoons chopped flat-leaf parsley

1. Spread the lentils on a plate, a few at a time, and pick out any tiny stones, pieces of grit, or chaff. Although not always necessary, it is better to soak lentils in cold water for about 4 hours, since sometimes they have been in storage for a long time and their skin has become tough. Soaking is unnecessary for Puy lentils or *lenticchie di Castelluccio*.

2. Rinse the soaked lentils under running water and put them in a saucepan, preferably an earthenware pot. Add the garlic, onion, bay leaves, vinegar, and enough water to cover the lentils by about 1 inch. Bring to a boil, turn down the heat so that the water simmers gently, and cook, covered, until the lentils are very tender. How long this takes depends on the quality of the lentils and storage time. But they should be ready well within 1 hour. Drain, reserving the liquid.

3. Remove and discard the bay leaves and puree the lentils through a food mill set with the small-hole disk or rub through a sieve. I do not recommend the food processor because it will not get rid of the skin of the lentils. Add enough of the lentil cooking liquid for the puree to be quite soft. Transfer to a clean saucepan and add the oil, salt, and plenty of pepper. Taste, check seasonings, and keep warm over a flame tamer or in a bain-marie or double boiler while you prepare the fish.

4. Trim all the gray skin and membrane from the fish. If left on they would cause the fish to shrink. Cut the monkfish into 1-inch morsels and pat dry with paper towels.

5. Chop the herbs and garlic and put into a large nonstick pan with the oil. Sauté for 1 minute, then add the fish and cook over moderate heat for 2 minutes, shaking the pan frequently. Turn the fish over and cook for 1 minute more. Splash with the wine and let it bubble away for a minute or so while turning the fish over once or twice. Add the tomatoes and cook for 2 minutes. Season with salt and plenty of pepper to taste.

6. To serve, heat a large dish (a round one is prettiest) and spoon the lentil puree around the outside of the dish. Place the fish in the middle of the lentil ring, sprinkle with parsley, and serve at once.

PREPARATION

The lentil puree can be made up to 3 days in advance and refrigerated, tightly covered. It can also be frozen. Heat it up very slowly either in a bain-marie or double boiler or in a saucepan on a flame tamer over low heat. The fish must be cooked just before you sit down at the table. Keep it warm in the pan with the lid on tight.

SERVES 8

Macedonia di frutta con la neve al limone

Fruit Salad with Lemon Granita

2 pounds assorted fruit, such as
bananas, pears, peaches, apricots,
plums, grapes, cherries

4 passion fruits

3 tablespoons sugar, more or less,
according to taste

⅔ cup freshly squeezed orange juice

LEMON GRANITA

2 large lemons

½ cup sugar

1. Peel the bananas and core the pears. Slice the bananas and cut the pears into ½-inch cubes and put them in a glass bowl. Wash, peel, and pit the peaches; wash and pit the apricots and plums. Cut into the same size pieces as the pears and add to the bowl with all the juices that have accumulated while cutting the fruit. Wash the grapes and remove the seeds, if necessary. Cut large grapes in half. Add to the bowl. Wash and pit the cherries and add to the bowl. Cut the passion fruits in half, scoop out the inside, and add to the other fruit. Sprinkle with the sugar and pour the orange juice over the fruit.

2. Cover the bowl with plastic wrap and refrigerate for at least 5 hours. Mix 2 or 3 times during the chilling.

3. Wash 1 of the lemons and grate the peel. Squeeze both lemons. Combine 2 cups water with the sugar and lemon juice and bring to a boil. Add the grated peel and boil for 3 minutes. Leave aside to cool and then transfer the mixture to a shallow metal pan. Freeze until almost set.

4. Break the mixture into chunks and process until it forms small crystals. Return to the freezer. After about 2 hours break the mixture up again with a fork and then return to the freezer. Just before serving, break up the granita with a fork and spread it all over the top of the fruit salad. Serve at once.

PREPARATION

The fruit salad is best prepared no more than 4 hours in advance. The granita can be prepared up to 24 hours in advance.

SERVES 8

DINNER FOR TWELVE

Passato di pomodoro
Tomato Soup

~~~

Petti di cappone alla Stefani
Chicken Breasts Seventeenth-Century Style

~~~

Prugne al vino
Plums Stewed in Wine

~~~

Gelato di mascarpone
Mascarpone Ice Cream

A sit-down dinner for twelve people is quite demanding, so the menu must be well thought out. If you have no one to help serve, I suggest you divide the second and third courses between two dishes, so that each end of the table can pass one around. Another excellent way is to put the dishes on the sideboard and let guests help themselves.

Perhaps because I am Italian, I have never taken to the idea of serving food already placed on the plate. It isn't done in Italy, except for some special antipasti and a few desserts. So if you are entertaining *all'italiana,* allow your guests to serve themselves.

The tomato soup is fresher and lighter than most; choose good ripe tomatoes to make your vegetable broth. The rice flour gives a less gluey texture to the soup than ordinary flour; rice flour can be bought in health food stores. The soup can be served cold on a hot summer evening.

The second course is based on a seventeenth-century recipe by Bartolomeo Stefani. I first had it at the restaurant Il Cigno in Mantua, where it has been recreated with great success. Stefani was the chef of Ottavio Gonzaga, and his book *L'arte di bene cucinare* was published in 1662. He was a great cook who had a flair for adapting traditional Mantuan country recipes to suit the table of his patron. He was also the first cook to discard the heavily spiced food of the Middle Ages and early Renaissance in favor of cooking with a lighter touch, flavored with herbs and flowers. It was cooking of a brilliant inventiveness, one that modern Italian chefs are keen to revive.

The original recipe calls for capon breasts, capon being moister and tastier than chicken. The recipe also works very well with large chicken breasts.

I serve the chicken breasts with green beans or carrots and cauliflower, dressed with enough extra-virgin olive oil to give them a shine. I put the green beans and cauliflower florets alongside the chicken if I am using an oval dish, in a mound in the middle if I am using a round dish. When you cook the vegetables, be sure not to overcook—or undercook—them. (See my note on page 319 concerning green beans.)

The dessert is plums stewed in wine and served with a rich mascarpone ice cream. This ice cream can be made without an ice-cream machine. I prefer to bake the plums instead of cooking them in a pan because they swell up during the baking and look very round and smooth. To preserve this look you should remove them just before the skin bursts. The plums are perfect by themselves. With the mascarpone ice cream, however, the dish rises to a new plane. It is an exquisite combination of flavors.

Passato di pomodoro
Tomato Soup

6 to 7 shallots	salt and freshly ground black pepper
½ cup extra-virgin olive oil	6 cups vegetable broth
1 carrot	4 tablespoons rice flour
4 celery stalks	½ cup tiny fresh basil leaves or marjoram leaves, torn
4 pounds ripe tomatoes	
12 garlic cloves, unpeeled	freshly grated parmesan
1½ tablespoons sugar	croutons (optional)

1. Chop the shallots and sauté them in the oil for 5 minutes. Chop the carrot and the celery and add to the onion. Cook for another 5 minutes or so.

2. Meanwhile cut the tomatoes into wedges and add to the pan together with the garlic, sugar, salt, and pepper. Cook for 20 minutes, then puree through a food mill. (A food processor is not suitable because the tomatoes and the garlic cloves are unpeeled.)

3. Return the puree to the pan, add the broth, and simmer for 15 minutes more. Add the rice flour in a thin stream while beating the soup with a small wire whisk or a fork. Cook for 10 minutes over very low heat. Taste and check the seasoning.

4. Pour the soup into individual soup bowls. Decorate with the basil leaves. Serve the cheese separately. If you want the soup to be more filling, hand around a bowl of croutons.

PREPARATION

The soup can be made up to 3 days in advance and refrigerated. It also freezes well.

SERVES 12

Petti di cappone alla Stefani
Chicken Breasts Seventeenth-Century Style

6 boneless and skinless chicken breasts

4 cups chicken broth or Italian broth (page 338)

1½ cups dry white wine

SWEET-AND-SOUR SAUCE

4 tablespoons brown sugar

½ cup dry white wine

½ cup golden raisins

4 teaspoons grated lemon peel

5 tablespoons balsamic vinegar

2 teaspoons salt

freshly ground black pepper

½ cup extra-virgin olive oil

1. Wipe the chicken breasts and remove any visible fat. Put them in a single layer in a large sauté pan and cover with the broth and wine, or use two pans, dividing the chicken, broth, and wine. The pieces should fit closely together. Poach until the breasts are cooked through, about 30 minutes, depending on their size. Leave to cool in the liquid.

2. For the sauce, combine the sugar and the wine in a small saucepan and bring very slowly to a boil. Simmer until the sugar has completely dissolved. Remove from the heat and add the raisins and lemon peel. Let cool, then strain into a bowl. Reserve raisins and lemon peel.

3. Add the balsamic vinegar, salt, and pepper to the liquid in the bowl. Pour in the oil gradually, whisking to form an emulsion. When you have added all the oil, mix in the raisins and lemon peel. Taste and adjust seasoning.

4. About 3 hours before you want to serve the dish, lift the cold chicken breasts out of the broth and place them on a cutting board. (Keep the broth for a soup.) Slice about ½ inch thick. Lay the slices on a very large dish or 2 smaller ones. Spoon the sauce over the chicken and cover the dish with plastic wrap. Do not refrigerate, since the chicken is best at room temperature.

PREPARATION

The chicken breasts can be poached up to 2 days in advance and refrigerated, covered, in their liquid. Before cutting, wipe off any solidified fat. The sauce can be prepared up to 1 week in advance and kept covered in the refrigerator.

SERVES 12

Prugne al vino
Plums Stewed in Wine

―――

3 pounds red plums	*10 peppercorns*
1½ cups dry white wine	*3 bay leaves*
1¼ cups sugar	*½ teaspoon ground cinnamon*

1. Preheat the oven to 325° F.

2. Wash the plums and put them in a single layer in a shallow ovenproof dish.

3. In a saucepan, heat the wine, sugar, peppercorns, bay leaves, and cinnamon. When the wine starts to boil pour over the plums, cover the dish with foil and tie the foil under the rim of the dish. Put the dish in the oven and bake for 20 to 30 minutes, checking after 20 minutes. The plums should be just soft but whole and beautifully plumped up. When they are ready, taste one plum. If not sweet enough, add a little more sugar. Serve at room temperature.

PREPARATION

The plums can be refrigerated for up to 5 to 6 days. You can also freeze them.

SERVES 12

Gelato di mascarpone
Mascarpone Ice Cream

3 cups mascarpone | *4 egg yolks*
1½ cups confectioners' sugar, sifted | *8 tablespoons amaretto*

1. Beat the mascarpone with the confectioners' sugar. Beat in the egg yolks and the amaretto until well blended.

2. Spoon into the bowl in which you want to serve it and cover with plastic wrap. Freeze for at least 6 hours.

3. Remove from the freezer and put in the refrigerator about 1 hour before serving.

PREPARATION

This ice cream can be made up to 2 weeks in advance.

SERVES 12

A BUFFET PARTY FOR TWENTY-FIVE

Vitello tonnato alla milanese
Veal in Tuna Sauce

∼

Mousse di prosciutto cotto
Truffle-flavored Ham Mousse

∼

I ricchi e i poveri
Shrimp and Bean Salad (page 100)

∼

Petti di cappone alla Stefani
Chicken Breasts Seventeenth-Century Style (page 126)

∼

Insalata di pasta, fontina, noci, e sedano
Pasta Salad with Fontina, Walnuts, and Celery

∼

Conchiglie rosse ripiene di spaghettini in insalata
Radicchio Leaves Filled with Spaghettini

∼

Insalate varie
Assorted Salads

∼

Torta di patate e mandorle
Potato and Almond Cake (page 49)

∼

Gelato di ricotta
Ricotta Ice Cream

∼

Pere alla crema del Lario
Poached Pears with Pear Liqueur Cream

∼

Macedonia di frutta con la neve al limone
Fruit Salad with Lemon Granita (page 122)

*T*here now seem to be two kinds of supper party: one, rather informal, with one or two large dishes, often hot, served as a main course; the other with quite a few dishes, usually cold, put out for the guests to help themselves. This menu falls into the second category, which is the more old-fashioned and formal kind of buffet party. You will find some of the recipes in other menus. I have gathered them here to provide a good assortment and give the right balance to the buffet. But there are also a few recipes to be found only in this menu, including the *vitello tonnato.*

Vitello tonnato is a very elegant summer dish, the one most northern Italian hostesses would serve at a supper party. It is usually accompanied with a bowl of cold rice dressed with some extra-virgin olive oil. In the old days it was traditionally served on August 15, *Ferragosto,* the Feast of the Assumption. My recipe comes from my mother. It is the traditional recipe from Milan, where the sauce is made with cream instead of mayonnaise (the version with mayonnaise is from Piedmont).

Every time I make it I think of the time my mother's *vitel tonné* (as it is called in Milanese dialect) finished on the dining room floor. It was at a family luncheon at the beginning of World War II, and my mother had managed to find the right veal roast, quite a triumph since meat was scarce. The dish was brought in by our maid Augusta, who was a real show-off when waiting on the table. She loved to dress up with a frilly apron, cap, and white gloves and would make her entry into the dining room as if she were on stage, carrying large dishes poised delicately on one hand, and taking tiny steps. That day she tripped over the carpet, and suddenly there was a sticky tan mess on the floor. My Aunt Esther got up, scooped up the meat, and said in dialect, "Ma l'è trop bun e mi me l' magni istess." (But it's too good and I'm going to eat it anyway.) Augusta, by now in tears, was asked to pick up the rest, clean off the sauce, and tell the cook to reconstruct the dish with the sauce that was left over. The *vitel tonné* reappeared a few minutes later, beautifully decorated with lemon butterflies and cornichon fans, just as it had been before.

Because it is difficult to find the right cut of veal, I have often used chicken instead, cooking it whole in the same way and cutting it into pieces when cold (the weight would be about 3½ pounds, and the cooking time the same as for the veal). But what you really need is good tuna. Buy Italian or Spanish tuna preserved in olive oil, which is available in specialty shops.

The recipe for the ham mousse comes from Signora Gay, the octogenarian mother of a great friend of mine in Milan. Ten years ago she moved to Milan from her native Turin to be nearer her daughter. But once a week she makes the 100-mile journey back to Turin to buy her poultry and meat, because, she says, "La carne e i polli a Milano non sono buoni come a Torino." (The meat and chicken in Milan are not as good as in Turin.) Such is the high standard of Signora Gay's table, where the ingredients are her prime concern. And how right she is. Her cooking is light but full of flavors, which are achieved through careful timing, absolute precision, and great care, and not by taking the easy way out—adding cream and butter. The mousse is proof of her light touch and feel for the balance of ingredients.

For this type of party you need many different salads, as well as a large bowl of green salad. My version of this is on page 325. There are many other recipes for salads throughout this book, and I would suggest you choose the most seasonal.

I have also included recipes for my favorite pasta salads, really two out of the only four pasta salads I like. Pasta salads are all the rage outside Italy but not with me, nor with most Italians. We prefer our pasta hot. At a large party like this though, a few cold pasta dishes are always popular. Cold pasta must be slightly undercooked and tossed with an olive oil dressing, not a mayonnaise- or cream-based sauce.

The ricotta ice cream is from a recipe kindly given to me by Caroline Liddell and Robin Weir and is included in their new book, *Ices,* published by New English Library. The authors write, "Both the flavor and the texture are clearly ricotta," and indeed they are. I have tried the recipe with several kinds of ricotta, and the ice cream is always delicious.

Another dessert for this dinner is a platter of poached pears with a pear liqueur cream, a recipe from Lake Como. *Crema del Lario* is an unusual hybrid of Italian and English cooking. Lario is another name for Lake Como, which was a fashionable resort for the English before World War I. They must have taught local cooks to prepare syllabub, to which the cook added a personal touch, in this case pears. Then the cream was flavored with a local pear eau de vie instead of sherry or Madeira.

Vitello tonnato alla milanese
Veal in Tuna Sauce

1 veal roast, about 3 pounds
1 carrot, cut up in chunks
1 celery stalk, cut up in chunks
1 medium onion, stuck with 2 cloves
1 bay leaf
a few parsley stems
salt
6 peppercorns, bruised
⅔ cup dry white wine
1⅓ cups chicken broth

TUNA SAUCE
8 ounces (¾ cup) tuna packed
in olive oil

6 anchovy fillets
6 tablespoons heavy cream
1 teaspoon sugar
4 tablespoons lemon juice
4 tablespoons extra-virgin olive oil
freshly ground black pepper

2 tablespoons fresh tarragon leaves
DECORATION
1 lemon
several cornichons

1. Have the butcher tie the veal in a neat shape. Put it in a casserole with the carrot, celery, onion, bay leaf, parsley stems, a little salt, and the peppercorns. Pour in the wine and half the broth and bring slowly to a boil. Cover the pan tightly and cook for about 1½ hours until the meat is tender. Remove from the heat and leave to cool in the pan. When the veal is cold, cut into ½-inch slices and lay them, slightly overlapping, on a serving dish.

2. Remove the bay leaf and the parsley stems from the cooking juices. Puree all the cooking juices and the vegetables in a food processor. Transfer the puree to a bowl.

3. Put the tuna and the anchovies in the food processor. Add a few tablespoons of the remaining broth and process for 1 minute or so. Scrape the bits down from the side of the bowl and add a few tablespoons of the puree, the cream, and the sugar. Process again, while gradually adding the lemon juice and the olive oil. Taste a few times and correct the sauce to your liking. You might not need to add all the lemon juice, or you might want a little more. Add salt if

necessary and a good grinding of pepper. The sauce should have the consistency of heavy cream. If necessary, add more broth. Coat the veal slices with a few tablespoons of the sauce. Cover with plastic wrap and refrigerate.

4. When you are ready to serve, spoon a little more sauce over the veal and transfer the rest of the sauce to a bowl, to be passed around separately. Coarsely chop or cut the tarragon and scatter over the veal. Decorate with the lemon cut into butterflies and cornichons cut into fans.

PREPARATION

The dish is best made 2 or even 3 days in advance.

SERVES 6 TO 8

Mousse di prosciutto cotto
Truffle-flavored Ham Mousse

2 egg whites

4 tablespoons dry sherry or dry marsala

2½ cups Italian broth (page 338), thoroughly defatted

about 1 tablespoon gelatin, as necessary

thick béchamel made with 1 tablespoon butter, 1 tablespoon flour, and ⅔ cup whole milk

¾ pound lean ham

2 to 3 teaspoons truffle paste

½ cup heavy cream, lightly whipped

freshly ground black pepper

1. Put the egg whites and sherry in a saucepan and add the broth. Bring to a simmer while beating with a balloon whisk. Stop beating, turn the heat down as low as possible, and leave for about 15 minutes. The broth should just break some bubbles on the surface. Do not boil.

2. Strain the broth very carefully through a sieve lined with a piece of cheese-cloth folded double. Taste for salt, remembering that food served cold needs more seasoning. You may find that the broth does not need any added gelatin. To test it, put a tablespoon of broth on a saucer in the freezer for 10 minutes. If it sets, no gelatin is needed. If not, dissolve some of the gelatin in a little of the broth and stir back into the broth. Test again and keep adding gelatin until you achieve the right consistency.

3. Pour enough jelly into a 5-to-6-cup rectangular loaf pan to come about ¾ inch up the side of the pan. Put the pan into the refrigerator for the jelly to set while you prepare the mousse.

4. Make the béchamel in the usual way, following the directions on page 106, but do not add any salt. Cook very gently for 15 minutes or so, using a bain-marie or double boiler or a flame tamer. When ready, cool in a bowl of ice water.

5. Put the ham in the food processor and process until very finely chopped. Transfer to a bowl and mix in the truffle paste. Truffle paste varies from brand to brand. Taste after you have added a little and add more if you want the truffle flavor to come through more strongly. Stir in the béchamel as soon as it is cold. Stir in the cream. Season with a generous amount of pepper; salt should not be necessary.

6. Take a 2-to-3-cup rectangular loaf pan and press the mousse into it, being sure to eliminate any air pockets. Put the mousse in the refrigerator to cool thoroughly. When the jelly in the first pan is set, slide a spatula around the mousse. Turn it onto a plate, then turn it into the pan with the aspic layer; the mousse should fall into the larger pan. Pour some more jelly around the mousse, cover with plastic film, and refrigerate.

7. Before your guests arrive, unmold the aspic onto an oval dish. This is easier if you immerse the pan in a bowl of hot water for 15 to 20 seconds. Keep in the refrigerator until the last minute and decorate the dish with a sprig of bay or a sprig of holly or ivy if you are serving it at Christmas.

PREPARATION

The whole dish can be prepared up to 3 days in advance and refrigerated.

SERVES 8

Insalata di pasta, fontina, noci, e sedano
Pasta Salad with Fontina, Walnuts, and Celery

———

1 pound small ziti or other medium tubular pasta	4 tablespoons walnuts
salt	the heart of 1 large celery head (3½ cups)
6 tablespoons mild olive oil	2 tablespoons walnut oil
½ pound fontina or Emmentaler	freshly ground black pepper
½ pound bel paese	handful celery leaves
½ pound strong gorgonzola	

1. Cook the pasta in plenty of salted boiling water and drain when very al dente. Refresh under cold water, drain again, and transfer to a large bowl. Pat dry with paper towels. Toss with the olive oil and leave to cool completely.

2. Cut the 3 cheeses into small cubes and add to the pasta together with the walnuts.

3. Remove any strings from the celery stalks with a knife or a swivel-action peeler. Cut the stalks into thin strips and add to the bowl. Toss with the walnut oil and plenty of pepper. Taste and add salt if necessary. Set aside for 1 hour or so for the flavors to combine.

4. Sprinkle the celery leaves over the top to make the salad look pretty.

PREPARATION

The pasta can be cooked and tossed with oil up to 6 hours in advance. The other ingredients can be prepared up to 1 day in advance but should be added no longer than 2 hours in advance.

SERVES 8

Conchiglie rosse ripiene di spaghettini in insalata

Radicchio Leaves Filled with Spaghettini

---

2 or 3 large radicchio heads	*2 dried chilies*
1 pound spaghettini	*freshly ground black pepper*
salt	*1½ cups (½ pound) large black olives,*
½ cup extra-virgin olive oil	*such as kalamata, pitted*
¾ cup flat-leaf parsley leaves	*6 tablespoons small capers*
2 garlic cloves	*8 hard-boiled eggs, shelled*

1. Remove the core of the radicchio and unfurl the outside leaves very gently so that they remain whole. You will need about 15 leaves (keep the rest of the radicchio for a green salad). Wash the leaves, dry thoroughly, and place on one or two large dishes.

2. Cook the spaghettini in plenty of salted water. It cooks quite quickly. When serving it cold, you should drain it when you think it is still on the undercooked side. Drain and refresh it under cold water. Drain again, then transfer to a large bowl. Pat dry with paper towels. Toss with half of the oil and allow to cool.

3. About 2 hours before you want to serve the pasta, chop together, by hand or in a food processor, the parsley, garlic, and chilies. Add the mixture to the spaghettini and toss thoroughly with the rest of the oil. Taste and add salt and pepper if necessary.

4. Fill each radicchio leaf with a forkful or two of spaghettini. Sprinkle with the olives and capers. Cut the eggs in wedges and decorate each radicchio shell or the dish with them.

PREPARATION

The radicchio leaves can be prepared up to 1 day in advance and kept in the fridge in a covered container. The pasta can be cooked and partly dressed with the oil up to 8 hours in advance but should be dressed no more than 4 hours in advance.

SERVES 8

Gelato di ricotta
Ricotta Ice Cream

—————

1²/₃ cups whole milk	*2¹/₄ cups ricotta*
1 cup sugar	*²/₃ cup heavy cream, well chilled*
3 egg yolks	*1 tablespoon dark rum*

1. Combine the milk and half the sugar in a medium saucepan and bring to a boil. Meanwhile, in a medium heatproof bowl combine the egg yolks with the remaining sugar and beat, preferably with a hand-held electric mixer, until the mixture is pale and thick enough to hold its shape when a ribbon of it is trailed across the surface. Pour in the hot milk in a thin stream, whisking steadily. Place the bowl over a pan of simmering water or return the custard to the saucepan and put it on a flame tamer so that it is not in direct contact with the heat.

2. Use a small wooden spoon or spatula to stir the custard frequently. It will take 25 to 30 minutes to reach 185° F. and thicken. To see if the custard has thickened sufficiently, dip the spoon in and look at the way the sauce coats the back of the spoon. If it forms only a thin film, draw a line across; it should hold a clear shape. If not, continue cooking until the custard coats the back of the spoon more thickly and holds a clear line. Remove the pan from the heat and plunge the base in cold water.

3. Gradually beat in ricotta and continue to beat vigorously until the custard is almost smooth. (Don't worry if a few small lumps remain; these will break down in the churning process.) When the custard is cold, remove, cover, and chill in the refrigerator.

4. When chilled, stir the cream and rum into the custard. Pour into the ice-cream machine and churn, following the manufacturer's instructions, until the mix has frozen to a consistency firm enough to serve or store. Quickly scrape into plastic freezer boxes and cover with wax paper and a lid. Once frozen, allow 25 to 30 minutes in the refrigerator to soften sufficiently to serve.

SERVES 8

Pere alla crema del lario
Poached Pears with Pear Liqueur Cream

---

8 ripe, firm pears	4 cups red wine
6 tablespoons lemon juice	3 teaspoons grated lemon peel
2½ cups sugar	⅔ cup Poire William eau de vie or Italian grappa alla pera
1 3-inch-long cinnamon stick	6 cups heavy cream

1. Peel, quarter, and core the pears. To prevent discoloration, drop them immediately into a bowl of cold water with a few drops of lemon juice added.

2. Put half the sugar and the cinnamon in the wine and heat gently until the sugar has dissolved. Add the pears and cook until tender, about 10 to 15 minutes.

3. While the pears are cooking, combine the remaining sugar with the lemon peel, remaining lemon juice, and the liqueur. Stir until the sugar has dissolved.

4. Whip the cream until it forms stiff peaks, then slowly fold the liqueur mixture into it.

5. Lift the pears out of the wine syrup (you can save the syrup to flavor a fruit salad) and place in a large glass bowl. Spoon the cream on top and chill for 1 hour.

PREPARATION

The pears can be cooked up to 3 days in advance and refrigerated. They can also be frozen; I freeze them in a covered container in the syrup. The dessert must be finished no more than 1 hour before serving.

SERVES 12

AUTUMN

A VENETIAN LUNCH FOR FOUR

1 4 4

Risotto coi peoci

Risotto with Mussels

❦

Radicchio alla trevisana

Broiled Radicchio and Belgian Endive

❦

Formaggio e frutta

Cheese and Fruit

DINNER FOR SIX

1 5 4

Peperoni ripieni della Zia Renata

Peppers Stuffed with Eggplant and Croutons

❦

Pasticcio di pesce

Fish Lasagne

❦

Insalata verde

Green Salad (page 325)

❦

Ananas e arancie

Pineapple and Oranges

A VEGETARIAN LUNCH FOR EIGHT

1 4 8

Torta di porri

Leek and Rice Torta

❦

Insalata agra di barbabietola

Beet, Watercress, and Grapefruit Salad

❦

Noci, uva, e grana

Walnuts, Grapes, and Parmesan

A SICILIAN DINNER FOR SIX

1 6 2

Caponatina di melanzane

Caponata with Chocolate

❦

Il timballo del Gattopardo

The Pie from *The Leopard*

❦

Insalata di finocchi, cicoria belga, ed arancie

Fennel, Belgian Endive, and Orange Salad

❦

Cassata siciliana

Sicilian Cassata

DINNER FOR EIGHT

1 7 2

Passato di sedano
Cream of Celery Soup

Maiale al latte
Loin of Pork Braised in Milk

Cachi al sugo di lime
Persimmons with Lime Juice

DINNER FOR TEN

1 8 4

Il fiore di melanzane alla senape
Broiled Eggplant with Lemon-Mustard Dressing

Coniglio con le Cipolle
Braised Rabbit

Purè di patate
Mashed Potatoes

Le carote di Ada Boni
Italian-style Carrots (page 329)

Torta di ricotta e mandorle con la salsina di arancia
Ricotta and Almond Cake with Orange Sauce

AN AUTUMN DINNER FOR EIGHT

1 7 8

Risotto con la zucca
Pumpkin Risotto

Cervo alla casalinga
Venison Stew with Onions

Polenta
Polenta (page 332)

Funghi al funghetto
Sautéed Mushrooms (page 328)

Coppette di pompelmo e uva
Grapefruit Cups with Grapes

A BUFFET SUPPER FOR TWELVE

1 9 0

L'insalata di Luisetta
Vegetable, Grapefruit, and Shrimp Salad

Tiella di pesce
Apulian Fish Pie

Insalata di sedano, carote, e mela al sapor di coriandolo
Celery, Carrot, and Apple Salad with a Wine and Cilantro Dressing

Torta di riso
Rice Cake

Insalata autunnale di frutta
Autumn Fruit Compote

A VENETIAN LUNCH
FOR FOUR

Risotto coi peoci
Risotto with Mussels

~~~

Radicchio alla trevisana
Broiled Radicchio and Belgian Endive

~~~

Formaggio e frutta
Cheese and Fruit

When we had an apartment in Venice, I went every morning on my pilgrimage by gondola-ferry across the Canal Grande from Ca' d'Oro to the Rialto market. The Rialto market is a sight not to be missed by anyone visiting Venice. It stretches along a few *calli* (alleys) and *campielli* (squares) around the bridge and along the Grand Canal. There are stalls selling lace and tablecloths and others selling bags, wallets, and purses, but the most spectacular are those stalls piled high with the choicest fruits and the greatest selection of vegetables you have ever seen, as well as fish stalls with crawling crustaceans and slender silvery fish, so many different species and kinds that you could spend the morning studying them. But as I stood there, entranced by the sheer abundance and variety of it all, I would be reminded by the jostlings of more down-to-earth Venetian housewives that I had lunch to make.

After searching for whatever looked best, I finished up, as often as not, giving in to my longing for seafood, and returned home with bags of shellfish for lunch and dinner. In keeping with the local cuisine, rice was the natural accompaniment to the seafood.

Risotto was followed by *radicchio alla trevisana* whenever it was in season. The radicchio was the long *radicchio di Treviso* (Treviso is a small town north of Venice), the best radicchio for grilling. It has a slightly bitter flavor that is brought out by heating it. I have never seen *radicchio di Treviso* in England or the United States, but I love grilled radicchio so much that I make it with the round *radicchio di Chioggia,* together with one or two heads of Belgian endive, which goes beautifully with it.

The cheese platter would certainly include the delicious Asiago, a semifat cheese made principally in the province of Vicenza. A bowl of fruit in season is an informal end to the meal.

Risotto coi peoci
Risotto with Mussels

------

3 pounds mussels

1 cup dry white wine

⅓ cup olive oil

3 shallots or 1 medium onion, very finely chopped

salt

4 cups fish broth (page 340) or vegetable broth

1 celery stalk, with leaves

1 garlic clove

1¼ cups Arborio rice

4 tablespoons chopped flat-leaf parsley

salt and freshly ground black pepper

1. Clean the mussels, following the directions on page 158. Throw away any that remain open after you have tapped them on a hard surface. They are dead and should not be eaten.

2. Put the wine in a large sauté pan, add the mussels, and cover the pan. Cook over high heat until the mussels open, 3 or 4 minutes. Shake the pan every now and then. As soon as the mussels are open, remove the meat from the shells and discard the shells. Strain the cooking liquid through a sieve lined with cheesecloth, pouring it slowly and gently so that most of the sand and debris remains at the bottom of the pan.

3. Pour the oil into a wide heavy saucepan, add the shallots and a pinch of salt, and sauté until the shallots are soft and just beginning to color.

4. Heat the broth to the simmer and keep it simmering all through the cooking.

5. While the shallot is cooking, chop the celery and garlic together, then add to the shallot. Sauté for another minute or so. Add the rice and, as we say in Italian, *tostatelo* (toast it in the oil), turning it over and over for a couple of minutes. Pour over the mussel liquid and stir well. When the liquid has been absorbed, add the broth, a ladleful at a time. Stir very frequently. When the rice is done, remove the pan from the heat, stir in the mussels and the parsley, and season with salt, if necessary, and with a generous grinding of black pepper. Transfer to a heated dish and serve immediately.

PREPARATION

The mussels can be cleaned and opened up to 1 day in advance. They must be kept in the refrigerator. The risotto should be made just before serving. However, you can half-cook it ahead of time and finish it just before serving, following the directions on page 219.

SERVES 4

Radicchio alla trevisana
Broiled Radicchio and Belgian Endive

1 medium radicchio head (about 1 pound)
2 small Belgian endives (about ½ pound)

⅓ cup extra-virgin olive oil
salt and freshly ground black pepper

1. Wash the radicchio and the Belgian endive and dry very thoroughly. Cut the radicchio into quarters and the Belgian endive in half, both lengthwise.

2. Oil the broiler pan and lay the vegetables in it. Pour over the olive oil and season with salt and a lot of pepper. Leave for 20 minutes, then cook under a slow, preheated broiler until the leaves soften, turning the pieces so that they cook all around. Serve warm or at room temperature.

PREPARATION

You can wash and dry the radicchio and Belgian endive up to 1 day in advance and refrigerate wrapped in a dish towel. The vegetables can be broiled a few hours in advance and kept, covered, at room temperature.

SERVES 4

A VEGETARIAN LUNCH FOR EIGHT

Torta di porri

Leek and Rice Torta

～

Insalata agra di barbabietola

Beet, Watercress, and Grapefruit Salad

～

Noci, uva, e grana

Walnuts, Grapes, and Parmesan

I can heartily recommend the pie of this simple lunch. The original was made with zucchini and was served to me by a friend in Genoa. When I arrived, I heard a great thumping noise coming from the kitchen where I found my friend, a distinctly aristocratic woman, bent double, bashing the bottom of the pie dish against the tiled floor. "This is how Ligurian peasants dislodge their vegetable pies!" she explained.

When I came back to London, the zucchini were tired-looking and very expensive. So I thought of making the pie with the young leeks that were just coming into the shops. It turned out to be delicious. In the spring and summer when young zucchini are available, substitute them for the leeks, adding a raw sweet onion, very finely sliced, to the zucchini and the rice. The quantities and method are the same. Although such vegetable pies are usually made with *pasta frolla* (short dough or *pâte brisée*) in Italy, I think phyllo pastry is the perfect container. It's also quicker, since you buy it already made!

The salad is clean and fresh, a perfect mixture of the acidity of the grapefruit, the sweetness of the beet, and the peppery fragrance of the watercress.

The last course, if it could be called such, was a favorite of my father's. In spite of his sophisticated tastes in other matters, the food he loved best was peasant food. I remember him telling me that the dish he usually had at Savini, the famous restaurant in Milan where he often went for supper after an evening at La Scala, was *polenta e baccalà* (polenta and salt cod), or *polenta pasticciata* (polenta baked in layers with béchamel and luganega, a coarse-ground sausage). If truffles were in season, the chef would add a few slices to the polenta— peasant food no longer! And, in the real peasant tradition, my father used to eat bread with everything. My children, brought up in England, where bread is eaten only with certain foods, were amazed to see Nonno, as they called their grandfather, eating bread with bunches of grapes at the end of the meal. Although I find bread and grapes too limited, I do like a combination of walnuts, grapes, parmesan, and bread. It is a perfect blend of flavors, the bread being the unifying note.

This menu, which is perfect for any lunch, vegetarian or otherwise, is also good for an informal supper.

Torta di porri
Leek and Rice Torta

———

1½ pounds leeks	*¾ cup extra-virgin olive oil*
salt	*freshly ground black pepper*
4 eggs	*½ cup freshly grated parmesan*
¾ cup Arborio rice	*½ pound frozen phyllo pastry, thawed*

1. Cut away and discard all but the white part and the inside of the green part of the leeks. Cut into very thin rounds, about ⅛ inch. Wash thoroughly, removing all the earth. If the leeks are large and have a strong smell, leave them for about 1 hour in plenty of salted cold water. Drain and put in a bowl.

2. Lightly beat the eggs and add to the bowl. Add the rice, half the oil, 2 teaspoons salt, plenty of pepper, and the parmesan. Mix very thoroughly (I use my hands). Set the bowl aside for a couple of hours, but toss again whenever you think of it because the liquid sinks to the bottom and you want the leek and rice mixture to have a fair share of it.

3. Preheat the oven to 350° F.

4. Oil a 10-inch springform pan and lightly flour it. Shake out the excess flour. Pour the rest of the oil in a small bowl.

5. Carefully unfold the phyllo leaves, one at a time, keeping the remaining leaves covered. Phyllo dries and cracks very easily. Lift out and lay 1 leaf over the bottom and up the sides of the prepared pan, allowing the ends to hang over the outside of the pan. Lightly brush the leaf all over with oil and cover with another phyllo leaf. Lay it across the previous one so that the sides of the pan are covered all around. Brush with oil and lay 2 more leaves in the same way.

6. Fill the pan with the leek mixture. Fold the overhanging phyllo back over the top, one strip at a time, to make a lid. If the phyllo is not long enough, lay 4 more sheets over the top, brushing each sheet with oil. Cut them to fit inside the pan and fold the overhanging edge over to form a ridge around the edge. If necessary, cut some of the pieces with scissors and patch any that need it so that the filling is evenly covered. Bake for 45 to 50 minutes.

7. Let the pie cool for 10 minutes, then remove the side of the pan and turn it over onto a baking sheet. Put the pie back in the oven, upside down, for 5 minutes to dry the bottom. Turn onto a round serving dish and serve.

PREPARATION

The pie is best served warm, a couple of hours after baking. It is also very good made 1 day in advance, left out of the refrigerator, and served at room temperature.

SERVES 8

Insalata agra di barbabietola
Beet, Watercress, and Grapefruit Salad

6 medium beets, cooked (about 2 pounds)

6 tablespoons extra-virgin olive oil

salt and freshly ground black pepper

2 grapefruit

8 scallions, white parts only, thinly sliced

2 bunches watercress (6 to 8 ounces each)

1. Peel and slice the beets. Put in a bowl and toss with 2 tablespoons of the olive oil, a little salt, and a lot of pepper. Pile on a dish.

2. Peel the grapefruit, divide into segments, and remove the membranes. Cut each segment in half and scatter over the beets, together with scallions.

3. Wash and dry the watercress. Remove the long stems and divide into short sprigs.

4. Surround the beets with watercress. Drizzle the remaining olive oil over the watercress and sprinkle with salt and pepper.

PREPARATION

The vegetables and the grapefruit can be prepared up to 1 day in advance and kept separately in the refrigerator in airtight containers. The dish can be arranged up to 1 hour in advance and covered with plastic wrap, but dress the watercress just before serving.

SERVES 8

Noci, uva, e grana
Walnuts, Grapes, and Parmesan

This is the sort of dish you must offer in generous proportions. After all, whatever is left over will not be wasted. Buy 2 pounds of walnuts, 3 pounds of green grapes, a good wedge of parmesan, at least 1 pound, and some crusty Italian or French bread.

Divide the grapes into small bunches. Put the bunches in a colander and run them under cold water. Dry thoroughly with paper towels. Put the parmesan in the middle of a large round dish and surround it with the walnuts and the grapes. Put the dish in the middle of the table so your guests can help themselves. If your table is oval or rectangular prepare two smaller dishes to place at each end of the table.

SERVES 8

DINNER FOR SIX

Peperoni ripieni della Zia Renata
Peppers Stuffed with Eggplant and Croutons

~

Pasticcio di pesce
Fish Lasagne

~

Insalata verde
Green Salad (page 325)

~

Ananas e arancie
Pineapple and Oranges

My Aunt Renata, a Milanese, had all the characteristics I associate with good cooks. She was plump, cheerful, and amusing, but temperamental. Her husband, Zio Carlo, was a diehard Neapolitan forced by circumstance to live in northern Italy. Sitting in his house in drizzling, gray Lombardy as a child, I used to listen to his descriptions of colorful vegetables ripened in the real sun, of the lively fish market at Pozzuoli, where at least ten different kinds of clam could be had at any time, of the abundance of food always ready for anyone who happened to drop in, a sure sign of the hospitality and warmth of southern Italians.

These stuffed peppers were one of Zia Renata's specialties, combining her cooking skills with his fond memories. The croutons were added by Zia Renata during wartime, to make the dish more nourishing and to use up stale bread; they were so successful they became an integral part of the dish.

To save time, I tried baking the peppers instead of grilling them, but they get too floppy. The best method is to grill them over charcoal, which gives them its special flavor. Failing that, do them directly over a flame, or if you cook with electricity, use the broiler hot enough to burn the skin without softening the flesh too much.

The second course is one of the best pasta dishes ever. Because of the time it takes, and its cost, I like to serve it as the centerpiece of a dinner. It also makes a most successful buffet dish twinned with a dish of lasagne layered with meat *ragù*.

After these two courses, relax and bring to the table the best seasonal salad, enhanced by a few leaves of arugula or a bunch of chopped herbs from the garden. The basic recipe for an Italian green salad is on page 325.

Cheese is optional. In Italy cheese is seldom served at night because it is too heavy. We have a saying: "Il formaggio è oro alla mattina, argento a mezzogiorno e piombo alla sera" (Cheese is gold in the morning, silver at midday, and lead at night).

The dessert is light, fresh, easy, and very attractive, but it does need good fruit, since it is not spruced up in any way. When you buy the pineapple make sure the skin is not blemished or bruised. Smell it: it should smell of pineapple. Choose large navel oranges. If you are not entirely happy with the fruit, sprinkle it with a little sugar and a couple of tablespoons of grappa or an orange liqueur to bring out the flavor.

In the last few years I have had many such perfect endings to good dinners in Italy.

Peperoni ripieni della Zia Renata
Peppers Stuffed with Eggplant and Croutons

———

1½ pounds eggplant

salt

6 red and yellow bell peppers

vegetable oil for frying

4 slices white bread, 1 or 2 days old, cut into ½-inch cubes

6 tablespoons extra-virgin olive oil

1 garlic clove

1 dried chili, seeded and crumbled

4 anchovy fillets

½ cup chopped flat-leaf parsley

2 tablespoons capers, rinsed and dried

freshly ground black pepper

12 black olives, for decoration (optional)

1. Peel the eggplants, cut them into ½-inch cubes, place in a colander, and sprinkle with salt. Let stand for at least ½ hour.

2. Meanwhile, grill the peppers over a direct flame or under the broiler. Keep a watch on them and turn them over so that they blacken evenly. When the peppers are cool enough to handle, peel them and cut them in half lengthwise. Remove and discard the cores, seeds, and ribs. Place in an oiled baking dish.

3. Preheat the oven to 400° F.

4. Heat the vegetable oil and when very hot add the bread and fry until gold. Remove with a slotted spoon and transfer to paper towels to drain.

5. Rinse the eggplant cubes and dry them with paper towels. Heat 4 tablespoons of the olive oil and add the eggplant. Sauté until cooked, about 6 minutes, stirring frequently.

6. Chop the garlic, chili, and anchovy fillets and add to the eggplant with half the parsley. Cook for 1 minute. Remove from the heat and add the capers and croutons. Taste and adjust seasoning.

7. Fill the peppers neatly with the eggplant mixture. Sprinkle with the remaining chopped parsley and drizzle with the remaining olive oil. Bake for 10 minutes. Remove from the oven and let rest for 30 minutes or so; stuffed vegetables are much nicer just warm. Scatter the olives, if using, in the dish before serving.

PREPARATION

The peppers can be grilled up to 3 days in advance and refrigerated. The croutons can be made up to 2 days in advance and refrigerated. They also freeze well. You can sauté the eggplant up to 2 days in advance and refrigerate it. Stuff the peppers just before putting them in the oven, or the croutons will become soggy.

SERVES 6

Pasticcio di pesce
Fish Lasagne

———

	RED SAUCE
2 pounds mussels	3 tablespoons unsalted butter
1 small onion	2 shallots or 1 small onion, very finely chopped
4 garlic cloves	
⅔ cup dry white wine	1 dried red chili, seeded and crumbled
½ pound squid	1 garlic clove, peeled and chopped
salt	¾-inch piece gingerroot, peeled and very finely sliced
1 bay leaf	
1½ pounds monkfish	2 tablespoons tomato paste
1 pound shrimp in the shell	½ cup dry sherry
½ pound scallops, preferably bay scallops	⅓ cup heavy cream
	⅓ cup sour cream
WHITE SAUCE	
1¾ cups whole milk	lasagne made with 1½ cups unbleached flour and 2 eggs or 1 pound storebought fresh lasagne or ¾ pound dried lasagne
1 bay leaf	
5 tablespoons unsalted butter	
6 tablespoons flour	
salt and freshly ground black pepper	

1. Scrub the mussels under running water, knock off the barnacles, if any, and tug off the beard. Wash in several changes of water. Throw away any mussels that remain open when tapped on a hard surface; they are dead and must not be eaten.

2. Put the onion, garlic, and wine in a wide shallow pan. Add the mussels, cover with a lid, and cook over high heat until the mussels open. Shake the pan frequently. Remove the meat from the shells as soon as they open, but do not force them or they will break. Put the meat in a large bowl and discard the shells. Strain the liquid left in the pan through a sieve lined with cheesecloth or paper towels into another large bowl and reserve.

3. Clean the squid or have the fishmonger do it for you. Wash thoroughly and then cut the bodies into thin strips no more than 2 inches long. Cut the tentacles into morsels. Pour 2½ cups water into a medium saucepan, add salt and the bay leaf, and bring to a boil. Drop in the squid and simmer very gently until just tender. I cannot give a precise time because it depends on the size of the squid. Lift the squid out of the liquid with a slotted spoon and add to the mussels.

4. Skin the monkfish, if necessary, and cut into small cubes. Drop into the squid water and cook for 3 minutes. Lift the monkfish out of the water and add to the other fish, reserving the cooking liquid.

5. Wash the shrimp, remove the heads and shells, and devein. If large, cut into pieces and add them to the bowl with the fish. Put the heads and shells into the fish cooking liquid and bring to a boil. Simmer for about 5 minutes and then strain into the bowl containing the mussel liquid. Reserve.

6. Wash the scallops, and cut sea scallops into horizontal slices; leave bay scallops whole. Add to the bowl.

7. For the white sauce, measure about 1¾ cups of the fish stock and put it in a saucepan. Add the milk and the bay leaf and heat to just below the boiling point. Melt the butter in a heavy saucepan and blend in the flour. Cook over low heat, stirring constantly for 40 seconds, remove from the heat, and gradually stir in the milk and stock mixture. Return the pan to the heat and bring to a boil. Add salt and pepper to taste and simmer over very low heat for at least 20 minutes, stirring frequently. If you have time, cook the sauce, covered, in a bain-marie or double boiler over very low heat for about 45 minutes or put the saucepan on a flame tamer. In either case, you don't need to watch the sauce; it's enough to stir it every now and then.

8. For the red sauce, heat the butter gently with the shallots or onion in a small saucepan and sauté until soft. Add the chili, garlic, and ginger and sauté for 30 seconds more. Stir in the tomato paste and cook for a few more seconds, mixing the whole time. Pour in the sherry, about ½ cup of the fish stock, and the two creams. Stir thoroughly, bring to a boil, and let the sauce simmer gently for 10 minutes. Mix a couple of tablespoons of the tomato sauce into the white sauce. Add all the fish, cooked and uncooked, to the red sauce and simmer for a couple of minutes. Taste and check seasoning.

continued

9. Make the pasta dough following the directions on page 333. Cut out and cook the lasagne as described on page 316.

10. Preheat oven to 375° F.

11. To assemble the dish, grease a 10-x-8-inch baking dish, preferably metal, with a little butter and spread 2 or 3 tablespoons of the pink sauce without fish over the bottom. Cover with a layer of lasagne, overlapping as little as possible. Spread 2 or 3 tablespoons of the fish and its sauce on top and cover with a second layer of lasagne. Build up these layers, finishing with lasagne on top. Spread the pink sauce without fish all over the top. Bake for about 20 to 35 minutes, depending on whether it was just made or was made in advance and is cold. When ready, the sauce on top should be bubbling with some patches of crust. Remove from the oven and leave to stand for at least 5 minutes before serving.

PREPARATION

The fish can be prepared up to 1 day in advance, covered, and refrigerated. The fish stock must be refrigerated. The whole dish can be made up to 1 day in advance, covered with plastic wrap, and refrigerated. Do not freeze.

SERVES 6

Ananas e arancie
Pineapple and Oranges

~~~~~~

1 large ripe pineapple | *6 to 8 large navel oranges*

1. Peel the pineapple and slice ¼- to ½-inch thick. Peel the oranges to the quick, removing all the pith, and slice.

2. Put the pineapple slices on a large dish. I use a round dish so that everything is round. Cover each pineapple slice with a slice of orange. Cover with plastic wrap and refrigerate. Serve straight from the refrigerator.

PREPARATION

I don't like to prepare fruit too long in advance; 6 to 8 hours is the maximum.

SERVES 6

A SICILIAN DINNER FOR SIX

Caponatina di melanzane
Caponata with Chocolate

~

Il timballo del Gattopardo
The Pie from *The Leopard*

~

Insalata di finocchi, cicoria belga, ed arancie
Fennel, Belgian Endive, and Orange Salad

~

Cassata siciliana
Sicilian Cassata

*C*aponata, one of the peaks of Sicilian cooking, demonstrates very clearly a main characteristic of that cuisine. A simple local ingredient, in this case eggplant, is embellished and enriched until the end result is an opulent and almost baroque achievement. In some areas of Sicily tiny octopus, *bottarga* (dried roe of tuna or grey mullet), or even a small lobster is added. In Palermo, caponata becomes more Arab in concept and execution with the addition of almond and cinnamon. And to make it even more grandiose, in Catania it is often covered with *la salsa di San Bernardo,* a sauce based on toasted bread-crumbs mixed with grated chocolate, toasted almonds, sugar, and vinegar. The sauce was supposedly created by monks in the monastery of San Bernardo.

Caponata is usually served as an antipasto, although in that case it would not precede the *timballo* that follows here. In fact, in a truly Sicilian meal the *timballo* would be served first. But I can hardly imagine, in this day and age, anyone wanting to start the meal with such a substantial dish, and so I have made it the *secondo.*

The *timballo* is my interpretation of the one offered by the fictional Prince Fabrizio Salina to the notables of the town of Donnafugata in Sicily in 1860. This is how Giuseppe Tomasi di Lampedusa describes it in his famous book *The Leopard:* "The burnished gold of the crusts, the fragrance of sugar and cinnamon they exuded, were but preludes to the delights released from the interior when the knife broke the crust; first came a mist laden with aromas, then chicken livers, hard-boiled eggs, sliced ham, chicken, and truffles in masses of piping-hot, glistening macaroni, to which the meat juice gave an exquisite hue of suède."

After that I would suggest a salad, and when I think of Sicily I always think of this one. It is based on one of the most Sicilian of all fruits, the orange. It is a fresh, astringent salad, perfect after the rich *timballo.*

I end the meal with the Sicilian cassata. This is the traditional festive dessert in Sicily.

Caponatina di melanzane
Caponata with Chocolate

———

3 pounds eggplant

salt

vegetable oil for frying

1 bunch celery

½ cup olive oil

2 white onions, sliced

1 tablespoon sugar

2 cups smooth tomato sauce or peeled, seeded, and pureed plum tomatoes

1 tablespoon grated semisweet chocolate

freshly ground black pepper

⅔ cup red wine vinegar

8 tablespoons capers, rinsed

12 to 15 green Sicilian olives

1. Peel the eggplants and cut into ¾-inch cubes, place in a colander, and sprinkle with salt. Put a weight on top and leave to drain for at least 1 hour. Rinse, squeeze, and dry with paper towels.

2. Heat 1 inch of vegetable oil in a wok or frying pan. When the oil is very hot (a small piece of stale bread should turn brown in 40 seconds), slip in as much eggplant as will fit in a single layer and fry until golden brown on all sides, turning halfway through the cooking. Adjust the heat if the eggplant begins to burn. Lift it out of the oil and drain on paper towels. Repeat until all the eggplant is fried.

3. Remove the outer stalks and the leaves from the celery and keep them for another dish. Use only the heart. Remove the coarse outer threads with a potato peeler if necessary. Cut into 1½-inch-long matchsticks. Fry the celery stalks until golden crisp in the same oil used for the eggplant. Drain on paper towels.

4. Heat the olive oil in a clean sauté or frying pan and add the onion, 2 pinches of salt, and 1 pinch of sugar. Cook for about 5 to 7 minutes, until soft and just colored. Add the tomato sauce, the rest of the sugar, the chocolate, a little salt, and a generous grinding of pepper. Cook over high heat for about 2 minutes, then add the vinegar and the capers.

5. Pit and quarter the olives. Put the eggplant and celery back in the pan and add the olives. Cook over low heat for 30 minutes. Taste and adjust seasonings. Spoon the caponata into a serving bowl and allow to cool. Serve at room temperature with plenty of good bread.

PREPARATION

Caponata is better made at least 1 day in advance. It can be made up to 3 days in advance and kept refrigerated, but remember to bring it back to room temperature before serving, so that the subtle flavor can be fully appreciated.

SERVES 6 TO 8

Il timballo del Gattopardo
The Pie from *The Leopard*

2 cups unbleached flour

1 teaspoon salt

1 egg

1 egg yolk

½ cup sugar

8 tablespoons (1 stick) unsalted butter, cut into small pieces

FILLING

½ cup dried porcini (about 1 ounce)

5 tablespoons unsalted butter

2 ounces luganega or other sweet, coarsely ground pork sausage, skinned and cut into small pieces

¼ pound boneless chicken breast, skinned and cut into ½-inch cubes

¼ pound chicken livers, trimmed and cut into small pieces

⅔ cup dry white wine

salt and freshly ground black pepper

pinch ground cloves

pinch ground cinnamon

generous pinch of grated nutmeg

1 tablespoon truffle paste (optional)

2 ounces prosciutto, thickly sliced

⅔ cup cooked peas (about 4 ounces)

½ cup freshly grated parmesan

¾ pound penne or short ziti

⅔ cup strong meat stock

1 tablespoon white flour

3 tablespoons dried breadcrumbs

2 hard-boiled eggs, shelled

1 egg yolk and 2 tablespoons milk for glazing

1. For the pastry, sift the flour with the salt into a mound on a work surface. Make a well in the center and add the egg, the egg yolk, 2 tablespoons water, and the sugar. Mix lightly, then add the butter. Blend together by pushing small pieces of dough away from you, using the heel of your hand. If the dough is too dry, add a little more cold water. Gather the dough into a ball and wrap in foil or plastic wrap lightly dusted with flour. Chill in the refrigerator for at least 1 hour. The pastry may also be made in a food processor.

2. Meanwhile, soak the dried porcini in 1 cup hot water for 30 minutes. Lift out carefully and rinse gently under cold running water. Dry and cut into small pieces. Strain the soaking liquid through a sieve lined with paper towels. Set aside.

3. Put 3 tablespoons of the butter and the luganega in a small heavy frying pan and sauté for 7 minutes, breaking up the sausage with a fork. Add the chicken and sauté for 2 minutes, stirring frequently, then mix in the chicken livers. Cook for 2 minutes or so, then add the wine and boil fast for 1 minute to evaporate the alcohol. Add salt and pepper to taste and about 4 tablespoons of the porcini soaking liquid.

4. Reduce the heat and cook until nearly all the liquid has evaporated. Add a couple of tablespoons of hot water and continue cooking for about 5 minutes, stirring occasionally. The meat should cook in very little liquid but not cook dry. Check the seasonings.

5. Meanwhile melt 1 tablespoon of the remaining butter in a small heavy sauce-pan. Add the chopped porcini and cook over low heat for about 2 minutes. Add the clove, cinnamon, nutmeg, and salt and pepper to taste. Add a couple of tablespoons of the porcini soaking liquid. Cook, stirring occasionally, for 5 minutes, then pour the sauce into the pan with the sausage and chicken mixture. Mix well and cook for 5 minutes more. Transfer the contents of the pan with all the cooking juices to a bowl, add the truffle paste, and mix well. Cut the prosciutto into thin short strips and add to the bowl together with the peas and all but 2 tablespoons of the parmesan. Mix well. Set aside for the flavors to combine.

6. Cook the pasta in plenty of salted boiling water until very al dente. It will finish cooking later, in the oven.

7. While the pasta is cooking, heat the stock. Blend the remaining butter with the flour and add it bit by bit to the simmering stock, waiting until each bit has been incorporated before adding the next. When all the mixture has been added, remove from the heat and set aside.

8. Drain the pasta and turn into a large bowl. Toss with the stock mixture.

9. About 1 hour before you want to cook the dish, remove the dough from the refrigerator and allow to become pliable at room temperature.

10. Heat the oven to 425° F.

11. Generously butter an 8-inch springform pan. Roll out about one-third of the dough into an 8-inch circle on a piece of wax paper. Turn it over onto the bottom of the pan and peel off the paper. For the sides of the pan, roll out half

continued

of the remaining dough in a wide strip on wax paper. Be sure it is wide enough to reach the top of the pan or even beyond. Seal the bottom and sides with cold water. Sprinkle the breadcrumbs and the remaining cheese over the bottom. Cover with a layer of pasta and then a layer of filling. Build up alternate layers, ending with pasta. Cut the eggs into wedges and push them here and there into the filling.

12. Roll out the remaining dough into a circle and cover the pasta. Seal the dough lid to the side strip with cold water. Brush the top of the pie with the egg yolk–milk glaze. If you wish, make a few decorations with the dough trimmings, brush with egg yolk and milk glaze, and fix to the top of the pie. Pierce the top with a fork in several places to let the steam escape. Bake for about 10 minutes. Turn the oven down to 325° F. and bake for 25 minutes more.

13. Remove from the oven and let stand for about 10 minutes. Unclip the tin and carefully transfer the pie, on the pan bottom, to a serving dish. Serve at once.

PREPARATION

The pastry dough can be prepared up to 3 days in advance and refrigerated. It can also be frozen. The filling can be made up to 1 day in advance and refrigerated. Assemble the *timballo* 30 minutes or less before baking.

SERVES 6

Insalata di finocchi, cicoria belga, ed arancie

Fennel, Belgian Endive, and Orange Salad

---

2 medium fennel bulbs, preferably round

3 navel oranges

4 Belgian endives

6 tablespoons freshly squeezed lemon juice

6 tablespoons olive oil

salt

24 small black olives, such as niçoise

1. Remove the stalks, feathery leaves, and any bruised or brown parts from the fennel bulbs. (Keep the stalks and leaves for a soup.) Cut the bulbs in half lengthwise, and then cut them across into thin slices. Wash the slices, drain, and dry thoroughly, then put them in a bowl.

2. Peel the oranges to the quick and thinly slice them on a plate so as not to lose any juice. Cut the smaller slices in half and the larger slices into quarters. Add to the fennel in the bowl, together with the juice collected on the plate.

3. Cut the Belgian endive crosswise into rings. Wash and dry thoroughly, then add to the bowl.

4. Beat the lemon juice and olive oil together, add salt, and pour over the prepared vegetables. Toss very well. Taste and adjust salt. (Pepper is never added to this kind of salad in Sicily; it would clash with the sweet fennel and orange.)

5. Transfer the salad to a deep dish and scatter the olives over it, or serve straight from the bowl.

PREPARATION

The vegetables can be sliced up to 1 day in advance and kept, wrapped in a dish towel, in the refrigerator. The oranges, too, can be prepared up to 1 day in advance and refrigerated in a covered bowl.

SERVES 6 TO 8

Cassata siciliana
Sicilian Cassata

2½ cups ricotta

⅔ cup heavy cream

½ cup sugar

½ pound (1 cup) mixed candied citrus peel, chopped

1 teaspoon ground cinnamon

2½ ounces semisweet chocolate, chopped

1 ounce (¼ cup) pistachio nuts, blanched, skinned, and chopped

½ cup marsala or rum

1 pound sponge cake, store bought or homemade (page 343), cut into ½-inch-thick slices

2⅓ cups confectioners' sugar

1 tablespoon lemon juice

½ pound candied fruit

1. Mix the ricotta thoroughly in a large bowl until smooth. Lightly whip the cream and fold it into the ricotta with the sugar. Add the candied peel, cinnamon, chocolate, pistachios, and half the marsala or rum. Mix very thoroughly.

2. Line the bottom of an 8-inch springform pan with parchment or wax paper. Cover with slices of cake, plugging any holes with bits of cake. Moisten with some of the remaining marsala or rum, using a pastry brush. Line the sides of the pan with sliced cake and moisten with more marsala or rum. Spoon in the ricotta mixture, cover with a layer of sliced cake and moisten with the rest of the marsala or rum. Cover with plastic wrap and chill for at least 3 hours.

3. To make the icing, put ¼ cup of confectioners' sugar and 2 tablespoons water in a small heavy saucepan and bring slowly to a boil, stirring constantly. This stock syrup, as it is called, helps make the icing run evenly. Put the rest of the sugar in the top of a double boiler, or into a saucepan that can fit inside a larger pan half full of simmering water. Very gradually add enough stock syrup to moisten and dilute to the consistency of heavy cream, working it in well with a wooden spoon. Add the lemon juice and continue cooking in the double boiler or bain-marie until just warm.

4. Unmold the cake and slowly pour the icing on the center of the cake, letting it run all over the surface and down the sides. Put the cake back in the refrigerator to allow the icing to set.

5. Just before serving, place the cake on a dish and decorate with the candied fruit. Serve chilled.

PREPARATION

Cassata must be made at least 8 hours before serving, but not more than 24 hours in advance.

SERVES 6 TO 8

DINNER FOR EIGHT

Passato di sedano
Cream of Celery Soup

~

Maiale al latte
Loin of Pork Braised in Milk

~

Cachi al sugo di lime
Persimmons with Lime Juice

*I*talian vegetable soups usually consist of seasonal vegetables cut into small pieces and cooked in stock or water, with some pasta or rice added at the end. When the vegetables are pureed, as in this soup, it is the result of French influence. Yet this pureed soup is typically Italian in flavor, since it is rounded out by ricotta instead of cream. The ricotta also gives the soup a rougher texture, which is emphasized by sautéed breadcrumbs.

Loin of pork braised in milk is a traditional dish from central Italy. I marinate the meat because I find that pork these days is often tasteless. The meat is then braised in milk, which turns into a thick, wickedly rich sauce studded with golden nuggets. With it I serve thick mashed potatoes to mop up the juices. The Italian-style carrots on page 329 are also a good accompaniment.

To cleanse the palate you need fruit, and the persimmons in lime juice are just tart enough to make your tongue tingle a little. Either the acorn-shaped Hachiya or the round Fuyu can be used in this dish. The Fuyu is less astringent.

Passato di sedano
Cream of Celery Soup

———

1½ medium bunches celery (about 1 pound)

5 tablespoons unsalted butter

2 tablespoons olive oil

3 potatoes, peeled and cut into small pieces

8 cups homemade broth, preferably Italian broth (page 338)

salt

4 slices whole wheat bread, crust removed and very lightly toasted

1 cup ricotta

freshly ground black pepper

freshly grated parmesan

1. Remove the strings and leaves from the celery stalks, wash thoroughly, and cut into pieces. Save the leaves for flavoring other dishes or for chopping into a salad.

2. Heat 2 tablespoons of butter and 1 tablespoon of oil. When the butter begins to foam, add the celery and the potatoes. Sauté very gently for 5 minutes, stirring frequently.

3. Meanwhile, bring the broth to a boil and pour over the sautéed vegetables. Add salt to taste and simmer for 30 minutes.

4. While the soup is cooking, make coarse breadcrumbs from the toasted bread. A food processor is ideal for the job. Heat the rest of the butter and oil in a small frying pan and when very hot, mix in the breadcrumbs and fry until all the fat has been absorbed and the crumbs are dark and crisp.

5. Puree the soup through a food mill, blender, or a food processor, and return to the pan. Bring the soup back to a boil. Remove from the heat. Break up the ricotta with a fork and add to the soup with the pepper. Mix well, taste, and adjust seasoning.

6. Ladle the soup into bowls and pass around the breadcrumbs and parmesan in separate bowls.

PREPARATION

Both the soup (without the ricotta) and the breadcrumbs can be prepared up to 2 days in advance. They can also be frozen. The ricotta must be added to the reheated soup just before serving.

SERVES 8

Maiale al latte
Loin of Pork Braised in Milk

1 boneless loin of pork, with a thin layer of fat (3½ pounds)

4 tablespoons vegetable oil

4 cloves, bruised

pinch ground cinnamon

sprig fresh rosemary

3 garlic cloves, peeled and bruised

salt

6 or 7 peppercorns, bruised

1 bay leaf

2 tablespoons unsalted butter

2 cups whole milk

freshly ground black pepper

1. Tie the loin in several places, if the butcher has not done it for you. Put the meat in a bowl and add 2 tablespoons of the oil, the cloves, cinnamon, rosemary, garlic, 1 teaspoon salt, the peppercorns, and the bay leaf. Coat the pork all over with the marinade, cover the bowl with a lid of some sort, and marinate for about 8 hours outside the refrigerator unless it is very hot. Turn the meat over in the marinade whenever you think of it.

2. Heat the butter and the rest of the oil in a heavy casserole large enough to hold the pork snugly. When the butter foam begins to subside, add the meat and brown well on all sides to a rich golden color.

3. Heat the milk to the boiling point and pour slowly over the meat. Sprinkle with salt and pepper, place the lid over the pan, slightly askew, and simmer for about 3 hours. Turn the meat over and baste about every 20 minutes. By the end of the cooking the meat should be very tender and the sauce should be a

continued

dark golden color and quite thick. If it is too thin, remove the meat to a side dish and boil briskly, uncovered, until it darkens and thickens. Transfer the meat to a carving board and let stand for about 10 minutes.

4. Meanwhile, skim off as much fat as you can from the surface of the sauce, add 2 tablespoons hot water, and boil over high heat for about 2 minutes, while scraping the bottom of the pan with a metal spoon. Taste and adjust seasonings.

5. Remove the string and carve the pork into ½-inch slices. Arrange the slices on a heated dish and spoon the sauce over the slices, or spoon only a little of the sauce and serve the rest separately in a warm sauceboat.

PREPARATION

The meat can be cooked up to 3 days in advance and kept, covered, in the refrigerator. It can also be frozen. Thaw completely before reheating. Carve the meat and cover with the sauce. Reheat very gently, covered, in a moderate oven for 15 minutes.

SERVES 8

Cachi al sugo di lime
Persimmons with Lime Juice

---

12 persimmons	*3 or 4 tablespoons sugar, according to*
4 limes	*taste and the sweetness of the fruit*

1. Wash the persimmons and dry. Slice them as you would an orange and lay the slices, slightly overlapping, on a serving dish.

2. One hour before serving, squeeze the limes and pour the juice over the persimmons. Sprinkle with the sugar and leave in the refrigerator, covered with plastic wrap, until ready to serve them.

PREPARATION

The fruits can be cut a few hours in advance and arranged on the serving dish. The dish must be covered with plastic wrap. The dressing must be spooned over no more than 1 hour before serving or the persimmons will macerate.

SERVES 8

AN AUTUMN DINNER
FOR EIGHT

Risotto con la zucca

Pumpkin Risotto

—————

Cervo alla casalinga

Venison Stew with Onions

—————

Polenta

Polenta (page 332)

—————

Funghi al funghetto

Sautéed Mushrooms (page 328)

—————

Coppette di pompelmo e uva

Grapefruit Cups with Grapes

Autumn offers an abundance of good produce. For me it is also the time when it is particularly enjoyable to start cooking again, after vacation and the warm weather. Slow-cooking dishes are autumnal, well suited to being accompanied by a steaming golden polenta. Game is in season, so I designed this menu around this typically Italian *secondo*. Polenta is the perfect foil for the succulent richness of the venison, cooked at length in the oven with plenty of onion. You might think the amount of onion overpowering, but when it is cooked for a long time very slowly, it becomes a golden-brown, slightly caramelized mush which absorbs and at the same time tones down the gaminess of the meat.

I've chosen mushrooms to go with it, the most autumnal of all accompaniments. In the recipe on page 328, I have suggested using a selection of mushrooms easily available in most supermarkets. The other accompaniment should be polenta (page 332), as it always is in Italy, or a puree of celery root and potato or of Jerusalem artichokes.

To precede this, a light buttery risotto is ideal, and for autumn, risotto with pumpkin is just right. Halloween pumpkins, the most commonly available, are not good to eat. I have tried many kinds of winter squash, and they were all quite good. Pumpkins and other hard squash have an elusive, sweet flavor that is hard to capture. When they are good, this flavor comes to life in a risotto. For me, it rates as one of the best dishes of the Lombard tradition, as interpreted here in my mother's recipe.

As the first two courses of this menu are quite substantial, you will only need fruit to finish the meal. Grapefruit cups filled with grapes fill the bill, very refreshing as well as seasonal.

Risotto con la zucca
Pumpkin Risotto

2³/₄ quarts homemade Italian broth (page 338)

6 tablespoons unsalted butter

8 shallots or 3 onions, very finely chopped

salt

1 teaspoon sugar

½ cup chopped flat-leaf parsley

1½ pounds cleaned pumpkin or hard squash, rind and seeds removed, cut into ½-inch cubes

2½ cups Arborio rice

freshly ground black pepper

½ cup heavy cream

½ cup freshly grated parmesan

extra freshly grated parmesan for serving

1. Heat the broth to the simmering point.

2. Heat the butter and the shallots in a large heavy saucepan and add 1 teaspoon of salt, which will help them to soften without browning, and the sugar. Cook for about 5 minutes. Add half of the parsley and continue cooking for 5 minutes more, stirring very frequently.

3. Add the pumpkin and cook until just tender, anywhere from 5 to 20 minutes, depending on the variety. For the longer-cooking ones, you may have to add 1 or 2 ladlefuls of hot broth to the pan. When the pumpkin is tender (when pricked with the point of a knife), stir in the rice and sauté for 1 or 2 minutes until the grains are well coated in butter. Pour in about 2 cups of simmering broth and stir very thoroughly. Bring the liquid to a lively boil, turn off the heat and cover the pan tightly.

4. About 15 minutes before serving, bring the broth back to the simmer. Add a knob of butter. Mix 2 ladlefuls of hot broth into the rice and continue cooking, gradually adding 1 ladleful of broth at a time, until the rice is ready. If you use up all the broth before the rice is cooked, add boiling water. This risotto should be more creamy and runny than others, half way between a thick soup and the usual risotto. Season with pepper and taste for salt.

5. Stir in the cream and the parmesan. Turn off the heat and leave for 1 minute for the cheese to melt and the flavors to blend.

6. Give the risotto a vigorous stir and heap it up on a heated round dish. Sprinkle with the remaining parsley and serve at once, passing the extra cheese separately in a bowl.

PREPARATION

Prepare the risotto through Step 3 no more than 1 hour in advance. Start Step 4 shortly before serving.

SERVES 8

Cervo alla casalinga
Venison Stew with Onions

———

3¼ pounds venison	*2 tablespoons olive oil*
MARINADE	*5 tablespoons unsalted butter*
2⅔ cups dry white wine	*3 pounds white onions, sliced*
2 tablespoons olive oil	*1 tablespoon sugar*
2 bay leaves	*salt and freshly ground black pepper*
2 carrots	*1¼ to 1½ cups strong meat stock*
1 large onion	*½ teaspoon ground cinnamon*
2 celery stalks	*½ teaspoon ground cloves*
2 garlic cloves, peeled and bruised	*½ nutmeg, grated*
10 juniper berries, bruised	
1 teaspoon black peppercorns, bruised	

1. Cut the venison into small slices or large strips about ½ inch thick. (I find that this type of meat becomes less dry if cut into strips rather than chunks or cubes.) Put the meat in a bowl and add all the ingredients for the marinade. Cover and leave in a cool place overnight. Except at the height of summer or in a warm climate, there is no need to refrigerate the meat for this short amount of time. In fact, leaving it at room temperature will help make the meat more tender.

2. The next day, heat the oil, butter, and sliced onions in a casserole and cook slowly until they soften. Sprinkle with the sugar and turn the heat up. The onion will caramelize slightly and turn golden brown. Season with salt and pepper and add the meat stock, cinnamon, cloves, and nutmeg. Cover the casserole and cook over very low heat for about 30 minutes, stirring occasionally.

3. Preheat the oven to 300° F.

4. Remove the meat from the marinade and dry with paper towels. Strain the marinade and discard the vegetables.

5. Transfer about half the onion from the casserole to a side plate. Lay the venison over the remaining onion in the casserole, season with salt and pepper, and cover with the onion previously lifted out. Heat the marinade and add to the casserole. Add more heated white wine if necessary so that the meat is just covered. Cook in the oven for about 1½ to 2 hours, or until the venison is very tender.

PREPARATION

The meat can be marinated up to 3 days in advance, in which case it must be refrigerated. The dish can be prepared up to 2 days in advance and refrigerated. If necessary, skim the fat from the surface of the stew before reheating.

SERVES 8

Coppette di pompelmo e uva
Grapefruit Cups with Grapes

---

4 grapefruits	*sugar to taste*
1 pound seedless grapes	*3 tablespoons kirsch*

1. Wash and dry the grapefruits and cut them in half. Remove the flesh and the thin skin between the segments, and the central pith. Put the cleaned pieces of grapefruit in a bowl. Chill the shells.

2. Wash and dry the grapes and add to the bowl. Sprinkle with about 3 or 4 tablespoons of sugar and splash with kirsch. Taste and adjust the sugar.

3. Cover the bowl with plastic wrap and chill for 2 to 3 hours, stirring the mixture 2 or 3 times while it chills. Put half a grapefruit shell on each plate and fill with the fruit mixture.

PREPARATION

If necessary you can prepare the grapefruit 1 day in advance and keep, covered, in the refrigerator. Mix the fruits together and add the kirsch and the sugar not more than 3 hours before serving.

SERVES 8

DINNER FOR TEN

Il fiore di melanzane alla senape

Broiled Eggplant with Lemon-Mustard Dressing

⎯⎯

Coniglio con le cipolle

Braised Rabbit

⎯⎯

Purè di patate

Mashed Potatoes

⎯⎯

Le carote di Ada Boni

Italian-style Carrots (page 329)

⎯⎯

*Torta di ricotta e mandorle
con la salsina di arancia*

**Ricotta and Almond Cake
with Orange Sauce**

*R*abbit is a sure winner, served in this golden onion sauce sharpened by wine vinegar. Serve it with buttery mashed potatoes to sop up the juices and with the carrots on page 329.

The dinner opens with a very attractive eggplant dish that looks like a pale sunflower. The flavor, however, has nothing pale about it; the lemony mustard dressing sinks into the grilled eggplant. Whenever I eat eggplant I am surprised at how well it blends with other ingredients but keeps its own individual flavor. It reminds me of a great character actor who is superb in totally different roles, and yet they all seem to have been written just for him.

I am sure you must have eaten a ricotta dessert of one sort or another if you are at all keen on Italian cooking, as it is very popular with Italians. But I doubt if you ever had one like this. The cake can be served as it is with a cup of tea or with coffee and liqueurs after dinner. But at the end of a meal, as here, I prefer to pass around an orange sauce. Heavy cream is also good, especially if you flavor it with a couple of spoonfuls of Grand Marnier and sweeten it with confectioners' sugar.

Il fiore di melanzane alla senape
Broiled Eggplant with Lemon-Mustard Dressing

———

3 pounds eggplant	*3 garlic cloves, peeled and chopped*
salt	*4 tablespoons freshly squeezed lemon juice*
⅔ cup extra-virgin olive oil	
3 tablespoons Dijon mustard	*4 tablespoons vegetable broth*
3 tablespoons chopped fresh mint	*sprigs fresh mint for garnish*

1. Wash the eggplants and cut them lengthwise into slices about ⅓ inch thick. Lay the slices on a slanting wooden board and sprinkle them generously with salt, preferably coarse salt. Leave to drain for at least 1 hour, then rinse and dry thoroughly with paper towels.

2. Heat the broiler. Line the pan with aluminum foil and brush the foil with a little olive oil. Lay the eggplant slices on the foil, brush with some more oil, and place the pan under the broiler. Broil for about 5 minutes on each side until soft and beginning to change color. If the eggplant slices are browning too fast, turn the heat down. They are ready when they can be pierced easily with a fork.

3. Meanwhile, put the mustard, mint, garlic, lemon juice, vegetable broth, and a little salt in the food processor. Set it in motion and gradually add the remaining oil through the funnel to make a smooth, emulsified dressing. Taste and check the seasoning.

4. Reserving the best-looking slices of eggplant of the same size, arrange a layer of slices in a circle. Spread a little dressing on top, then cover with another layer of eggplant slices. Continue building up the dish, finishing with the best slices. Set aside. Reserve a few spoonfuls of dressing. Cover with plastic wrap and refrigerate for at least 6 hours.

5. Before serving, coat with the remaining dressing and decorate the dish with a few sprigs of fresh mint in the middle of the eggplant "flower."

PREPARATION

The dish must be prepared at least 6 hours in advance for the flavors to blend. I like to serve it on the following day. I think it is at its best then.

SERVES 10

Coniglio con le cipolle
Braised Rabbit

———

4 pounds white onions	*7 pounds rabbit pieces*
½ cup olive oil	*½ cup red wine vinegar*
salt	*freshly ground black pepper*
⅔ cup meat stock	*4 tablespoons balsamic vinegar*
4 tablespoons sugar	

1. Thinly slice the onions. Put them in a heavy casserole with the oil, 2 teaspoons salt, and 6 tablespoons stock. Cover the casserole with the lid and cook for about 1½ hours over very low heat until the onions are reduced to a golden mush. Turn the heat up to moderate, mix in the sugar, and cook for 15 minutes more to caramelize the onion slightly. Stir frequently.

2. Preheat the oven to 300° F.

3. Wash and dry the rabbit pieces and add to the casserole. Check that there is enough liquid before adding them. If necessary, add a couple of tablespoons of stock. Turn the pieces of rabbit over a couple of times, then pour in the wine vinegar. Season with plenty of pepper and 2 teaspoons of salt.

4. Cook for 5 minutes over moderate heat, then cover the casserole and place it in the oven. Cook until the rabbit is done, about 1 hour or more. Stir in the balsamic vinegar and cook on top of the stove for a few minutes, turning the pieces over once or twice. Taste and check the seasoning. Serve from the casserole or transfer to a heated bowl.

PREPARATION

The dish can be prepared up to 3 days in advance and refrigerated. Reheat in a moderate oven for 20 minutes.

SERVES 10

Torta di ricotta e mandorle con la salsina di arancia
Ricotta and Almond Cake with Orange Sauce

---

1 cup almonds	*5 tablespoons potato starch*
2¼ cups ricotta	*confectioners' sugar*
¾ cup sugar	ORANGE SAUCE
3 to 4 drops pure almond extract	*3 large juice oranges*
7 eggs, separated	*1 cup sugar*
2 tablespoons grated orange peel	*½ lemon*
3 tablespoons Grand Marnier (optional)	

1. Butter and line a 10-inch springform pan with parchment paper.

2. Preheat the oven to 350° F.

3. Blanch the almonds for 30 seconds in boiling water. Peel them, dry with paper towels, and chop in the food processor to a fine grain but not a powder.

4. Push the ricotta through a food mill or a sieve into a bowl. Add the sugar and beat hard until creamy and smooth. Mix in the almonds, the almond extract, and the egg yolks, one by one, beating hard after each addition. Mix in the orange peel and the Grand Marnier, if using.

5. Beat the egg whites until stiff and fold into the ricotta mixture a little at a time alternately with the potato starch. Use a metal spoon and a high movement to incorporate more air. Spoon the mixture into the prepared pan and bake for about 40 minutes, or until set. A toothpick inserted into the middle of the cake should come out very lightly moist. Allow to cool in the pan and then place on a round serving plate. Sprinkle lavishly with confectioners' sugar just before serving.

6. For the sauce, wash and scrub the oranges thoroughly. Remove the peel, taking off only the orange part. Juice the oranges and set aside. Cut the peel into julienne strips and put in a small saucepan. Cover with cold water, bring to a boil, and cook until they are soft and slightly transparent. Drain.

7. Put the sugar and 4 tablespoons water in the same pan and bring very slowly to a boil. When the sugar has dissolved, add the orange and lemon juices. Stir in the strips of peel and simmer for 1 or 2 minutes. Serve cold in a sauceboat or a bowl.

PREPARATION

The cake is best made the day it is to be eaten. If necessary it can be made up to 1 day in advance. The orange sauce can be made up to 1 week in advance and refrigerated in an airtight container.

SERVES 10

L'insalata di Luisetta

Vegetable, Grapefruit, and Shrimp Salad

~~~

Tiella di pesce

Apulian Fish Pie

~~~

Insalata di sedano, carote, e mela al sapor di coriandolo

**Celery, Carrot, and Apple Salad
with a Wine and Cilantro Dressing**

~~~

Torta di riso

Rice Cake

~~~

Insalata autunnale di frutta

Autumn Fruit Compote

I like buffet suppers. When you find the conversation grinding to a halt, you can simply say, "I must go and have some more of that delicious meat," and move on. It is always very pleasant to be able to change eating partners with each course. But at this sort of supper you must serve food that does not need a knife, so that you can sit anywhere, or even stand, and go on eating while you chat. I like to make it a three-course meal, just as if we were sitting at the table.

This is a fish-based menu. The *primo* is a light and refreshing salad, modern in its combination of flavors. The *secondo* is a robust dish brimming with Mediterranean aromas. It is a version of an earlier recipe of mine for *tiella di pesce alla pugliese* (baked fish and potatoes Apulian style). These southern Italian *tielle* are made with raw potatoes that absorb the flavor of the fish or meat with which they are baked.

The special salad I suggest is particularly suitable for a party in autumn. The other salad should be a green salad, which you will find on page 325.

The rice cake is as typically Italian as rice pudding is American or English. The two are based on the same ingredients, but they are treated differently to produce a very different result. *Torta di riso,* of which there are as many variants as there are cooks, is a real cake, firm yet moist. It is served unmolded and cold, perhaps tepid, but never hot. It is made with short-grain Italian rice, which absorbs the milk, and is flavored with characteristic Italian flavorings.

The other dessert, the autumn fruit compote, is a rich mixture of fruit cooked in wine and lavishly scented with spices, a dish reminiscent of Renaissance cooking, when spices were sprinkled with a generous hand. The two sweets are different, yet they go well enough together to be served on the same plate.

L'insalata di Luisetta
Vegetable, Grapefruit, and Shrimp Salad

———

2 pounds shrimp

2 shallots, cut in half

1 celery stalk, cut in pieces

6 peppercorns

3 parsley stems

2 dill or fennel sprigs

2 bay leaves

2 tablespoons olive oil

½ cup dry white wine

salt

¼ pound arugula

the heart of 1 curly endive

¾ pound green beans, steamed or boiled

the hearts of 2 celery heads (2 cups)

8 small tomatoes

2 pink grapefruits

¾ pound very small zucchini

1 cup extra-virgin olive oil

6 tablespoons raspberry vinegar, if available, or cider vinegar

freshly ground black pepper

1. Put the shrimp in a pan and cover with cold water. Add the shallot, celery, peppercorns, parsley, dill, bay leaves, 2 tablespoons of the olive oil, wine, and 1 teaspoon salt and bring to a boil. Boil for 1 minute, then drain and refresh under cold water.

2. Clean, trim, and wash the arugula and the heart of endive. Cut into very fine strips and spread out on a large oval dish. Cut the beans into 1½-inch pieces, the celery into very thin strips, and the tomatoes into thin wedges and place them over the greens.

3. Peel the grapefruit to the quick, separate into segments, and remove the membrane between them. Cut the segments in half and scatter over the dish.

4. Wash and dry the zucchini and cut into thin rounds. Add to the dish.

5. Shell the shrimp and devein if necessary. Keep about 6 of the best for garnish, cut the others into small pieces, and put them here and there among the vegetables.

6. Beat the oil and vinegar together in a bowl with a fork, add salt and pepper, and pour over the salad. Decorate with the reserved shrimp and serve at once.

PREPARATION

All the vegetables can be prepared up to 4 hours in advance, but they should be placed on the dish no more than 1 hour in advance. Dress the salad just before serving.

SERVES 10

Tiella di pesce
Apulian Fish Pie

4 pounds mussels	*salt and freshly ground black pepper*
1¹⁄₃ cups dry white wine	*6 tablespoons chopped flat-leaf parsley*
10 garlic cloves, peeled and bruised	*2 dried chilies, seeded and crumbled*
2 lemons, cut into wedges	*¹⁄₂ pound hard pecorino, grated*
1 pound fillet of cod	*10 fennel seeds, pounded to coarse powder*
2 pounds fillet of haddock	
4 pounds new potatoes	*2 pounds ripe tomatoes, peeled, seeded, and sliced*
1¹⁄₂ cups olive oil	

1. Clean the mussels, following the directions on page 158. Throw away any that remain open when you tap them on a hard surface. They are dead and should not be eaten.

2. Put the wine, 4 of the garlic cloves, and the lemons in a large sauté pan. Bring to a boil and boil for 2 minutes. Add about half the mussels, cover the pan with a lid, and leave them to steam open. Shake the pan every now and then, to turn the mussels over. When they are open, remove the pan from the heat.

3. Remove the mussels from their shells and put them in a bowl, opening them over the pan so that you collect the juices. Discard the shells. Repeat with the remaining mussels.

continued

4. Strain the mussel liquor through a sieve lined with cheesecloth into a bowl. Set aside.

5. Skin the cod and haddock fillets, if necessary, and cut into pieces.

6. Peel the potatoes and cut them into wafer-thin slices, using the food processor fitted with a fine blade disk. Put the potatoes in a bowl of cold water and rinse them to get rid of some of the starch. Drain, dry very thoroughly, and put in a bowl. Toss with 2 tablespoons of the oil and season with salt and pepper.

7. Preheat the oven to 400° F.

8. Mix together in a bowl the parsley, chilies, cheese, and fennel. Slice the remaining garlic cloves and add to the mixture. Add salt to taste.

9. Grease a large lasagne dish or a shallow baking dish with a little oil. Cover the bottom with half the potatoes. Make a layer with half the tomatoes. Sprinkle with a third of the herb and cheese mixture and place the fish and the mussels on top. Sprinkle with half the remaining herb and cheese mixture and pour over half the remaining olive oil and half the mussel liquor. Cover with the remaining potatoes, then with the remaining tomatoes. Sprinkle with the remaining herb mixture and dribble the rest of the olive oil and the mussel liquor over all.

10. Cover the dish with foil and place in the oven for 25 minutes. Remove the foil and continue cooking until the potatoes are tender. Let stand for 5 minutes before serving, for the flavors to blend.

PREPARATION

The pie is better made the day it is to be eaten, although the fish can be prepared up to 1 day in advance and refrigerated in a covered container.

SERVES   12

Insalata di sedano, carote, e mela al sapor di coriandolo

Celery, Carrot, and Apple Salad with a Wine and Cilantro Dressing

the hearts of 2 large white celery heads (2 cups)

7 medium carrots

2 Granny Smith apples

4 tablespoons lemon juice

½ cup dry white wine

⅓ cup extra-virgin olive oil

salt and freshly ground black pepper

3 tablespoons chopped fresh cilantro leaves

1. Remove the outer stalks of the celery and use only the hearts. Save the stalks for another purpose. Wash the tender stalks and remove strings if necessary. Slice into very thin strips and put in a bowl.

2. Peel, wash, and dry the carrots. Cut them into matchsticks and add to the bowl, using the food processor fitted with the matchstick disk.

3. Peel and cut the apple into the same size matchsticks. Add to the bowl. Sprinkle with a little lemon juice to prevent the fruit from discoloring.

4. Heat the wine, half the oil, and the remaining lemon juice and simmer very gently for 5 minutes to evaporate the alcohol. Pour over the vegetables about 1 hour before you want to serve the salad.

5. Toss with the rest of the oil and season with salt and plenty of pepper. Sprinkle with the chopped cilantro just before serving.

PREPARATION

Do not prepare the vegetables more than half an hour before the sauce is poured over them, as they will discolor.

SERVES 12

Torta di riso
Rice Cake
———

3⅓ cups whole milk	*½ cup pine nuts*
1 cup plus 2 tablespoons sugar	*4 eggs, separated*
strip of lemon peel, yellow part only	*3 tablespoons chopped candied orange, lemon, and citron peel*
1-inch piece of vanilla bean, split in half	*1 teaspoon grated lemon peel*
2-inch piece of cinnamon stick	*3 tablespoons rum*
salt	*butter and dried breadcrumbs for the pan*
¾ cup Arborio rice	
1 cup almonds, blanched and peeled	*confectioners' sugar for decoration*

1. Put the milk, 2 tablespoons of the sugar, the lemon peel, vanilla bean, cinnamon stick, and a pinch of salt in a saucepan and bring to a boil.

2. Add the rice and stir well with a wooden spoon. Cook, uncovered, over very low heat for about 40 minutes, until the rice has absorbed the milk and is soft and creamy. Stir frequently during the cooking. Set aside to cool.

3. While the rice is cooking, preheat the oven to 350° F.

4. Spread the almonds and the pine nuts on a baking tray and toast them in the oven for about 10 minutes. Shake the tray once or twice to keep them from burning. Cool a little, then coarsely chop the nuts by hand or in the food processor, but do not reduce them to powder.

5. Remove the lemon peel, the vanilla bean, and the cinnamon stick from the rice and spoon the rice into a mixing bowl.

6. Incorporate the egg yolks one at a time into the rice, mixing well after each addition. Add the remaining sugar, the nuts, candied peel, grated lemon peel, and rum, combining thoroughly.

7. Beat the egg whites until stiff and fold into the rice mixture.

8. Butter an 8-inch springform pan, line the base with wax or parchment paper, and butter the paper. Sprinkle all over with the breadcrumbs and shake off the excess. Spoon the rice into the pan and bake for about 45 minutes, until a thin skewer or toothpick inserted in the middle of the cake comes out just moist. The cake will also have shrunk from the sides of the pan.

9. Leave the cake to cool in the pan, then remove the band and turn the cake over onto a dish. Remove the base of the pan and the paper, place a round serving dish over the cake, and turn it over again. Sprinkle lavishly with confectioners' sugar before serving.

PREPARATION

The cake must be made at least 1 day in advance. It can be kept for a few days in the refrigerator, wrapped in foil. Remove from the refrigerator at least 2 hours before serving, to bring it back to room temperature.

SERVES 12

Insalata autunnale di frutta
Autumn Fruit Compote

3 lemons

1 bottle sweet white wine

5 tablespoons clear honey

½ teaspoon ground ginger

¼ teaspoon ground cloves

½ teaspoon freshly grated nutmeg

½ teaspoon ground cinnamon

3½ ounces (¾ cup) pitted prunes

1½ cups hot tea

¾ cup golden raisins

¾ cup dried apricots

10 dried figs or ¾ cup pitted dates

1 pound tart apples, such as Granny Smiths

1 pound pears

⅔ cup almonds, blanched, peeled, and cut into slivers

½ cup pine nuts

lightly whipped cream or yogurt (optional)

1. Peel the lemons, yellow part only, and juice them. You should have ¾ cup of juice. Put the peel, juice, wine, honey, and spices in a saucepan. Bring to a boil and simmer very gently for 20 minutes.

2. Meanwhile, put the prunes in a bowl. Cover with the tea and leave to soak for 20 minutes.

3. Soak the raisins, apricots, and figs in warm water for 15 minutes, then dry thoroughly and cut the apricots and figs into strips. Do the same to the prunes.

4. Peel the apples and pears, cut into small cubes, and put in a saucepan. Pour over the wine mixture and cook gently until the fruit is tender. Add the dried fruit, almonds, and pine nuts. Cook for 5 minutes, more, stirring every now and then.

5. Allow to cool in the pan and then transfer to a bowl. Serve cold, with a bowl of cream or yogurt, if you like.

PREPARATION

This dessert must be made at least 1 day in advance (2 or 3 days would be even better) and chilled. This allows time for the flavors to blend.

SERVES 12

WINTER

A VEGETARIAN LUNCH FOR FOUR

203

Pasta asciutta e ceci
Pasta with Chick Peas

Piatto rustico
Vegetable Casserole

Albicocche, arancie, e banane al vino
Dried Apricots, Oranges, and Bananas in
Wine Syrup

A TUSCAN LUNCH FOR TWELVE

212

Crostini alla toscana
Chicken Liver Canapés

Arista alla toscana
Roast Pork with Rosemary and Fennel

Fagioli all'uccelletto
Sautéed Cannellini Beans and Tomatoes

Insalate di stagione
Seasonal Salads

Formaggio
Cheese

Panforte e vinsanto
Sienese Fruit and Spice Cake with Vinsanto

LUNCH FOR SIX

208

Bigoli in salsa
Whole-Wheat Spaghetti with Onion and
Anchovy Sauce

Trance di nasello al forno
Baked Hake

Spinaci all'agro
Lemon Spinach (page 331)

Formaggio e frutta
Cheese and Fruit

DINNER FOR SIX

217

Risotto al Gorgonzola
Risotto with Gorgonzola

Coniglio al rosmarino
Rabbit with Tomato and Rosemary Sauce

Patate in umido
Braised New Potatoes

Panna cotta
Molded Cream Dessert (page 36)

A VEGETARIAN DINNER FOR SIX

2 2 3

Pasticcio di tagliatelle, pomodori, e mozzarella

Baked Tagliatelle with Tomato Sauce and Mozzarella

~

Sformato di patate e carote

Potato and Carrot Mold

~

La bonissima

Walnut and Honey Pie

~

Frutta di stagione

Fruit of the Season

DINNER FOR EIGHT

2 3 1

Tagliatelle alle cozze e porri

Tagliatelle with Mussels and Leeks

~

Insalata veronese

Celery Root, Belgian Endive, and Radicchio Salad

~

Formaggio

Cheese

~

Torrone molle

Soft Chocolate Nougat

DINNER FOR TEN

2 3 7

Insalata di cavolfiore alla salsa bianca

Cauliflower Salad with Anchovies and Pine Nuts

~

Bollito misto

Italian Boiled Dinner

~

Salsa rossa

Red Sauce

~

Salsa verde

Green Sauce

~

Salsa d'api

Walnut Sauce

~

La torta di cioccolato di Julia

Chocolate and Nut Cake

~

Arancie caramellate

Oranges in Caramel Syrup

CHRISTMAS DINNER FOR TEN

247

Mousse di prosciutto cotto
Truffle-flavored Ham Mousse (page 134)

~~~

Stracciatella al sapor di limone
Lemon, Egg, and Parmesan Soup (page 290)

~~~

Tacchino arrosto ripieno
Stuffed Roast Turkey

~~~

Ripieno di frutta
Fruit Stuffing

~~~

Ripieno di castagne
Chestnut and Sausage Stuffing

~~~

Patate arrosto
Roast Potatoes (page 326)

~~~

Le Caramellone natalizie con crema allo zenzero
Christmas "Crackers" with Ginger Custard

NEW YEAR'S EVE SUPPER FOR TEN

256

Bresaola con la rucola
Bresaola with Arugula (page 45)

~~~

Il gran raviolo
One Egg Ravioli in Clear Broth

~~~

Zampone allo zabaione
Zampone with Zabaglione

~~~

Lenticchie in umido
Green Lentils with Sage

~~~

Bomba di panna e marrons glacés
Marron Glacé Bombe

~~~

Ananas e arancie
Pineapple and Oranges (page 161)

Pasta asciutta e ceci

Pasta with Chick Peas

~

Piatto rustico

Vegetable Casserole

~

Albicocche, arancie, e banane al vino

Dried Apricots, Oranges, and Bananas in Wine Syrup

One of my godsons is a strict vegetarian and after inviting him to lunch one day, I found myself momentarily at a loss. What could I cook for him? As I looked into my refrigerator and cupboard for inspiration I realized that all the dishes going through my mind contained either an egg, or a cupful of milk, or two tablespoons of parmesan . . . all ruled out. Eventually I decided on the following three dishes, and Tom was delighted with the result.

The first course, on further reflection, was not a problem, since pasta or rice with vegetables was the obvious solution, and for that I have recipes galore. Narrowing them down, I chose pasta with chick peas, a nourishing dish that can also be made with cannellini beans.

The *piatto rustico* is based on a recipe that had just been given to me by a friend from Umbria. I decided to serve the vegetables in a hollowed-out round loaf of bread. It looks pretty and gives the dish more substance.

The dessert is fresh and you can accompany it, for less strict vegetarians or nonvegetarians, with the lemon meringues on page 342 and/or the almond crescents on page 341.

Pasta asciutta e ceci
Pasta with Chick Peas

3 cups cooked or canned chick peas
¾ pound small tubular pasta, such as shells
3 rosemary sprigs
2 garlic cloves, peeled

1 dried chili, seeded
6 tablespoons olive oil
½ pound ripe tomatoes, peeled, seeded, and chopped

1. Drain and rinse the canned chick peas, if using. If you have time, remove the skin.

2. Cook the pasta in plenty of salted boiling water.

3. While the pasta is cooking chop together the rosemary needles, the garlic, and the chili and put them, with 4 tablespoons of the oil, into a large sauté pan, preferably earthenware, which you can bring to the table. Sauté for a minute or so. Add the tomatoes and sauté for a couple of minutes. Add the chick peas, scooping them out with a slotted spoon in such a way that a little of the cooking liquid goes into the pan with them. If you are using canned chick peas, use some of the pasta water to moisten the mixture. Sauté for 5 minutes or so, coating the beans.

4. Drain the pasta when al dente and transfer quickly to the pan. Add the rest of the oil and stir-fry for about 1 minute. Serve immediately from the pan.

PREPARATION

Chick peas can be cooked up to 2 days in advance and refrigerated. They can also be frozen. The *soffritto* of herbs and garlic can be made a few hours in advance and reheated. The pasta must be cooked at the last minute.

SERVES 4

Piatto rustico
Vegetable Casserole

---

1 small eggplant (¼ pound)

salt

½ pound potatoes

1 small zucchini (about 6 ounces)

1 small red bell pepper (about 6 ounces)

½ pound white onions

1 garlic clove

1¼ cups coarsely chopped fresh or canned plum tomatoes

4 tablespoons olive oil

freshly ground black pepper

2 teaspoons dried oregano

1 round loaf of bread, 6 to 8 inches in diameter

1. Peel the eggplant and cut into 1-inch chunks. Put in a colander and sprinkle with salt. Place a plate with a weight on it on top and let stand for 1 hour. Rinse the eggplant under cold water and dry with paper towels.

2. Preheat the oven to 325° F.

3. Peel the potatoes and cut into chunks. Cut the zucchini and pepper into similar size pieces. Peel the onion and cut into thick slices. Peel the garlic and cut into small slices. Put all the vegetables, including the tomatoes, into a casserole, add half the olive oil, 1 teaspoon salt, a generous grinding of pepper, and the oregano. Cover the casserole with the lid and cook in the oven until the vegetables are tender, about 1½ hours.

4. Remove from the oven and turn the heat up to 400° F. Cut the loaf of bread in half horizontally and make a container out of the bottom half by scooping out all the soft part. Brush the inside with the rest of the olive oil and put in the oven for about 8 minutes. Transfer the bread bowl to a round dish.

5. Taste the vegetables and check the seasoning. Spoon them with their liquid into the bread bowl and serve at once.

PREPARATION

The vegetables can be prepared up to 2 days in advance and refrigerated. Fill the bread just before serving, or it will become soggy.

SERVES 4

Albicocche, arancie, e banane al vino
Dried Apricots, Oranges, and Bananas in Wine Syrup

―‿―

½ pound dried apricots
1¼ cups dry white wine
3 tablespoons sugar
1 bay leaf
1 tablespoon lemon juice

2 bananas
2 oranges
3 tablespoons chopped toasted almonds (optional)

1. Soak the apricots for 1 hour in warm water. Drain. Put the wine, sugar, and bay leaf in a heavy saucepan and bring to a boil. Simmer for 5 minutes after the sugar has dissolved. Add the apricots. Cook until tender, which takes from 10 to 20 minutes. Remove the bay leaf and add the lemon juice.

2. When the apricots are cool, pour into a glass bowl. Cut the bananas into ¼- to ½-inch-thick rounds and mix into the apricots. Peel the oranges to the quick and slice ¼- to ½-inch thick. Reserve some of the best slices, cut the others in half, and mix into the other fruit. Lay the pretty slices on the top. Cover with plastic wrap and refrigerate for at least 1 hour.

3. If you are using the toasted almonds, sprinkle them over the top just before serving.

PREPARATION

The apricots can be soaked and cooked up to 2 days in advance and refrigerated. Add the bananas and oranges no longer than 4 hours before serving. Mix the bananas well to coat them in the syrup or they will discolor.

SERVES 4

LUNCH FOR SIX

Bigoli in salsa
Whole-Wheat Spaghetti with Onion and Anchovy Sauce

~~

Trance di nasello al forno
Baked Hake

~~

Spinaci all'agro
Lemon Spinach (page 331)

~~

Formaggio e frutta
Cheese and Fruit

In Italy we often serve two courses containing fish, as in this easy to prepare meal. It is arranged so that you need to leave your guests only for the time it takes to cook the spaghetti; even less if you cook it following the Agnesi method on page 335.

Bigoli, a specialty of Venice, is the only traditional Italian pasta made with whole wheat. Here I have used whole-wheat spaghetti, which has become widely available; the nutty flavor of it counterbalances the assertiveness of the anchovy sauce.

The second course is a contrast to the first, and yet it is fish again. So we have a harmony, yet at the same time a contrast resulting from the use of a different fish, from the way it is cooked, and from the flavorings. I use hake for this dish whenever I can find it, but cod, a fish of the same family, is a perfect substitute. Spinach goes well with this fish; I recommend the Italian way of preparing it (see page 331).

Cheese is usually served at luncheons in Italy; it is hardly ever served at dinner. The cheese is always followed by a bowl of seasonal fruit. If you want your lunch to be more formal, choose a sweet based on fresh fruit: the oranges and kiwi on page 64, or the pineapple and oranges on page 161, for example.

Bigoli in salsa
Whole-Wheat Spaghetti with Onion and Anchovy Sauce

3 ounces salted anchovies or 1 can (2 ounces) anchovy fillets packed in oil
milk
7 white onions, sliced paper thin (5 cups)

7 tablespoons olive oil
salt
1 pound whole-wheat spaghetti
3 tablespoons chopped flat-leaf parsley
freshly ground black pepper

1. If you are using salted anchovies, remove the bone and rinse under cold water. Divide into 2 fillets, put them on a small plate, and pour over enough milk to cover. If you are using canned anchovies, wipe them clean of oil and cover with milk.

2. Put the onion and half the oil in a sauté pan large enough to hold the pasta later. Cook slowly until the onion is soft and golden. Add 3 or 4 tablespoons warm water, stir, and simmer, covered, for 30 minutes, stirring at times. Add a little more water if the sauce becomes too dry. The onion should dissolve and become like a puree.

3. When the sauce is nearly ready, bring a large pot full of salted water to the boil. Drop in the spaghetti and cook until al dente. If you prefer, use the Agnesi method (page 335), which requires less last-minute attention.

4. While the pasta is cooking, coarsely chop the anchovy fillets and add to the onion sauce with 2 tablespoons of the milk. Mash with a fork to a paste, while cooking for 2 minutes over very low heat. Anchovies must be cooked over very low heat or they will acquire a bitter taste. Mix in the parsley, the remaining oil, and the pepper and remove from the heat.

5. Drain the pasta and turn immediately into the pan with the onion and anchovy sauce. Stir-fry for a minute, lifting the spaghetti high into the air so as to coat every strand.

6. Serve at once from the pan or transfer to a heated bowl. No grated cheese is served when pasta is dressed with a fish-based sauce.

PREPARATION

The sauce can be prepared up to 2 days in advance and kept in the refrigerator. Pasta must always be cooked just before it is served.

SERVES 6

Trance di nasello al forno
Baked Hake

6 fish steaks, about 1 inch thick and ½ pound each	2 tablespoons chopped fresh oregano or marjoram leaves
3 shallots, cut in half	salt and freshly ground black pepper
3 garlic cloves, bruised	4 tablespoons lemon juice
6 tablespoons extra-virgin olive oil	4 tablespoons chopped flat-leaf parsley
4 bay leaves	

1. Wash and thoroughly dry the fish steaks with paper towels. Roll them up neatly and tie them with string, so that they will keep a nice shape.

2. Put the shallots, garlic, olive oil, bay leaves, oregano or marjoram, and salt and pepper to taste in a baking dish large enough to hold the fish in a single layer. Coat the fish in the mixture on both sides and leave to marinate for 1 hour, turning the steaks over once or twice.

3. About half an hour before serving, heat the oven to 350° F. Place the dish in the oven and bake for 20 to 25 minutes, turning the steaks over gently halfway through the cooking.

4. When the fish is done, remove and discard the shallot, garlic, and bay leaves. Drizzle with the lemon juice and sprinkle with parsley. Serve at once.

PREPARATION

There is no last-minute problem with this dish. Just place it in the oven about 20 minutes before you want to serve it.

SERVES 6

A TUSCAN LUNCH FOR TWELVE

Crostini alla toscana
Chicken Liver Canapés

Arista alla toscana
Roast Pork with Rosemary and Fennel

Fagioli all'uccelletto
Sautéed Cannellini Beans and Tomatoes

Insalate di stagione
Seasonal Salads

Formaggio
Cheese

Panforte e vinsanto
Sienese Fruit and Spice Cake with Vinsanto

For about ten years in the 1970s we had a little house on a hill in Chianti and spent many happy holidays there. Then one morning when I was shopping in Gaiole, our local village, I realized that there were no fewer than seven British cars in the little village square. Chianti had become Chiantishire! Soon afterwards, we sold Cornia, our house, and bought an apartment in Venice.

While we were in Tuscany we had many pleasant times with our Italian neighbors, always over a glass or two, or more, of vinsanto. Sometimes we had lunch together, and this menu is typical of that sort of occasion. There is, I must admit, one less course in my menu than in those authentic Tuscan feasts because I have omitted the tagliatelle that followed the antipasto. So the antipasto becomes the first course here.

The crostini are part of the antipasto. You should also serve two or three of the following dishes: a platter of salami, prosciutto, mortadella, and other cold meats with pickled vegetables, some bruschetta (page 71), and/or a rustic lentil salad garnished with arugula and dressed only with olive oil, the very best you have.

The main course, the roast pork, can be served hot or cold; in Tuscany it is traditionally served cold. The strange name of this dish is a mystery. Many food historians and writers, myself included, used to subscribe to the theory that it comes from an episode that took place at a banquet during the Ecumenical Council in Florence in 1439. A Greek patriarch tasted the dish and supposedly exclaimed, *"Aristos!"* (the best). The story, however charming, has proved to be unfounded, since the dish *arista* is mentioned in a novella written by Franco Sacchetti a hundred years before the Council.

Another odd name is that of the *fagioli all'uccelletto, uccelletto* meaning small bird. Many theories have been advanced as to its origin. The only one I find convincing is that beans prepared in this way are the traditional accompaniment to *uccelletti.* The dish can also be made *in bianco* (without tomato).

The salad I leave to you, but whatever it is, make a lot and dress it with plenty of extra-virgin olive oil. My recipe is on page 325.

For dessert, serve a Tuscan pecorino with other Italian cheeses. At the same time put on the table two panfortes, the deliciously spiced and honeyed cakes from Siena. Although I have made panforte at home, I am convinced that the ready-made panforte available in many Italian and gourmet shops is better. Serve the panforte with a sweet vinsanto, a strong wine, as the Tuscans would do.

Crostini alla toscana
Chicken Liver Canapés

---

1 pound chicken livers

4 tablespoons olive oil

⅓ cup very finely chopped celery stalk

2 shallots, very finely chopped

2 small garlic cloves, peeled and chopped

3 tablespoons chopped flat-leaf parsley

1 tablespoon tomato paste

⅓ cup dry white wine

salt and freshly ground black pepper

1 tablespoon capers, rinsed and chopped

4 anchovy fillets, chopped

2 tablespoons unsalted butter

3 tablespoons extra-virgin olive oil or chicken stock mixed with vinsanto

French baguette

1. Remove the fat, gristle, and any greenish bits from the chicken livers. Wash, dry, and cut into small pieces.

2. Put the oil in a saucepan and when just hot, add the celery, shallots, garlic, and parsley and cook for 7 to 10 minutes, or until soft. Add the chicken livers and cook very gently until they lose their raw color. Mix in the tomato paste and cook for 1 minute. Raise the heat, pour over the wine, and reduce until nearly all the wine has evaporated. Lower the heat and add a little salt and plenty of pepper. Simmer gently for 10 minutes.

3. Preheat the oven to 400° F.

4. Remove the pan from the heat and add the capers and anchovies. Transfer the mixture to a chopping board and chop coarsely. If you use a food processor, be very careful not to reduce the mixture to a puree. Return the mixture to the saucepan and add the butter. Cook slowly for 2 minutes, stirring constantly.

5. Slice the bread; brush with the extra-virgin olive oil. Toast 6 to 7 minutes, until crisp. When cool, spread with the chicken-liver mixture and serve.

PREPARATION

The chicken-liver mixture can be made up to 1 day in advance. Cover and refrigerate.

SERVES 12

Arista alla toscana
Roast Pork with Rosemary and Fennel

6 garlic cloves, peeled

4 sprigs fresh rosemary, about 3½ inches long

2 teaspoons fennel seeds

salt and freshly ground black pepper

4½ pounds boneless loin of pork

4 cloves

½ cup extra-virgin olive oil

⅔ cup dry white wine

1. Ask the butcher to give you the bones of the loin, if possible, and to tie the meat into a neat roll.

2. Chop together the garlic, rosemary, and fennel seeds, add salt and pepper, and mix well. Make small deep incisions in the meat, along the grain, and push the mixture into the meat. Pat the rest of the mixture all over the meat and stick with the cloves. Rub with half the oil and place in a bowl. Allow to stand for 4 to 5 hours at room temperature, loosely covered with foil.

3. Preheat the oven to 350° F.

4. Put the meat and the bones, if any, in a roasting pan and pour on the rest of the oil. Roast for 2 to 2½ hours, basting every 20 minutes or so. The meat is ready when it is very tender; a meat thermometer should read 150 degrees.

5. Turn up the heat to 425° F. for the last 10 minutes to brown the meat, then transfer it to a cutting board. Remove and discard the bones, if any. Let stand for 10 to 15 minutes before carving.

6. Remove as much fat as you can from the surface of the cooking liquid. Deglaze with the wine and ½ cup hot water, boiling briskly while scraping the bottom of the pan to loosen the residue. Reduce to about a third. (This very concentrated juice can also be eaten with the meat when it is cold. In that case, refrigerate the sauce, remove the fat on top, and serve the soft jelly underneath.) To serve the pork hot, remove the string from the meat, carve, and place it neatly on a serving dish. Spoon the deglazing liquid over it.

PREPARATION

To serve the pork hot, you must cook it at the last minute, like any other roast. To serve it cold, cook it up to 2 days in advance and refrigerate it, well wrapped

continued

in foil. Remove from the refrigerator at least 2 hours before serving to bring back to room temperature.

SERVES 12

Fagioli all'uccelletto
Sautéed Cannellini Beans and Tomatoes

⅓ cup extra-virgin olive oil

2 sprigs fresh sage

2 sprigs fresh rosemary

10 unpeeled garlic cloves, washed and dried

1 pound ripe tomatoes, preferably plum tomatoes, peeled and coarsely chopped

salt and freshly ground black pepper

4 cups cooked or canned cannellini beans (two 16-ounce cans)

1. Put three-quarters of the oil, the sage, rosemary, and garlic in a pot, preferably earthenware, that you can put directly on the heat. Sauté until the herbs begin to sizzle.

2. Add the tomatoes to the pan. Season with salt and pepper and cook until the oil separates, about 20 minutes. Rinse and drain the canned cannellini, if using. Add the beans to the pan and continue cooking for about 15 minutes, until everything is well blended.

3. Before serving, pour over the remaining olive oil and check seasoning.

PREPARATION

The dish can be prepared up to 2 days in advance. Cover and refrigerate. Gently reheat, or bring back to room temperature if you want to serve the dish cold with cold meat.

SERVES 12

DINNER FOR SIX

Risotto al Gorgonzola
Risotto with Gorgonzola

———

Coniglio al rosmarino
Rabbit with Tomato and Rosemary Sauce

———

Patate in umido
Braised New Potatoes

———

Panna cotta
Molded Cream Dessert (page 36)

Risotto is easier to make in small quantities, so I suggest that if you are not an experienced risotto maker, start by making it for four before attempting larger quantities.

Rabbit is now readily available almost everywhere. It is a white meat, less fat than chicken, and it lends itself to being prepared in any number of different ways. The sauce for this dish has the herby tomato taste everybody associates with traditional Italian cooking. It is often served in central Italy, where the recipe comes from. If you want to serve a vegetable with it, I suggest the lemon spinach on page 331 or, better still, a green salad to follow, as in my recipe on page 325.

Dessert could be the molded cream pudding on page 36 or your favorite apple tart.

Risotto al Gorgonzola
Risotto with Gorgonzola

---

4 shallots or 2 small onions

5 tablespoons unsalted butter

salt

6 cups vegetable or chicken stock

2 cups Arborio rice

1 cup dry white wine

12 ounces dolce latte Gorgonzola, cut into small pieces

freshly ground black pepper

½ cup chopped flat-leaf parsley

1. Mince the shallots or onions and sauté them in the butter in a large heavy saucepan. Add a pinch of salt to release the moisture and keep them from browning. Cook gently for 7 minutes or so, stirring frequently.

2. Meanwhile heat the stock to the simmer.

3. Add the rice to the shallots and stir well for 1 or 2 minutes, coating the grains with butter. Turn the heat up and pour in the wine. Let it bubble away, then begin to add the stock little by little. As each ladleful of stock is absorbed, add another ladleful. Halfway through the cooking, mix in the Gorgonzola. Stir constantly until the cheese has melted. Continue gradually adding stock until the risotto is ready. If you have used up all the stock before the rice is done, use hot water to finish the cooking. When adding stock toward the end of the cooking, add only very little at a time. The rice should cook at a lively simmer. When the rice is done, tender yet with an inner firmness, about 20 minutes, season with plenty of pepper. If necessary, season also with salt, although the salt from the cheese may be enough.

Transfer to a heated bowl, sprinkle with parsley, and serve immediately.

PREPARATION

The sautéed onion can be prepared in advance and reheated. Other than that, for a perfect result you should cook the risotto just before serving it. There is another method, which works quite well. Sauté the onion, then sauté the rice and add about 1 cup of stock. As soon as the stock comes back to a boil, turn off the heat and leave the pot with the lid firmly on. When you go back to finish the dish, you will find the rice dry and half cooked. Add a lump of butter and proceed with the cooking; it will take about 10 minutes.

SERVES 6

Coniglio al rosmarino
Rabbit with Tomato and Rosemary Sauce

4¹/2 pounds rabbit pieces
¹/2 lemon, cut into wedges
4 tablespoons olive oil
3 garlic cloves, finely chopped
1 onion, roughly chopped
1 cup dry white wine
salt and freshly ground black pepper

TOMATO AND ROSEMARY SAUCE

2 to 3 shallots or 1 small onion, very finely chopped

4 sprigs fresh rosemary, 5 inches long, needles very finely chopped

4 tablespoons extra-virgin olive oil

1¹/2 pounds tomatoes, peeled and seeded, or 1¹/4 cups canned plum tomatoes, drained

1 to 1¹/2 dry chilies, according to taste, seeded and very finely chopped

salt

1. Trim any gristle or fat from the rabbit pieces and rub with lemon. Heat the oil in a large heavy sauté pan and brown the rabbit on all sides. Push it to the side of the pan and add the garlic and onion. Cook over low heat until the onion is soft, stirring frequently.

2. Heat the wine in a small saucepan.

3. Bring the rabbit back to the middle of the pan, turn the heat up, and splash with wine. Boil briskly for 1 minute or so to evaporate the alcohol content, then season with salt and pepper. Cover the pan and cook for 20 minutes over very low heat. Turn the rabbit over 2 or 3 times and, if necessary, add a little hot water during the cooking.

4. For the sauce, sauté the shallots and rosemary gently in the olive oil for 5 minutes. Coarsely chop the tomatoes and add to the pan. Add the chili and salt to taste. Cook, uncovered, over low heat for 10 minutes. Adjust the seasonings.

5. Pour the sauce over the rabbit. Stir quickly, scraping the cooking juices and mixing them into the sauce, and continue cooking until the rabbit is done. Taste and check seasoning. Transfer to a heated dish and serve.

PREPARATION

The rabbit and the sauce can be prepared 1 day in advance and refrigerated. If necessary they can be frozen together, then thawed and very gently reheated.

SERVES 6

Patate in umido
Braised New Potatoes

———

2 pounds new potatoes

2 tablespoons unsalted butter

4 tablespoons olive oil

2 ounces pancetta or unsmoked streaky bacon, chopped (⅓ cup)

1 onion, finely chopped

2 garlic cloves, finely chopped

1 tablespoon fresh marjoram or ½ tablespoon dried marjoram

1¼ tablespoons tomato paste dissolved in 7 tablespoons hot water

salt and freshly ground black pepper

1. Peel and wash the potatoes, and cut them into 1-inch cubes. Steam them for about 5 minutes.

2. While the potatoes are cooking, put the butter, oil, and pancetta in a heavy saucepan and cook for 1 minute. Add the onion and the garlic and sauté gently for 5 minutes, stirring very frequently. Mix in the partly cooked potatoes, turning them over very gently to coat them with fat, and cook for 3 to 4 minutes.

3. Add the marjoram, the dissolved tomato paste, and the salt and pepper. Stir well and cook, covered, until the potatoes are tender, turning them over often during the cooking. Use a fork to turn the potatoes over; this breaks them up less than a spoon, although some are bound to break a little. Taste, adjust the seasoning, and serve with the rabbit. If you are using an oval dish put the potatoes alongside the rabbit; put them in the middle if you have a large round dish.

PREPARATION

Potatoes never take kindly to being reheated, but they can be kept hot for 30 minutes or so in a very low oven.

SERVES 6

A VEGETARIAN DINNER
FOR SIX

Pasticcio di tagliatelle, pomodori, e mozzarella
Baked Tagliatelle with Tomato Sauce and Mozzarella

~

Sformato di patate e carote
Potato and Carrot Mold

~

La bonissima
Walnut and Honey Pie

~

Frutta di stagione
Fruit of the Season

*T*his baked tagliatelle dish is fresh and very Mediterranean, with mozzarella oozing from underneath the ribbon of pasta and a splash of red sauce flavored with oregano.

For the second course we move to the northwestern regions of Italy, Lombardy and Piedmont, where the cuisine reflects the proximity of France. The mold is the sort of dish that is currently appearing in many fashionable restaurants. My *sformato* comes from my mother's *ricettario* (recipe book). It is a recipe that uses béchamel, which has become the Cinderella among sauces. I cannot understand why béchamel has been demoted; it is a versatile sauce with excellent flavor. In Italy a vegetable mold is usually served without a sauce, but if you want to pass one around, I would suggest the fontina and cream sauce on page 48.

With the *sformato* I like to serve spinach, good young spinach sautéed in butter, and large croutons. I cut slices of white bread diagonally across and bake them, moistened with melted butter, in a medium-hot oven for 7 minutes or so. If you prefer, you can fry the bread triangles in butter. Unmold the *sformato* on a round dish, and heap the spinach into the hole and around the dish, alternating with the croutons.

The dessert is *La bonissima,* and *bonissima* (very good) it certainly is. The pastry I use is made with hard-boiled egg yolks and potato starch. It is a soft and buttery pastry, quite different from the usual *pâte sucrée.* It can be difficult to roll out, but if you do it on a sheet of wax paper, you will manage quite easily.

If you would like to enrich the pie, pass around a bowl of crème fraîche or heavy cream with it. *La bonissima* will become *bonissimissima!*

To end the meal, a bowl of seasonal fruit is perfect.

Pasticcio di tagliatelle, pomodori, e mozzarella

Baked Tagliatelle with Tomato Sauce and Mozzarella

---

tagliatelle made with 2¼ cups unbleached flour and 3 eggs or 1½ pounds fresh storebought tagliatelle or 1 pound dried egg tagliatelle

½ pound fresh mozzarella

4 tablespoons extra-virgin olive oil

2 garlic cloves, peeled and very finely sliced

1 dried chili

freshly ground black pepper

2 teaspoons dried oregano

3 cups tomato sauce (page 336)

salt

2 tablespoons unsalted butter

6 tablespoons freshly grated parmesan

1. Make the fresh pasta following the directions on page 333.

2. Coarsely chop the mozzarella, put it in a deep dish, and pour over 2 tablespoons of the oil. Add the garlic, chili, a generous grinding of pepper, and 1 teaspoon of the oregano. Let stand to absorb the oil at least 30 minutes or up to 2 hours.

3. Preheat the oven to 350° F.

4. Gently heat the tomato sauce, if necessary.

5. Cook the tagliatelle in plenty of boiling salted water. If fresh, it will only take 1 to 2 minutes to cook. Drain, reserving 1 cup of the pasta water. Return the pasta immediately to the saucepan and add the butter and the remaining oil. Mix well, then add the hot tomato sauce and the parmesan.

6. Remove and discard the chili from the mozzarella and add the mozzarella to the pasta. Toss very well and, if the pasta appears too dry, add a couple of tablespoons of the pasta water. Taste, adjust the seasoning, pour into a greased shallow baking oven dish, and sprinkle the remaining oregano over the top.

7. Cover with foil and bake for 10 minutes. Let stand for 3 or 4 minutes for the flavors to blend before serving.

continued

PREPARATION

The dish can be prepared up to 1 day in advance and refrigerated, well covered with foil. It could, if necessary, be frozen. The sauce can be made up to 2 days in advance and refrigerated. It can also be frozen very satisfactorily. The tagliatelle can be made a few days in advance and stored, when completely dry, in an airtight container.

SERVES 6

Sformato di patate e carote
Potato and Carrot Mold

POTATO PUREE

1½ *pounds Russet potatoes*

⅔ *cup whole milk*

4 *tablespoons unsalted butter*

3 *tablespoons freshly grated parmesan*

salt and freshly ground black pepper

grated nutmeg

1 *egg*

1 *egg yolk*

CARROT PUREE

1½ *pounds carrots, peeled, washed, and cut in chunks*

salt

BÉCHAMEL

1 *cup whole milk*

3 *tablespoons unsalted butter*

4 *tablespoons flour*

1 *egg*

1 *egg yolk*

3 *tablespoons freshly grated parmesan*

grated nutmeg

freshly ground black pepper

dried breadcrumbs

4 *tablespoons unsalted butter*

1. Wash the potatoes and cook them in their skins. Do not put any salt in the water, as it tends to break them up. Drain the potatoes as soon as they are done. Peel the potatoes while still warm and puree them back into the saucepan, using a food mill fitted with the small-hole disk. Heat the potatoes slowly, stirring constantly, to dry them.

2. Meanwhile, heat the milk. Add to the potatoes with the butter, parmesan, salt and pepper, and a generous grating of nutmeg. Beat hard until the puree is smooth. Beat in the egg and the egg yolk. Taste and check seasonings and set aside.

3. While the potatoes are cooking, cook the carrots in salted water until done.

4. While the potatoes and carrots are cooking make the béchamel. Heat the milk just to the simmer. Melt the butter in a heavy saucepan and stir in the

continued

flour. Cook for 1 minute, then remove the pan from the heat. Add the milk gradually while beating vigorously to incorporate. When all the milk has been absorbed, return the pan to the heat and bring to a boil. Add salt and cook over very low heat for 15 minutes, stirring frequently.

5. Preheat the oven to 375° F.

6. Drain and dry the carrots with paper towels. Puree, using a food mill, back into the saucepan. Put the saucepan on the heat briefly to dry the puree. Add the béchamel and allow to cool for a few minutes, then add the egg and egg yolk. Stir in the cheese, nutmeg, and pepper, and check the salt.

7. Grease the bottom of a one-quart ring mold with some of the butter. Cut a piece of wax paper to fit in the bottom of the mold. Generously butter the paper and the sides of the mold. Sprinkle with the dried breadcrumbs and shake off the excess.

8. Melt the remaining butter in a little saucepan.

9. Half-fill the mold with the carrot puree, leveling it with the back of a moistened metal spoon. Spoon the potato puree on top and smooth it with the wet spoon. Sprinkle with breadcrumbs and drizzle with melted butter. Put the mold in a roasting pan. Pour enough boiling water into the pan to come two-thirds of the way up the side of the mold. Place the pan in the oven and cook until set, about 25 minutes. A toothpick inserted in the middle of the mold should come out dry.

10. Remove from the oven and let stand for 5 minutes. Run a small spatula around the side of the puree to loosen it, then turn it upside down onto a dish. Shake the mold a little and lift it off. Peel off the paper.

PREPARATION

The carrot and potato mold can be prepared several hours in advance, but it cannot be refrigerated because the flavor of the potatoes changes with chilling.

SERVES 6

La bonissima
Walnut and Honey Pie

—————

PASTRY	*GLAZE*
1¼ cups flour	*1 egg yolk*
½ cup potato starch	*1 tablespoon milk*
½ teaspoon salt	
¼ cup sugar	*1½ cups crème fraîche or heavy cream (optional)*
10 tablespoons cold unsalted butter, cut into small pieces	
2 large hard-boiled egg yolks	
FILLING	
1½ cups walnuts	
1 cup honey	
2 teaspoons grated lemon peel	
4 tablespoons dark rum	
2 tablespoons dried breadcrumbs	
1 tablespoon sugar	

1. Sift the flour, potato starch, and salt into a mixing bowl. Add the sugar and butter. Rub the butter into the mixture with the tips of your fingers until the mixture is like small crumbs. Push the egg yolks through a sieve or a food mill fitted with the smallest-hole disk directly into the bowl. Work the mixture together, then turn the dough onto a lightly floured surface and gather into a ball as quickly as you can. Wrap the dough in plastic wrap and refrigerate for at least 30 minutes. (To make the dough in a food processor, put the flour, sugar, and butter in the workbowl, process for a few seconds, then add the yolks, cut into small pieces, and process until a ball forms; add 2 tablespoons cold water, if necessary, to form a ball.)

2. While the pastry is chilling, blanch the walnuts for 30 seconds in boiling water. Lift them out of the water a few at a time and remove the skin; they are easier to peel when hot. Drain on paper towels. Coarsely chop the walnuts by hand or in the food processor.

continued

3. Heat the honey in a saucepan and mix in the walnuts and lemon peel. Cook gently until the mixture is hot and the walnuts are well coated with honey. Remove the pan from the heat, mix in the rum, and set aside to cool.

4. Preheat the oven to 350° F.

5. Butter an 8-inch springform pan and flour lightly all over.

6. Remove the dough from the refrigerator and cut off about a third of it. Put a piece of wax paper on the work surface, shake a little flour over it, and roll out the smaller portion of dough on the paper. Lift the paper and turn the circle over onto the bottom of the pan. Peel off the paper. Roll out strips of dough about 2 inches wide on wax paper. Line the sides of the tin. Sprinkle the breadcrumbs and sugar over the bottom. Spoon in the filling. Roll out the rest of the dough on wax paper and turn it over to cover the pie. Prick it to let the steam escape. With the remaining dough, make a narrow ribbon and place around the edges to seal.

7. Mix together the egg yolk and milk and brush the top of the pie all over. If you want, make some cut-out shapes with any remaining pastry to decorate the pie. Brush these as well with the glaze.

8. Bake for about 30 to 40 minutes until the pastry is golden. Cool in the pan, then transfer to a round dish. Serve with crème fraîche.

PREPARATION

The pie can be prepared up to 2 days in advance.

SERVES 6

DINNER FOR EIGHT

Tagliatelle alle cozze e porri
Tagliatelle with Mussels and Leeks

~~~~~

Insalata veronese
Celery Root, Belgian Endive, and Radicchio Salad

~~~~~

Formaggio
Cheese

~~~~~

Torrone molle
Soft Chocolate Nougat

*E*ight is a good number for guests, less good for hosts. It needs a well-planned menu that, like this one, has only one dish to attend to just before eating.

In Italy pasta is only served as a first course, except, very occasionally, for some baked pasta dishes. Another maxim is summed up in the saying "la pasta non aspetta nessuno" (pasta waits for no one), which means that it must be eaten the moment it is dressed. For this dish, you can use a good Italian brand of dried egg tagliatelle. The Italian brands are usually better than the so-called fresh tagliatelle you find in supermarkets. Best of all is to make your own. Mussels and leeks are an excellent combination, and the pasta gives the dish more substance.

In the old days I would have hesitated to write a recipe for eight people containing mussels. Who would stand at the kitchen sink for hours on end to clean enough dirty, sandy, barnacled, and bearded mussels? The mussels we buy now are usually farmed. The farms are on rafts or ropes, and as a result the mussels are quite clean when they reach our sinks.

Cheese is seldom served at dinner in Italy, except on very informal occasions, but here I think it fits. You can pass around the cheese platter with the salad; it is a salad that goes particularly well with cheese.

The dessert is rich, but the rest of the meal is not. It is absolutely delicious and very easy to make.

Tagliatelle con cozze e porri
Tagliatelle with Mussels and Leeks

———

tagliatelle made with 3½ cups unbleached flour and 5 eggs or 2 pounds fresh tagliatelle or 1¼ pounds dried tagliatelle

4 pounds mussels

1½ cups dry white wine

2 pounds leeks, preferably small, young leeks

8 tablespoons (1 stick) unsalted butter

salt and freshly ground black pepper

1⅓ cups heavy cream

1. Make the tagliatelle following the directions on page 333.

2. Scrub the mussels. Under running water, knock off any barnacles, and tug off the beard. Wash in several changes of cold water. Throw away any mussel that remains open when tapped on a hard surface; it is dead and must not be eaten. You should cook this quantity of mussels in two batches. Use a large pan.

2. Pour the wine into a large pan with a tight-fitting lid, bring to a boil, and add half the mussels. Cover and cook over high heat until the mussels open. Shake the pan frequently. When the mussels are open, remove from the heat. Remove the mussels from the shells as soon as they open, but do not force them open or they will break. Do this over the pan to collect the juices. Put the mussels in a bowl and discard the shells. Cook the second batch of mussels.

3. Filter the pan liquid through a sieve lined with cheesecloth into a saucepan. Reduce the liquor over high heat until about 1 cup is left. Set aside.

4. Trim the leeks, cutting away the roots and about 2 or 3 inches from the top, depending on how fresh they are. Cut all the white part of the leeks, and the tender green heart, into thin rounds. Wash very thoroughly, removing any grit stuck between the leaves. Drain.

5. Put 6 tablespoons of the butter in a very large sauté pan. Heat until the butter has melted, then add the leeks and cook, turning them over in the butter, for 5 minutes. Add 4 tablespoons of the mussel liquor, cover the leeks with a sheet of buttered wax paper, put the lid on the pan, and cook very gently for about 45 minutes, until the leeks become a puree. Keep a watch on the cooking

continued

and add a couple of tablespoons of mussel liquor whenever the leeks get too dry. Add the mussels and the remaining mussel liquor. Taste and add salt and a generous amount of pepper.

6. Cook the pasta, keeping in mind that fresh pasta takes far less time to cook than dried pasta. While the pasta is cooking, heat the cream in a small saucepan. When the pasta is al dente, drain, reserving 1 cup of pasta water. Transfer the pasta immediately to a heated bowl.

7. Add the remaining butter, the hot cream, and the mussel and leek sauce. Toss thoroughly and, if the dish appears too dry, add a few tablespoons of pasta water. Serve immediately.

PREPARATION

The leeks can be cooked up to 1 day in advance and refrigerated. The mussels can also be cleaned and opened 1 day in advance. Put them in a bowl with the strained liquor, cover with plastic wrap and refrigerate. The pasta must be cooked just before serving.

SERVES 8

Insalata veronese
Celery Root, Belgian Endive, and Radicchio Salad

DRESSING

3 tablespoons lemon juice

1 teaspoon English mustard powder

½ cup extra-virgin olive oil

salt and freshly ground pepper

1 medium celery root

3 Belgian endives

3 medium heads radicchio

1. For the dressing, put the lemon juice in a small bowl and mix in the mustard. Add the oil in a very thin stream while beating with a fork to emulsify. Season to taste with salt and pepper.

2. Peel the celery root and cut into julienne strips. This is easily done in a food processor fitted with the julienne disk. Toss with some of the dressing and put in a bowl. Cover with plastic wrap and leave in the refrigerator for 2 to 3 hours.

3. Cut the Belgian endives and the radicchio into ½-inch strips. Wash and dry thoroughly and toss with the remaining dressing. Put the celery root in the middle of a serving dish and spoon the salad mixture around it.

PREPARATION

The celery root can be cut and dressed 1 day in advance and refrigerated. The endives and radicchio can be washed and cut 1 day in advance and kept, wrapped in a clean dish towel, in the vegetable drawer of the refrigerator.

SERVES 8

Torrone molle
Soft Chocolate Nougat

½ pound (2 sticks) unsalted butter, at room temperature

1 cup plus 2 tablespoons sugar

¼ pound (⅔ cup) cocoa powder

1 whole egg

1 egg yolk

¾ cup almonds

¼ pound plain cookies, such as digestive or Petit Beurre

3 tablespoons dark rum

DECORATION

candied violets (optional)

candied almonds (optional)

whipped cream (optional)

1. Cream together the butter and sugar until light and fluffy. Add the cocoa, a spoonful at a time, and beat hard until it has been completely incorporated. This takes a little time and some beating. Use a food processor if you have one.

2. Lightly beat together the egg and the egg yolk and add to the creamed butter, stirring until well blended.

3. Blanch the almonds for 30 seconds in boiling water. Peel and coarsely chop them. Add to the butter mixture. Crumble the biscuits with a rolling pin and add to the mixture together with the rum. Mix very thoroughly.

4. Line a 4-cup loaf pan with wax paper and spoon the mixture into it. Press it down well to eliminate any air pockets and level the top with a spatula. Cover with plastic wrap and refrigerate for at least 4 hours.

5. To serve, turn the *torrone* out onto an oval dish. If you like, decorate it with candied violets and almonds or surround it with whipped cream, using a pastry bag fitted with a fluted nozzle. Cut the *torrone* with a sharp knife into slices about ½ inch thick.

PREPARATION

The torrone can be made up to 2 days in advance and refrigerated. It can also be frozen.

SERVES 8

DINNER FOR TEN

Insalata di cavolfiore alla salsa bianca

Cauliflower Salad with Anchovies and Pine Nuts

———

Bollito misto

Italian Boiled Dinner

———

Salsa rossa

Red Sauce

———

Salsa verde

Green Sauce

———

Salsa d'api

Walnut Sauce

———

La torta di cioccolato di Julia

Chocolate and Nut Cake

———

Arancie caramellate

Oranges in Caramel Syrup

*T*he centerpiece of this dinner is the *bollito misto*. It is the ideal dish for when you have a lot of people to feed, since, at its best, it contains many different kinds of meat. This Italian boiled dinner is made in all northern Italian regions; if you go there, keep a lookout for a restaurant that serves it—it's a sure sign of the very best establishment. A trolley with many compartments will be wheeled to your table for you to choose a thick slice of beef, a small chunk of veal, a slice or two of cotechino and one of tongue, a chicken leg, and a few boiled vegetables. All the meats are immersed in steaming stock, giving off a rich and intense aroma that holds promise of the delights to come.

Bollito misto is a convivial dish, which must be offered in generous quantities, accompanied by at least two sauces and a *mostarda di frutta*. There are quite a few of these *mostarde* on the market; the most popular is *mostarda di Cremona. Mostarda* consists of various candied fruits preserved in a thick syrup of white wine and honey, highly spiced with mustard. To tell the truth, I am quite happy to do without the other sauces and have only *mostarda,* but since it is not to everyone's taste—and may be difficult to find in the United States—I am including recipes for three traditional sauces. The honey and walnut sauce is quite exceptional.

The recipe for *bollito misto* is for ten to twelve people, but you can scale it down by omitting the cotechino, for instance. When I do *bollito* for the family, I cook only a piece of brisket and one or two pieces of osso buco. The trimmings are the same, although I would do just one sauce or simply put my best olive oil on the table, with the jar of *mostarda di Cremona. Bollito misto* is always accompanied by boiled vegetables, including potatoes, carrots, and onions.

The first course of this menu is a cauliflower salad that I have adapted from a recipe by Vincenzo Corrado, a Neapolitan cookery writer of the eighteenth century. Cauliflower and anchovies always make a successful combination of flavors. The pine nuts add their own delicate flavor.

For dessert I have chosen a melt-in-the-mouth chocolate cake, the pièce de résistance of my daughter Julia. The oranges are for careful eaters—and for the very greedy who like to indulge in two desserts.

Insalata di cavolfiore alla salsa bianca
Cauliflower Salad with Anchovies and Pine Nuts

2¼ to 2½ pounds small cauliflower florets (3 medium heads)

⅔ cup extra-virgin olive oil

¾ cup pine nuts

6 salted anchovies or 12 anchovy fillets in oil

2 tablespoons white wine vinegar

3 tablespoons lemon juice

salt and freshly ground black pepper

6 tablespoons chopped flat-leaf parsley

1. Wash the cauliflower thoroughly, then cook the florets in plenty of salted water until tender when pricked with a fork but not soft. Drain thoroughly and spread out on paper towels. Pat dry and transfer to a bowl or a dish. Toss gently with 2 tablespoons of the oil while the cauliflower is still hot, so that it absorbs the oil better.

2. Roast the pine nuts briefly in a nonstick pan to bring out the flavor.

3. Clean and rinse the salted anchovies or drain the anchovy fillets from the oil. Put the anchovies in a mortar with the pine nuts. Pound the mixture with the vinegar, lemon juice, and salt and pepper, using the pestle. Stir in the remaining oil with a fork to form an emulsion. The sauce can also be made in a food processor.

4. Spoon the sauce over the cauliflower, cover with plastic wrap and leave for 1 hour. Sprinkle with chopped parsley and serve at room temperature.

PREPARATION

The cauliflower can be cooked and the sauce prepared up to 1 day in advance. Pour 1 tablespoon of oil over the cauliflower while still hot. Pour the sauce over the cauliflower no more than 1 hour before serving, or the cauliflower will "cook" in it.

SERVES 10 TO 12

Bollito misto
Italian Boiled Dinner

1 large onion, stuck with 1 clove

3 celery stalks, cut into pieces

2 leeks, cut into pieces

2 carrots, cut into pieces

2 pounds fresh beef brisket

3 ripe fresh tomatoes or 3 canned tomatoes without their juice

5 or 6 black peppercorns, lightly crushed

several parsley stems

salt

3 pieces of osso buco

1 fresh chicken (about 4½ pounds), preferably a stewing hen

1 cotechino sausage (about 1 pound)

1. Put the onion, celery, leeks, and carrots in a stockpot, cover with cold water, and bring to a boil. Add the beef and bring back to a boil. Lower the heat —the broth should just be simmering. Remove the foam that comes to the surface during the first few minutes of cooking. Add the tomatoes, pepper-corns, parsley, and some salt. Cover the pan and simmer for 1½ hours.

2. Add the osso buco, and simmer for 1 hour more. Put in the chicken and cook for 1½ to 2 hours, depending on whether it is a roaster or a boiler. If you are using precooked cotechino, follow the manufacturer's instructions. If the cotechino is not precooked, soak it in cold water for a few hours, then prick the cotechino with a thin needle in a few places, and wrap with cheesecloth, tying each end with a piece of string. Put in a saucepan, cover with water, bring to a boil and cook gently for 2½ hours.

3. When you serve the *bollito,* lift one piece of meat at a time out of the broth and carve only as much as you need to go around for the first helping. Keep the rest in the broth to keep it from getting dry. If you have also cooked the cotechino, transfer it to the stockpot with all the other meats.

4. Put the carved meat on a large heated platter and bring it to the table with dishes of boiled potatoes, carrots, onions, and other seasonal roots, all cooked separately, and sauces such as red sauce (page 241), green sauce (page 242), and walnut sauce (page 243) in bowls.

PREPARATION

You can partially cook the *bollito misto* 1 day in advance, without the chicken. Bring the *bollito* back to a boil and add the chicken.

SERVES 10

Salsa rossa
Red Sauce

3 tablespoons olive oil	3 garlic cloves, peeled
1 pound ripe fresh tomatoes, cut into quarters	1 or 2 dried chilies, according to taste, seeded
1 teaspoon tomato paste	1 clove
2 onions, coarsely chopped	pinch of cinnamon
1 carrot, coarsely chopped	salt
1 celery stalk, coarsely chopped	1 tablespoon red wine vinegar

1. Put half the oil and all the other ingredients except the vinegar in a saucepan with a very heavy bottom. I use an earthenware pot that can be put directly on the heat. Cook over the lowest possible heat for 1 to 1½ hours, adding a little hot water if necessary.

2. Puree through a food mill or sieve. If you use a food processor, you must peel the tomatoes before you cook them.

3. Return the puree to the pan and add the rest of the oil and the vinegar. Cook for 30 minutes more, then taste and check the seasoning. Let the sauce cool a little before serving. It can also be served at room temperature.

PREPARATION

This sauce can be prepared up to 3 days in advance, covered, and refrigerated. It also freezes very well.

MAKES 1 CUP

Salsa verde
Green Sauce

⌐⌐⌐⌐

⅔ *cup fresh white breadcrumbs*	*1 hard-boiled egg, shelled*
1 to 1½ tablespoons red wine vinegar	*6 anchovy fillets in oil, drained, or 3 salted anchovies, boned and rinsed*
1 garlic clove	*2 teaspoons Dijon mustard*
⅔ *cup flat-leaf parsley leaves*	¾ *cup extra-virgin olive oil*
4 tablespoons fresh tarragon	*freshly ground black pepper*
2 tablespoons capers, rinsed and drained	*salt*
6 cornichons or 1 additional tablespoon capers	

1. Put the breadcrumbs in a bowl and pour the vinegar over them. Set aside.

2. Peel the garlic clove, cut it in half, and remove the hard central core, if necessary. This is the part that has a pungent flavor instead of a sweet flavor.
   Chop the garlic, parsley, tarragon, capers, cornichons, hard-boiled egg, and anchovies together. Put this mixture into another bowl.

3. Squeeze the vinegar out of the bread and add the bread to the herb mixture, working it in with a fork. Add the mustard, then gradually add the olive oil, beating the whole time. Season with a generous amount of pepper. Taste and add salt if necessary; the anchovies and capers may have made the sauce salty enough. You might want to add a little more vinegar, depending on the strength of the vinegar and how you like the sauce.

4. The sauce can be made in the food processor. Put the soaked and squeezed-out breadcrumbs, the garlic, parsley, tarragon, capers, cornichons, egg, and anchovies in the bowl of a food processor. Turn the machine on and add the oil through the beaker, and then add the mustard and process again for 30 seconds. Add salt and pepper to taste.

PREPARATION

This green sauce can be made up to 3 days in advance and kept, covered, in the refrigerator.

MAKES 1 CUP

Salsa d'api
Walnut Sauce

———

¼ cup walnuts

3 tablespoons broth from the bollito

3 tablespoons honey

1½ tablespoons English mustard, prepared

1. Blanch the walnuts in boiling water for 20 seconds. Drain and peel them.

2. Put the walnuts in a food processor, add the broth and the honey, and process to a coarse puree. Add the mustard and process again for a few seconds to mix it in thoroughly.

PREPARATION

The sauce can be prepared up to 2 days in advance and kept, covered, in the refrigerator.

MAKES ½ CUP

La torta di cioccolato di Julia
Chocolate and Nut Cake

2 cups hazelnuts
2½ cups walnuts
½ pound semisweet chocolate
6 tablespoons brandy
2 tablespoons ground cinnamon
2 tablespoons whole milk
1 cup sugar

5 large eggs, at room temperature, separated
1½ tablespoons very finely chopped orange peel
confectioners' sugar
heavy cream, whipped (optional)

1. Preheat the oven to 400° F.

2. Spread the hazelnuts out on a baking sheet and toast for 5 minutes. Let cool, then rub them between the palms of your hands or with a rough cloth, to remove the papery skin. Do this in the sink or, better still, outdoors, to avoid having little bits of hazelnut skin flying all over the kitchen.

3. Put the hazelnuts and walnuts in the food processor. Cut the chocolate into small pieces and add to the nuts. Process until the mixture is of a grainy consistency, not ground fine.

4. Transfer the mixture to a bowl, then stir in the brandy, cinnamon, milk, and sugar. Mix thoroughly. Add the egg yolks gradually, one at a time, blending them in very well. Add the orange peel.

5. Generously butter a 10-inch springform pan. Sprinkle with flour and shake off any excess.

6. Beat the egg whites until stiff but not dry. Fold the egg whites, a few tablespoons at a time, into the chocolate mixture with a large metal spoon.

7. When all the egg whites have been folded in, spoon the mixture into the prepared pan and bake for about 1 hour. The cake is ready when a toothpick inserted in the middle comes out dry. Unclip the band and turn the cake onto a wire rack. Remove the base and leave until cold.

8. Before serving, sprinkle lavishly with confectioners' sugar. The cream is optional, but it certainly makes the cake even more luscious.

PREPARATION

The cake is better eaten as soon as it is cool. But it can be made up to 1 day in advance.

SERVES 10 TO 12

Arancie caramellate
Oranges in Caramel Syrup

10 to 12 navel oranges	3 tablespoons Grand Marnier or
1 cup sugar	Cointreau

1. Scrub the oranges and dry thoroughly. Remove the peel of 3 of the oranges, leaving all the pith on the fruit. Cut 3 wide strips of skin from a fourth orange. Put all the oranges in the freezer to harden while you make the syrup.

2. Cut the peel from the 3 oranges into julienne strips about 1 inch long and put them in boiling water. Boil for 5 minutes. Drain and refresh under cold water and set aside.

3. Put the sugar, the 3 wide orange strips, and ⅔ cup water in a small saucepan and cook over low heat. When the syrup begins to boil, turn the heat up slightly and continue boiling until the syrup begins to turn pale gold at the edge of the pan. Remove the wide orange strips and add the julienne strips. Boil for 5 minutes, stirring constantly, until the julienne becomes slightly transparent. Add the Grand Marnier, stir, and remove from the heat.

4. Take the oranges out of the freezer and peel carefully with a small sharp knife, removing all the pith. Cut the oranges across into thin slices and put them in a glass bowl or deep dish. Do this on a plate so that you can collect the juice and pour it over the oranges at the end.

5. Spoon the syrup and the julienne over the oranges and chill for at least 2 hours.

PREPARATION

You can cut the oranges and make the syrup up to 1 day in advance, and keep, covered, in the refrigerator. Pour the syrup over the oranges no longer than 6 hours before serving.

SERVES 10 TO 12

Mousse di prosciutto cotto

Truffle-flavored Ham Mousse (page 134)

～

Stracciatella al sapor di limone

Lemon, Egg, and Parmesan Soup (page 290)

～

Tacchino arrosto ripieno

Stuffed Roast Turkey

～

Ripieno di frutta

Fruit Stuffing

～

Ripieno di castagne

Chestnut and Sausage Stuffing

～

Patate arrosto

Roast Potatoes (page 326)

～

Le caramellone natalizie con crema allo zenzero

Christmas "Crackers" with Ginger Custard

*O*ur 1990 Christmas dinner provided a good opportunity for a dress rehearsal for this menu, since I had to hand in the manuscript of this book just a few days later. All, I am glad to say, went well.

First came the ham mousse, followed by a light soup (page 290).

The turkey is my version of the turkey that was served at my aunt and uncle's prewar Christmas dinners in Milan. They were marvelous parties. The grown-ups, presided over by Nonna Irene looking like a miniature Queen Mary in widow's weeds and rows of pearls to her waist, sat at a vast table, while we children sat at a smaller table in a corner of the room. I was the youngest of all, a very light eater and totally overwhelmed by the occasion. My memories of the food are sketchy. I only remember red monsters with frightening claws, glistening brown turkeys, and on one of the sideboards a huge dome-shaped panettone surrounded by dishes and dishes of candied fruits, dried fruits, chocolates, chestnut truffles, marrons glacés, grapes, mandarin oranges, quince paste, and fruit jellies. But back to my 1990 Christmas dinner, which was spartan by comparison, yet ample enough for our shrunken stomachs and complex enough for the nonexistent domestic staff. I made two stuffings for the turkey, both based on original Milanese stuffings. The fruit stuffing for the cavity is there to keep the meat moist during the cooking; it is not very good to eat. Since I had a fairly small turkey, I had extra stuffing, which I cooked as in the recipe here. It made a very good relish to go with the turkey. The chestnut stuffing is also too much for a small bird, so I used the extra chestnut stuffing to make croquettes to serve with the bird.

With the turkey I served roast potatoes flavored with bay leaf, as in the recipe on page 326, Brussels sprouts, and parsnips, which I love. I partly boiled the parsnips and the sprouts and sautéed them separately in butter. Then I placed them together in a baking dish, flavored them with grated parmesan, and covered them with a velouté sauce.

When my children were young, I always served Christmas pudding. I don't think they liked it particularly, but they liked the tradition. In the recent past, breaking with English tradition, I have served oranges in caramel syrup (page 246) or just an orange jelly, plus the panettone, *torrone,* and other delicacies reminiscent of my Milanese Christmas.

This year I tried these small strudels. The recipe comes from Francesca Davoli, a talented young Roman cook. The look alone of these strudels, which are shaped like Christmas "crackers," testifies to Francesca's talent. The ginger custard really sets the crackers alight.

Tacchino arrosto ripieno
Stuffed Roast Turkey

1 small turkey (11 to 13 pounds)

salt and freshly ground black pepper

TURKEY BROTH

neck, gizzard, and heart of the turkey

1 carrot

1 onion

1 bay leaf

1 celery stalk

4 or 5 parsley stalks

6 peppercorns

1 teaspoon salt

⅔ cup red wine

5 cups fruit stuffing (page 251)

2 cups chestnut and sausage stuffing (page 252)

8 tablespoons (1 stick) unsalted butter

6 to 8 thick slices bacon, blanched

1 tablespoon flour

1. Wash the turkey thoroughly inside and out and wipe with paper towels. Season the cavity well with salt and pepper.

2. Put all the broth ingredients (up to and including the red wine) in a saucepan and cover with cold water by about 2 inches. Simmer gently for 2 hours, then strain. Set aside.

3. Meanwhile, make the stuffings. Loosely pack the fruit stuffing in the cavity of the bird. Sew closed the opening. Stuff the neck end of the turkey loosely with the chestnut and sausage stuffing and sew down the flap of skin. Spread 6 tablespoons of the butter all over the turkey, especially over the breast.

4. Preheat the oven to 450° F.

5. Lay a large sheet of foil in a roasting pan large enough to hold the turkey and place another sheet across it. Put 1 tablespoon of the remaining butter, cut up into small pieces, on the foil. Lay the turkey on top and cover the breast with the bacon. Wrap the foil loosely around the bird, leaving a pocket of air on top. Roast for 45 minutes, then turn the heat down to 325° F. and continue cooking until the bird is done. To test, insert a small pointed knife into the thickest part of the thigh. The juice that runs out should be clear, not bloody. A turkey of this size should take about 3½ hours. About half an hour before the end of the cooking time, unfold the foil and cut it off. Push the bacon down next to the turkey.

continued

6. Turn the heat up to 400° F. Baste the turkey and put it back in the oven to brown the breast. When the turkey is brown, transfer it, with the bacon, to a dish, cover with foil, and let stand at room temperature for at least 30 minutes, to allow the juices that have come to the surface to sink back into the meat.

7. Blend the flour with the remaining tablespoon of butter and set aside. Skim off as much of the fat in the turkey pan as you can. Heat the cooking juices and add some broth, according to how much gravy you like to serve. (Refrigerate or freeze the remaining broth.) Boil for 1 or 2 minutes and then add the flour and butter mixture in small bits, beating it in with a small balloon whisk. Taste and add salt and pepper as you wish. Transfer the gravy to 1 or 2 sauceboats.

8. Bring the turkey to the table to carve and serve. Give each person some chestnut and sausage stuffing, but not the fruit stuffing. Pass around the cooked leftover fruit stuffing as a relish.

PREPARATION

You can stuff the turkey up to 2 hours before putting it in the oven. Do not refrigerate. The broth can be made as soon as you have the turkey.

SERVES 8 TO 10

Ripieno di frutta
Fruit Stuffing

2 oranges

1 lemon

3½ cups fresh cranberries (12-ounce bag)

2 Granny Smith apples, peeled, cored, and cubed

3 red onions, thinly sliced

12 pitted prunes, cut into strips

4 garlic cloves, peeled

1⅓ cups red wine

1 teaspoon ground mace

1 teaspoon ground cloves

1 cup brown sugar

salt and freshly ground black pepper

1. Wash and dry one of the oranges and grate the rind into a large bowl. Peel both oranges and the lemon to the quick. Separate the segments and remove any white pith that's left and the papery skin between the segments. Place in a bowl together with all the other ingredients. Cover with plastic wrap and let stand for 1 to 2 hours.

2. Pack half the mixture into the cavity of the bird and sew up the opening.

3. Place the rest of the mixture in a saucepan and cook over low heat for about 1 hour. Stir occasionally and add water if it gets too dry. The mixture will be rather like a chutney by the end of the cooking. Taste and correct the seasoning.

PREPARATION

You can prepare the fruit in advance, but macerate it in the wine for no longer than 2 hours.

MAKES ABOUT 5 CUPS

Ripieno di castagne
Chestnut and Sausage Stuffing

½ pound fresh chestnuts

¼ pound pancetta

1 medium onion

4 celery stalks, with leaves

2 garlic cloves, peeled

½ cup flat-leaf parsley

12 fresh sage leaves

1 tablespoon fresh rosemary needles

2 tablespoons unsalted butter

¾ cup fresh white breadcrumbs

½ pound lean ground pork

½ pound sweet Italian pork sausage, peeled and crumbled

1 turkey liver, cleaned and chopped

3 tablespoons freshly grated parmesan

freshly ground black pepper

salt

1 egg (optional)

flour (optional)

oil (optional)

1. Buy large, hard, shiny chestnuts. Throw away any that have a rancid smell; you will notice the smell as soon as you begin to peel them. Peeling chestnuts is a labor of love, justified, however, by the result, since fresh chestnuts have a mealy richness that canned or dried chestnuts lack.

Wash the chestnuts, put them in a pan, cover with cold water, and bring very slowly to a boil. There is no need to make a cut in the shells if you start the chestnuts in cold water and bring the water slowly to a boil. Cook for 40 to 45 minutes, or until quite soft. To test, fish a chestnut out of the water, cool under running water, and squeeze between your thumb and forefinger. It should offer no resistance. Take a few chestnuts out of the water and peel, removing the outer skin and the thin brown inner skin. It is easier to peel chestnuts if they are hot.

2. Coarsely chop the pancetta, onion, celery, garlic, parsley, sage, and rosemary. You can do this in a food processor.

3. Melt the butter in a large frying pan and add the pancetta mixture, the breadcrumbs, ground pork, and sausage and stir-fry for 5 minutes. Add the liver and cook for 5 minutes more. Stir frequently to *insaporire* (let the mixture take the flavor).

4. Transfer to a bowl and add the parmesan, plenty of freshly ground pepper, and salt to taste. I cut up the chestnuts, cutting the large ones in half or even into quarters. Mix into the meat mixture. Taste and adjust the seasoning. Loosely pack the stuffing into the neck end of the turkey and sew down the flap of skin.

5. If you have any stuffing left over, chop it well in a food processor, adding 1 egg for binding. Shape small croquettes the size of limes and roll them in flour. Put the croquettes in the refrigerator to get firm. About 30 minutes before serving, place the croquettes on a well-oiled baking sheet. Brush with more oil and bake for 30 minutes.

PREPARATION

The stuffing can be prepared up to 2 days in advance and refrigerated in a closed container. It can also be frozen for 2 to 3 weeks; after that the chestnuts get too soft.

MAKES 2 CUPS

Le caramellone natalizie con crema allo zenzero

Christmas "Crackers" with Ginger Custard

3-inch-piece gingerroot

2 cups whole milk

4 large egg yolks

½ cup sugar

3 tart apples, such as Granny Smiths

2 tablespoons lemon juice

⅔ cup golden raisins

1 tablespoon dark rum

⅓ cup walnuts, blanched, peeled, and chopped

1 teaspoon ground cinnamon

3 tablespoons sugar

¼ cup dried breadcrumbs

8 tablespoons (1 stick) unsalted butter

10 to 14 ounces frozen phyllo pastry, thawed

confectioners' sugar

1. Peel the ginger and grate it, using the coarse hole of a grater.

2. Bring the milk to a simmer, remove the pan from the heat, stir in the ginger, and let stand for about 1 hour. Strain the milk through a fine strainer, discard the ginger, and return the milk to the pan.

3. Put the egg yolks in a bowl and gradually add the sugar while beating with a hand-held electric beater or a wire whisk. Beat for 2 to 3 minutes, until the mixture is pale yellow and forms a ribbon.

4. Meanwhile, bring the strained milk to a simmer. Pour it slowly over the egg mixture while continuing to beat. Transfer the mixture to a heavy saucepan and place over moderate heat. Cook, stirring slowly and constantly with a wooden spoon and reaching all around the bottom of the pan, until the sauce thickens enough to coat the back of the spoon, about 15 minutes. To see whether it is ready, dip the spoon in the custard and draw your finger across the back of it. If a clear line remains the custard is ready. If you have a candy thermometer, check that the temperature is no more than 170° F. Remove the pan from the heat and place it in a basin of cold water to cool quickly. Beat for the first minute, then beat occasionally. When cold, cover with plastic wrap and chill.

5. Peel, quarter, and core the apples. Cut each quarter in half lengthwise, then thinly slice it across. Put in a bowl and add the lemon juice, raisins, rum, walnuts, cinnamon, sugar, and breadcrumbs. Mix very thoroughly.

6. Melt 2 tablespoons of the butter in a nonstick frying pan. Add the apple mixture and sauté gently for 5 minutes, turning it over often. Set aside for about 1 hour for the flavors to blend.

7. Melt the remaining butter in a small saucepan. Brush a baking sheet with a little butter. Unroll the phyllo pastry and cut the leaves into 6- x 4-inch pieces. Take out 4 pieces and keep the rest of the phyllo pastry covered, or it will dry out and crack. Place a leaf of phyllo on the work top surface and brush with melted butter. Place the other 3 leaves on top of the first, brushing each generously with butter. Spread 1 scant tablespoon of filling on the top leaf, leaving 1 to 1½ inches at the end of the longer side uncovered. Roll up the pastry lengthwise. Twist the pastry ends like a "cracker," and crimp them. Place on the baking sheet. Repeat to make the other 9 crackers. Refrigerate for about 45 minutes.

8. Preheat the oven to 375° F.

9. When the oven is hot, bake for 20 minutes, or until the crackers are golden.

10. When the crackers have cooled slightly, sprinkle with confectioners' sugar and serve with the ginger custard passed around separately in a bowl. If you prefer, place the crackers on individual dessert plates and spoon a little custard around them.

PREPARATION

The custard can be prepared up to 2 days in advance and kept, covered, in the refrigerator. The crackers, like strudel, are best eaten freshly baked and warm. However, they can be made up to 2 days in advance and kept wrapped in foil. Reheat in a warm oven for 10 minutes.

SERVES 10

NEW YEAR'S EVE SUPPER FOR TEN

Bresaola con la rucola
Bresaola with Arugula (page 45)

Il gran raviolo
One Egg Ravioli in Clear Broth

Zampone allo zabaione
Zampone with Zabaglione

Lenticchie in umido
Green Lentils with Sage

Bomba di panna e marrons glacés
Marron Glacé Bombe

Ananas e arancie
Pineapple and Oranges (page 161)

The most memorable New Year's Eve supper I ever had was years ago in Naples. It was not long after the end of World War II, when the wounds of war were healing and people were beginning to enjoy life again. I went south from Milan to see in the New Year with family friends who had teenaged children my age.

New Year's Eve in southern Italy is a major event. Fireworks go off in all directions and car horns honk mercilessly, but I was not prepared for what happened just a few minutes after we had toasted the New Year. Our friend Mariarosa got up from the table, picked up her chair, went over to the window, opened it, and threw the chair down to the street. Her brother and sister did the same with some of the crockery on the table. I ran to the window to see people hurling their oldest belongings into the street; they were having a good housecleaning to welcome in the year 1948! Later in the night, people from *i bassi* (the slums) came around to pick whatever could be salvaged. I am told that nowadays this custom, which also existed in Rome, has almost died away.

In this menu I have included one dish from the supper I enjoyed that memorable night, the zampone. The other dishes were local in origin, such as pies made with local vegetables, as well as cheese and sausages. There were also delicious little sweet things, many of them fried at the last moment.

For my menu, a mainly northern Italian one, I thought it would be good to start with something that can be bought, like prosciutto or bresaola, and serve them with arugula and parmesan. Their pungent flavor makes them good stimulants to the appetite. The recipe, if you can call it that, is on page 45. To make the dish more festive, cut some young parmesan or grana padano into slivers and scatter them over the dish.

The soup is slightly complicated though far less so than the traditional Italian New Year's soup, *cappelletti in brodo.* Cappelletti are small, filled pasta shapes, and they take hours to make, even if you're an expert pasta maker. The soup I suggest is ideal, one beautiful large ravioli floating in a bowl of clear broth.

Zampone is the traditional festive dish in northern Italy. It consists of ground pork, flavored with nutmeg, cinnamon, and cloves, stuffed into boned pigs' feet. The ingenuity of zampone dates back to the siege of Modena by the papal army in 1511. There was plenty of pork but, legend has it, until someone thought of the pig's foot, no way of making a sausage.

Zabaglione is the sauce that is served with zampone in Modena. It may seem odd, but it is perfect. The heady alcoholic sweetness of the zabaglione cuts through the richness of the zampone. At a New Year's Eve supper, zampone is always accompanied by lentils, which are considered a sign of future prosperity, each lentil representing a gold coin. In Italy green lentils are the most popular kind. They are tasty and they keep their shape beautifully when cooked. I would also serve a dish of buttery spinach, another traditional accompaniment to zampone. You will need two zampone for ten people. If you can't find zampone, use the smaller cotechino sausages, allowing three to four pounds for ten people.

One of the two desserts, the pineapple and oranges on page 161, in the menu is fresh and refreshing, the other, the bombe, rich and luscious. I make it with broken marrons glacés, which you can buy in Italy. They are sold at a quarter of the price of perfect ones. Even if you are not planning a trip to Italy for the purpose of saving money on marrons glacés, I am sure this dessert definitely justifies the cost of the ingredients.

Il gran raviolo
One Egg Ravioli in Clear Broth

³/4 pound fresh spinach, cooked, or 1 package (10 ounces) frozen leaf spinach, thawed

6 tablespoons unsalted butter

1¹/2 cups ricotta

¹/3 cup freshly grated Parmigiano-Reggiano

¹/2 nutmeg, grated

salt and freshly ground black pepper

10 small eggs

10 cups Italian broth (page 338)

pasta dough made with 2²/3 cups unbleached flour, 4 eggs, and 1 teaspoon olive oil

extra Parmigiano-Reggiano for serving

1. Squeeze all the liquid out of the spinach with your hands and finely chop it. Melt the butter in a sauté or frying pan and add the spinach. Turn it over and over until it has absorbed all the butter, and cook for about 5 minutes. Transfer to a bowl and add the ricotta, the cheese, the nutmeg, and salt and pepper to taste. Mix very thoroughly with your hands. Taste and check the seasoning.

2. Make the pasta dough following the directions on page 333. Roll it out thinly. If you are using a machine, roll out as wide a sheet as possible. Roll out to the next-to-the last notch. If you are rolling out by hand, divide the dough into 5 balls and roll out 1 ball at a time, keeping the rest of the dough wrapped in a clean cloth. Cut the sheets into 4-inch circles. Fill each ravioli before you proceed to roll out more dough, or the dough will dry out and you will not be able to seal the ravioli. Place about 2 tablespoons of filling on every other circle. Shape the mixture into a ring, leaving a ²/3-inch border all around it, and room for the egg yolk in the middle. Break 1 egg and very carefully separate it, reserving the white for another purpose. Tip the yolk gently into the center of the ring of spinach. Using a pastry brush, moisten the edges of the circle with cold water. Place a plain circle on top, making sure that no air is trapped inside, and seal the edges tightly together. Continue until you have prepared all 10 ravioli.

3. Divide the broth into two large sauté pans and bring to a boil. Using a pancake turner, transfer as many ravioli as you can into the pans without overlapping. Bring the broth back to a boil, reduce to a simmer, and cook for 5 minutes.

continued

4. Lift each ravioli out of the broth very carefully and place in individual heated soup dishes. Cover with a little broth and keep warm while you finish cooking the ravioli. Fill each bowl with the broth. Serve with the extra Parmigiano-Reggiano passed around in a bowl.

PREPARATION

Prepare the ravioli as late as you possibly can, or the pasta will dry too much and take longer to cook; the egg yolks would then be overcooked. The ravioli must not be made more than 1 hour in advance. They must be cooked at the last moment.

SERVES 10

Zampone allo zabaione
Zampone with Zabaglione

2 zampone or 3 to 4 pounds cotechino sausages

4 egg yolks

4 tablespoons sugar

⅔ cup marsala

1. If you have bought zampone or cotechini *precotto* (partly cooked), follow the manufacturer's instructions. If your sausages are raw, soak them in cold water for a few hours. Prick them with a thin needle in a few places, wrap with cheesecloth, and tie each end with a piece of string. Put them in a saucepan and cover with water. Bring to a boil and cook gently for 2½ hours. Turn the heat off while you prepare the zabaglione.

2. Using a balloon whisk, beat the egg yolks with the sugar until creamy. Place in a double boiler or over a saucepan of simmering water and gradually add the marsala while beating constantly. When the custard thickens, remove from the heat. Transfer to a warm bowl and keep warm in a bain-marie or leave it in the double boiler until you bring it to the table.

3. Cut the sausages into ½-inch slices and place them, slightly overlapping, on an oval dish. Cover the dish with foil and keep it warm until you bring it to the table.

PREPARATION

Zampone is one of those marvelous foods that do not need any preparation. The zabaglione takes such a short time to prepare that there is no point in making it beforehand, with the risk of curdling or of serving it too cold. Do it before you sit down at the table and keep it warm in a bain-marie or double boiler.

SERVES 10

Lenticchie in umido
Green Lentils with Sage

——

3 cups green lentils (about 1½ pounds)   12 fresh sage leaves, chopped

6 cups chicken broth   2 tablespoons cider vinegar

7 tablespoons olive oil   salt and freshly ground black pepper

1½ onions, finely chopped

1. Spread out some of the lentils and remove any stones or grit. Repeat until you have checked them all. Rinse and drain the lentils. Soak them for about 4 hours in cold water.

2. Heat the broth or if you are cooking the zampone at the same time, use some of the cooking liquid plus some water.

3. Put the oil and the onion in an earthenware pot or a heavy-bottomed saucepan and sauté over medium heat until the onion is soft. Stir the sage into the onion, then add the lentils, stirring until they are well coated with oil. Add enough broth, sausage cooking liquid, or boiling water to cover the lentils. Bring to a boil, reduce the heat, cover the pan, and simmer for about 45 minutes to 1 hour. Add a little hot water from time to time if necessary, so that the lentils do not cook dry. Halfway through the cooking, stir in the vinegar and continue cooking until the lentils are tender. By the time they are ready, they should have absorbed nearly all the liquid.

4. Add salt and pepper to taste. Mix well and turn the lentils into the dish alongside the zampone and serve.

PREPARATION

Lentils are better done a day in advance. Refrigerate them in a covered container. They can also be frozen.

SERVES 10

Bomba di panna e marrons glacés
Marron Glacé Bombe

¾ pound marrons glacés

5 tablespoons dark rum

3 ounces best semi-sweet chocolate

3⅓ cups heavy cream

6 tablespoons confectioners' sugar, sifted

3 egg whites

1. Cut the marrons glacés into small pieces and put them in a bowl. Add the rum and leave to macerate for about 30 minutes.

2. Meanwhile, cut the chocolate into small bits. Do not use a food processor as it tends to reduce some of the chocolate to powder.

3. Whip the cream, then mix in the confectioners' sugar, the marrons glacés with the rum, and the chocolate pieces.

4. Beat the egg whites until stiff and fold into the mixture.

5. Spoon into a 5-cup bombe mold or any other 5-cup dome-shaped container. Cover with the lid or with foil and put in the freezer for at least 6 hours. Remove from the freezer 30 minutes before serving and leave outside. Unmold onto a round serving dish and decorate with a sprig of mistletoe.

PREPARATION

The bombe should be made 1 day in advance. It can be made and frozen up to 1 week in advance, although it gradually loses flavor.

SERVES 10

MY FAVORITE MENUS

DINNER FOR FOUR

269

Soffiato di riso all'aragosta
Rice and Lobster Soufflé

Petti di pollo farciti di carciofi
Chicken Breasts Stuffed with Artichokes

Pere alla crema del Lario
Poached Pears with Pear Liqueur Cream
(page 139)

A BALSAMIC VINEGAR–FLAVORED DINNER FOR SIX

280

Cicoria belga sul letto d'indivia
Roasted Belgian Endive with Balsamic Vinegar

Petti di anatra all'aceto balsamico
Duck Breasts with Balsamic Vinegar Sauce

Purè di sedano
Celery Puree

Gelato di fragola all'aceto balsamico
Strawberry Ice Cream Flavored with Balsamic
Vinegar

A HISTORICAL DINNER FOR SIX

274

Cozze all'italiana
Mussels Italian Style

Timballo di maccheroni alla Pampadur
Baked Penne with Chicken and Prosciutto

Mela in tortiglié
Apple Snow in a Ring

A LEMON-FLAVORED DINNER FOR EIGHT

288

Stracciatella al sapor di limone
Lemon, Egg, and Parmesan Soup

Vitello al limone
Veal with Lemon and Cream

Spinaci all'agro
Lemon Spinach (page 331)

Coppette di frutta al caramello
Fruit Salad in a Caramel Sauce

A BASIL-FLAVORED DINNER FOR EIGHT

294

Patate e fagiolini al pesto
Potatoes and Green Beans with Pesto

~~~

Dentice al forno
Baked Porgies with Tomatoes and Basil

~~~

Spinaci all'agro
Lemon Spinach (page 331)

~~~

Sorbetto di limone al basilico
Basil-Lemon Sorbet (page 109)

A MILANESE DINNER FOR EIGHT

299

Minestra mariconda
Parmesan and Parsley Dumplings in Broth

~~~

Manzo alla California
Beef Braised in Vinegar and Cream

~~~

Il panettone col mascarpone
Panettone with Mascarpone

DINNER FOR EIGHT

304

Minestra di cavolfiore
Cauliflower Soup

~~~

Brasato cotto a crudo
Braised Beef

~~~

Polenta
Polenta (page 332)

~~~

Funghi al funghetto
Sautéed Mushrooms (page 328)

~~~

Bônet
Amaretti Pudding

A BOLOGNESE FEAST FOR THIRTY

310

Maccheroni gratinati con la luganega e l'aglio
Baked Ziti with Sausage and Garlic

~

Lasagne verdi al forno
Baked Green Lasagne

~

Penne ai quattro formaggi
Penne with Four Cheeses

~

Tagliatelle gratinate al prosciutto cotto e piselli
Baked Tagliatelle with Ham and Peas

~

Insalata verde
Green Salad (page 325)

~

Insalata di fagiolini e pomodori
Green Bean and Tomato Salad

~

Finocchio al parmigiano
Fennel Salad with Parmesan

~

Crostata di conserva di amarena
Sour Cherry Jam Tart

~

La bonissima
Walnut and Honey Pie (page 229)

DINNER FOR FOUR

Soffiato di riso all'aragosta
Rice and Lobster Soufflé

—

Petti di pollo farciti di carciofi
Chicken Breasts Stuffed with Artichokes

—

Pere alla crema del Lario
Poached Pears with Pear Liqueur Cream (page 139)

*T*his menu is a perfect dinner for a small formal occasion.

The soufflé is not a real soufflé, so there's no danger of ending up with a *soufflé tombé*.

For the chicken breasts, the only real job is preparing the artichokes. Be sure to buy artichokes with no brown patches that are tightly closed and have silvery green leaves attached to the stem. The potatoes with parsley on page 327 make a good accompaniment to this dish.

After these two rich courses, I would serve a fruit dessert. If persimmons are still available when the first artichokes arrive, choose the recipe on page 177. Otherwise, the poached pears (page 139) are suitable. Both recipes would have to be halved.

Soffiato di riso all'aragosta
Rice and Lobster Soufflé

---

1 cooked lobster (about 1½ to 2 pounds)
1 cup long-grain rice
salt
3 tablespoons unsalted butter
½ cup heavy cream

3 eggs, separated
2 tablespoons chopped fresh dill
4 tablespoons freshly grated parmesan
freshly ground black pepper
1 tablespoon dried breadcrumbs

1. Ask the fishmonger to split the cooked lobster in half. Remove all the meat, including the small claws. Do this over a bowl to collect the juices. Cut the lobster meat into small cubes.

2. Meanwhile, cook the rice in salted boiling water. As soon as it is ready, drain and refresh under cold water. Put it back into the saucepan and add the butter, cream, egg yolks, dill, and 3 tablespoons of the parmesan. Mix thoroughly, then gently mix in the lobster and its juices. Taste and add salt and pepper.

3. Preheat the oven to 400° F. Generously butter an 8-cup soufflé dish and sprinkle with the remaining parmesan mixed with the breadcrumbs.

4. Beat the egg whites until stiff but not dry, then fold them gently into the rice mixture. Spoon the mixture into the dish and bake for 25 to 30 minutes.

PREPARATION

You can prepare the lobster meat 1 day in advance and refrigerate it. The rice should not be cooked longer than 6 to 8 hours in advance and must not be refrigerated. Assemble the dish no more than 30 minutes before cooking.

SERVES 4

Petti di pollo farciti di carciofi
Chicken Breasts Stuffed with Artichokes

2 boneless and skinless chicken breasts, cut in half

2 tablespoons lemon juice

salt and freshly ground black pepper

1 lemon, cut in half

2 medium artichokes (about 1 pound)

4 tablespoons olive oil

1 tablespoon chopped fresh mint

1 garlic clove, peeled and chopped

4 ripe tomatoes, peeled, seeded, and chopped

flour

3 tablespoons unsalted butter

1 cup chicken or beef broth

1. Cut the chicken breasts horizontally in half and then cut each half through almost to the other side. Open each slice like a book. Put them on a dish, drizzle with lemon juice, and season with salt and pepper. Leave to marinate for no longer than 1 hour while you prepare the artichokes.

2. Rub your hands with ½ lemon to protect them from the artichoke juice. Cut off the artichokes at the base and rub the cut parts with lemon. Break off the tough outer leaves. Snap off the top of each leaf by bending it back. Continue snapping off the tops until you get to the central cone of paler leaves. With a very sharp knife, cut off about 1 inch straight across the top of the artichoke. Every time you cut it, rub immediately with lemon and drop the pieces into a bowl of cold water with the juice of ½ lemon.

3. Quarter the prepared artichokes and remove the choke and the prickly purplish leaves at the base. Cut the artichokes down into thin wedges with one edge remaining attached to the bottom. Put in the bowl of acidulated cold water. Peel away the tough outside part of the stalks. Cut the tender inside into rounds. Add to the acidulated water. When everything is done, dry the artichokes thoroughly.

4. Put the oil and the artichoke wedges and rounds in a heavy sauté pan. Season with salt and pepper and cook gently for 3 minutes, turning them over frequently. Mix in the mint and garlic and sauté for another couple of minutes.

5. Add the tomatoes to the pan. Add a couple of tablespoons of hot water and cook, tightly covered, for about 30 minutes, adding more water as necessary. When done, the artichokes should feel quite tender when pricked with a fork. There should be no liquid left in the pan except for an oily tomato sauce.

6. Dry the chicken breasts with paper towels and put them on the work surface. Lay a large spoonful of the artichoke and tomato mixture on each breast half. Fold over and close it with 1 or 2 wooden toothpicks. Coat packet very lightly in salted flour.

7. Heat the butter in a large pan and when it is sizzling, add the chicken breasts and fry on each side. Meanwhile, heat the broth in a small saucepan. When the chicken breasts are pale gold, pour over half the broth and continue cooking over low heat for 15 minutes, adding 1 or 2 tablespoons hot broth if necessary. Taste and adjust seasoning.

8. Remove the toothpicks, transfer the chicken breasts to a heated dish, and spoon over the cooking liquids.

PREPARATION

The dish can be prepared totally up to 1 day in advance and refrigerated. Add a little knob of butter when you reheat it. The artichokes can be prepared and cooked up to 2 days in advance and refrigerated. They can also be frozen.

SERVES 4

A HISTORICAL DINNER
FOR SIX

Cozze all'italiana

Mussels Italian Style

———

Timballo di maccheroni alla Pampadur

Baked Penne with Chicken and Prosciutto

———

Mela in tortiglié

Apple Snow in a Ring

I am always fascinated by what people used to eat, and I love to adapt recipes from old books. This menu was inspired by three of my favorite writers from the past, all from southern Italy.

The first two recipes are typically Italian. The *primo,* mussels, is a popular dish to this day, and it is often made the same way as in this old recipe by Leonardi. Francesco Leonardi was a Roman who crowned a successful career by becoming chef to Catherine the Great. While he was very knowledgable about foreign methods, techniques, and produce, he also recorded simple Italian regional cooking, as in this recipe for mussels.

Contrary to what most Italians would do, I have decided to serve a pasta dish as a main course. But this *timballo* is no everyday pasta dish—it is a rich and delectable concoction. Vincenzo Corrado, its creator, dedicated it to Madame Pompadour, the *Pampadur* of the recipe title. Corrado was the first author to assimilate the terminology of French gastronomy, which by the eighteenth century had gained supremacy over all other cuisines. In his book *Il cuoco galante* he tried to graft French techniques onto the local cuisine, but the Italian feeling for simplicity and purity of ingredients is there, especially in the chapter "Il vitto pitagorico," devoted to vegetarian food, in which most of the recipes are very appealing to the modern palate.

Cucina teorico-pratica, from which I have taken the dessert, was written by Ippolito Cavalcanti, Duke of Buonvicino, at the beginning of the nineteenth century. The dessert interested me especially because I could see in it a connection with English nursery food. Perhaps Cavalcanti got the recipe from one of the many English ladies who spent the winter months in Naples. Cavalcanti gives apple snow an appealing shape and decorates it with *erbaggio,* sugar shapes mainly green in color. I have used chopped pistachio nuts instead. It is a good dessert, and one your friends will love for the familiar flavor hiding beneath an elegant disguise.

Cozze all'italiana
Mussels Italian Style

4 pounds mussels | *1 onion*
long Italian bread or French baguette | *3 garlic cloves*
½ cup extra-virgin olive oil | *1 cup dry white wine*
½ cup flat-leaf parsley leaves | *freshly ground black pepper*

1. Clean the mussels as described on page 158. Discard any mussel that remains open after you tap it on a hard surface.

2. Preheat the oven to 400° F.

3. Cut the bread into fairly thick slices and lay them on a baking sheet. Using a pastry brush, moisten the bread with a little oil. Bake for 6 to 8 minutes. Turn off the oven, leaving the bread in it to keep warm.

4. Pour the oil into a large saucepan large enough to cook the mussels later, or divide it between 2 pans, increasing the amount of oil by 1 tablespoon.

5. Chop the parsley, onion, and garlic together and add to the pan or pans. Turn the heat on and sauté for 1 minute. Add the wine and the pepper and cook briskly for a couple of minutes to evaporate the alcohol content. Transfer the mussels to the pan or pans. Cover tightly and cook until all the mussels are open. Shake the pan often.

6. As soon as the mussels are open, turn the heat off. If you are using an earthenware pan, bring it to the table. Otherwise, transfer the mussels and all the juices to a heated terrine or spoon the mussels directly into individual soup bowls. Place the toasted bread in the soup bowls first so that the mussels are ladled over it. Serve at once.

PREPARATION

Mussels cannot be reheated. You can clean them and leave them in a covered bowl up to a few hours in advance. The bread can be toasted up to 2 days in advance, wrapped in foil, and refrigerated. Remove from the refrigerator at least 2 hours before serving.

SERVES 6

Timballo di maccheroni alla Pampadur
Baked Penne with Chicken and Prosciutto

8 tablespoons (1 stick) unsalted butter

1 tablespoon olive oil

1 sprig fresh rosemary, about 3 inches long, or 1 teaspoon dried rosemary

1-pound piece boneless pork loin

1 cup dry white wine

salt and freshly ground black pepper

1 small boneless and skinless chicken breast, cut in half (½ pound)

¼ pound prosciutto, sliced ⅛-inch thick

1 pound penne

½ cup freshly grated parmesan

3 tablespoons dried breadcrumbs

3 egg yolks

1½ cups heavy cream

½ teaspoon ground cinnamon

1. Choose a small heavy casserole into which the pork will just fit. Put in 4 tablespoons of the butter, the oil, and rosemary and turn the heat to medium-high. As soon as the butter begins to color, add the pork and brown well on all sides. This will take about 10 minutes.

2. Turn the heat up to high and pour over the wine. Reduce by half, then turn the heat down to low so that the liquid simmers very gently. Sprinkle with salt and pepper. Cover the pan with a sheet of wax paper and put the cover on slightly askew. Cook for about 1½ hours, turning the meat over every 30 minutes and adding water if the pork is cooking dry. When the meat is very tender, remove from the pan and reserve for another meal.

3. Add a couple of tablespoons of warm water to the pan and bring to a boil, scraping the bottom of the pan with a wooden spoon to loosen the residue. Measure the liquid and if necessary add enough water to make ½ cup of liquid.

4. Heat 2 tablespoons of the remaining butter in a nonstick frying pan. Add the chicken breast and sauté very gently until done, about 15 minutes, turning the breast over halfway through the cooking. Season with a little salt and pepper and add a couple of tablespoons of water if necessary. Transfer the chicken breast with pan juices and the prosciutto, cut into pieces, to a food processor. Process until coarsely ground. If you do not have a food processor, chop coarsely by hand. Transfer the mixture to a bowl and add the pork juices. Mix thoroughly.

continued

5. Cook the penne in plenty of salted boiling water. Drain, turn immediately into the bowl with the meat mixture, and add the remaining butter and half the parmesan. Mix very thoroughly, then taste and adjust the seasoning.

6. Preheat the oven to 400° F.

7. Butter a baking dish and sprinkle all over with the dried breadcrumbs. Shake off the excess crumbs. Transfer the pasta into the dish and gently even it off.

8. Mix together the egg yolks, cream, cinnamon, the remaining parmesan, a little salt, and a generous amount of pepper. Spoon this sauce over the pasta and place the dish in the oven. Bake for about 15 minutes, until a golden crust forms. Remove the dish from the oven and let stand for 5 minutes before serving.

PREPARATION

The dish can be prepared without the topping up to 1 day in advance. Cover tightly and refrigerate. Add the egg and cream topping just before baking. Bake for 5 minutes longer to allow the cold pasta to heat through.

SERVES 6

Mela in tortiglié
Apple Snow in a Ring

⌐⌐⌐

2¼ *cups apple puree* | 3 *egg whites*
1 *vanilla bean* | ⅓ *cup sugar*
3 *tablespoons Maraschino, Alchermes,* | 2 *tablespoons chopped pistachio nuts*
Rosolio, or Crème de Cassis | 1 *cup heavy cream*
1 *teaspoon cinnamon* |
2 *teaspoons grated lemon peel* |

1. The apple puree must be thick and dry or it will not keep its ring shape. Sweeten it to taste, keeping in mind that it will be covered by a sweet meringue.

2. Split the vanilla bean in half, scrape out the seeds, and add to the puree with the liqueur, cinnamon, and lemon peel. Taste for sweetness and flavoring.

3. Beat the egg whites until stiff. Reserve 2 tablespoons of the sugar and set aside. Add one-third of the sugar to the egg whites. Continue beating, then add half of the remaining sugar. Beat well. The meringue will be beautifully glossy and silky. Sprinkle the rest of the sugar over the top and gently fold it into the meringue.

4. Shape the puree into a ring on an ovenproof round dish. If your puree is really stiff you can use a pastry bag with a large fluted nozzle attached.

5. Preheat the oven to 300° F.

6. Cover the puree with the meringue, using a thin metal spatula. Sprinkle with the reserved sugar and then with the chopped pistachio. Bake for 15 to 20 minutes, until the meringue is set and just colored.

7. Leave to cool, then chill. Before serving, whip the cream and fill the hole in the middle with some of the cream. Serve the rest of the cream separately.

PREPARATION

The puree can be totally prepared up to 3 days in advance and kept in the refrigerator in a closed container. The meringue must be prepared and baked no more than 1 hour before serving or it will get soggy.

SERVES 6

A BALSAMIC VINEGAR–FLAVORED DINNER FOR SIX

Cicoria belga sul letto d'indivia
Roasted Belgian Endive with Balsamic Vinegar

~

Petti di anatra all'aceto balsamico
Duck Breasts with Balsamic Vinegar Sauce

~

Purè di sedano
Celery Puree

~

Gelato di fragola all'aceto balsamico
Strawberry Ice Cream Flavored with Balsamic Vinegar

*A*fter reading my previous book *The Italian Pantry,* some of my friends remarked that balsamic vinegar must be one of my favorite ingredients. Well, yes it is. So I really enjoyed designing a menu round it.

Because of the way it is made, balsamic vinegar has a sweeter and deeper flavor than other vinegars. Wine vinegar is commonly made from dry wine; balsamic vinegar starts from cooked white Trebbiano grapes, which are picked very late. The result of the cooking of the must is that most of the water is evaporated and the sugar content rises. The amber syrup is then put in a wooden barrel. A long time later it is decanted into a succession of at least five other barrels. By law, this process of maturing must last for twelve years or more. Only then is the balsamic vinegar ready.

The expertise of the maker, the ideal climate of the provinces of Modena and nearby Reggio, and, finally, the approval of the "tasting masters" make this a very fine vinegar with a deep, velvety sweetness and a complex mixture of aromas. No wonder it has been a most highly regarded condiment since the Middle Ages. This is the *aceto balsamico tradizionale,* which is sold in Italy for stratospheric prices.

The balsamic vinegar you and I usually buy in shops outside Italy is something very different. It is still made from the boiled must of the Trebbiano grape, but it is produced in a much reduced span of time and its flavor is sometimes emphasized by caramelized sugar. In spite of not being the genuine article, this balsamic vinegar still can harmonize the many flavors in a seafood salad or blend with the robustness of raw meat in a carpaccio. Balsamic vinegar brings out aromas and scents with an intensity never previously detected.

This is what it does in the first and last courses of my menu. The bitterness of the Belgian endive and chicory is tempered, yet enhanced, by the vinegar. Strawberries dressed with balsamic vinegar are a classic dish of Emilia-Romagna, but, as far as I know, this ice cream is my own creation. I am rather proud of this recipe; I hope you will see why! If you want to serve a balsamic vinegar–flavored dinner when strawberries are out of season, I suggest you make the mascarpone ice cream on page 128, and simply put a little bottle of balsamic vinegar on the table. Pour a teaspoonful on each portion.

In the *secondo,* the balsamic vinegar is used in the sauce to cut through the richness of the duck, much as brandy, port, or Madeira often are. Duck breasts are easily available nowadays, though I prefer to buy a whole duck and remove the breasts, which are enough for my husband and myself. I then make a *ragù* for a dish of pasta with the rest of the meat and boil the carcass for some rich, well-flavored stock. But this takes time, and time, today, is often the least available ingredient. So I suggest you buy duck breasts, which are now sold in many butcher shops and better supermarkets. Some of these breasts are quite large, certainly enough for two people. The balsamic vinegar–flavored duck breasts go very well with celery puree or with the green lentils with sage on page 262. A second accompaniment could be grilled polenta (page 333), which you can prepare beforehand and reheat quickly in the oven for five minutes.

Cooking the duck is the only thing you have to do at the last minute, as the fist course is all ready on plates and the last is all ready in the freezer or refrigerator. In fact, this is another menu that might have been specially designed for the last-minute cook.

Cicoria belga sul letto d'indivia
Roasted Belgian Endive with Balsamic Vinegar

2 salted anchovies or 4 canned anchovy
fillets in oil

milk

8 firm Belgian endives of similar size

⅔ cup extra-virgin olive oil

salt and freshly ground black pepper

2 tablespoons pine nuts

4 tablespoons balsamic vinegar

½ pound chicory

3 hard-boiled eggs

1. Rinse the salted anchovies under cold water and remove the backbone. Drain the oil from the anchovy fillets. Pat dry. Coarsely chop the anchovies, put them in a small bowl, and cover with milk. This will soften the strong flavor.

2. Remove a thin slice from the root end of each Belgian endive and any brown edges from the outside leaves. Slice in half lengthwise and rinse under cold water. Lay on a slanting board, cut side down, to drain for half an hour. Dry them with paper towels.

3. Preheat the oven to 450° F.

4. Grease a baking sheet with a little of the oil. Lay the endives cut side up, on the tray, brush with olive oil, and season with salt and pepper. Bake for 10 minutes, until the inner core can be pierced with a fork. Transfer to a dish.

5. Remove the anchovies from the milk and put in a small frying pan with the remaining oil. Cook gently for 1 minute, mashing the anchovies with a fork. Keep the heat very low. Stir in the pine nuts and the balsamic vinegar. Sauté for 1 minute more, then add salt, if necessary, and a good deal of pepper. Spoon three-quarters of the hot sauce over the Belgian endive. Cover with plastic wrap and set aside for 2 hours.

6. Half an hour before you are ready to serve dinner, wash the chicory and dry thoroughly. Cut into very thin strips, the finer the better. Place on a serving dish and spoon over the remaining sauce. Do not mix the salad or you will spoil its appearance. Place the Belgian endives neatly on the bed of chicory and pour over all the juices from the dish it was on.

continued

7. Cut the hard-boiled eggs in half and remove the yolks (you can use the whites in a salad on another occasion.) Press through a sieve or a food mill fitted with the small-hole disk. Do this directly over the dish so that the egg mimosa will stay airy and light. Serve immediately.

PREPARATION

The only thing that is better done at the last minute is the pureeing of the egg yolks. The rest can be prepared up to 3 hours in advance. The Belgian endive can be baked up to 1 day in advance and kept covered.

SERVES 6

Petti di anatra all'aceto balsamico
Duck Breasts with Balsamic Vinegar Sauce

———

3 tablespoons unsalted butter
1 celery stalk, very finely chopped
1 shallot, very finely chopped
salt
4 tablespoons dry white wine
²/₃ cup duck stock or other strong meat stock

3 whole boneless duck breasts (about ¾ pound each)
freshly ground black pepper
1 tablespoon olive oil
4 tablespoons balsamic vinegar
1 tablespoon flour

1. Preheat the oven to 425° F.

2. Heat half the butter with the celery and the shallot in a saucepan. Add 2 pinches of salt. When the vegetables are just soft but not brown, pour over the wine and boil until the liquid is reduced by half. Add the stock and simmer gently for about 30 minutes.

3. While the sauce is simmering, score the skin of the duck breasts with the point of a sharp knife, deeply enough to penetrate into the flesh, and rub with salt and pepper. Grease a roasting pan with the oil and lay the breasts in it, skin side down. Roast for 15 to 20 minutes, according to how well cooked you like your duck.

4. Remove the skin from the duck. (It is delicious cut into small strips, fried, and sprinkled over a radicchio salad.) Put the duck on a plate and keep warm, covered with foil. Skim off the fat from the roasting pan. Put the pan on the heat and deglaze with the balsamic vinegar, boiling rapidly for 30 seconds, while scraping the bottom of the pan with a metal spoon. Pour into the sauce.

5. Blend together the remaining butter and the flour with the prongs of a fork. Swirl small dots of this mixture into the sauce. When the last bit of the mixture has melted, the sauce is ready. Taste for seasoning and transfer to a heated sauceboat.

6. Slice the duck breasts on a diagonal and transfer to a warm dish. Spoon over a little of the sauce. Serve the rest of the sauce separately.

continued

PREPARATION

The sauce can be prepared in advance and reheated before the deglazing juices are added.

SERVES 6

Purè di sedano
Celery Puree

—

1½ *bunches celery*

salt

2 *tablespoons olive oil*

1 *onion, finely chopped*

1 *tablespoon lovage, chopped, or 2 teaspoons celery seed, pounded*

½ *teaspoon dried oregano*

½ *cup white wine*

½ *cup vegetable stock*

1. Remove all the strings from the celery stalks. I find a potato peeler better than a knife for this job. Scrub and wash the stalks and cut into 2-inch pieces.

2. Bring a saucepan of salted water to a boil. Add the celery and cook for 5 minutes after the water has come back to the boil. Drain thoroughly. Chop the celery to a coarse puree. You can use a food processor but be careful not to make the celery too mashed up.

3. Put all the other ingredients in a saucepan and bring to a boil. Simmer for 10 minutes, then stir in the celery. Cook for 10 minutes more, stirring frequently. If the puree seems too thin, turn up the heat to evaporate some of the liquid. Taste, check seasoning, and serve.

PREPARATION

The puree can be prepared up to 1 day in advance and refrigerated in a covered container. Reheat slowly in a well-oiled heavy saucepan.

SERVES 6

Gelato di fragola all'aceto balsamico

Strawberry Ice Cream Flavored with Balsamic Vinegar

1 pound strawberries	*1½ tablespoons balsamic vinegar*
¾ cup sugar	*⅔ cup heavy cream*

1. Wash and hull the strawberries. Dry them with paper towels and put in a food processor with the sugar. Set the processor in motion and add the balsamic vinegar through the feed tube. Transfer the mixture to a bowl, cover it, and refrigerate for 2 to 3 hours. The sugar and vinegar will bring out the flavor of the fruit.

2. Whip the cream to soft peaks and fold into the strawberry mixture. Put in the ice-cream machine, following the manufacturer's instructions. If you do not have an ice-cream machine, put the mixture in a container and cover it. Stir the mixture once during the freezing. Remove from the freezer half an hour before serving and leave at room temperature.

PREPARATION

This, like any fruit ice cream, is best eaten within a day of being made.

SERVES 6

A LEMON-FLAVORED DINNER FOR EIGHT

Stracciatella al sapor di limone
Lemon, Egg, and Parmesan Soup

———

Vitello al limone
Veal with Lemon and Cream

———

Spinaci all'agro
Lemon Spinach (page 331)

———

Coppette di frutta al caramello
Fruit Salad in a Caramel Sauce

*S*ometimes I like to give my dinners a theme. In the previous menu it was balsamic vinegar; here it is lemon, an ingredient that improves so many dishes. This is an elegant and well-balanced menu and one of the easiest you could make.

The light soup needs a homemade Italian broth (my recipe is on page 338) made with meat and a few bones. I beg you to try the second course. The veal is expensive, but it goes a long way because there is no waste. Go to a good butcher and ask for a cut suitable for roasting. I like to serve the veal with buttery-soft mashed potatoes, but I have also served fresh tagliatelle as an accompaniment. I cook the pasta just before sitting down and keep it hot in the cooking pan, tossed with butter and a few tablespoons of the veal sauce. Spinach is the ideal vegetable; a recipe for lemon-flavored spinach is on page 331.

The little fruit salad gets a special flavor all its own from the lemony-orange caramel. Alternatively serve the basil-flavored lemon sorbet (page 109), or, in summer, the fruit salad with lemon granita (page 122).

Stracciatella al sapor di limone
Lemon, Egg, and Parmesan Soup

3 eggs
4 tablespoons semolina
6 tablespoons freshly grated parmesan
salt and freshly ground white pepper

2 tablespoons grated lemon peel
8 cups Italian broth (page 338)
3 tablespoons fresh marjoram leaves or fresh oregano

1. Beat the eggs lightly in a bowl. Add the semolina, parmesan, salt, pepper, and lemon peel. Beat thoroughly with a fork.

2. Heat the broth to simmering. Pour a couple of ladlefuls over the egg mixture, whisking with a fork or a balloon whisk.

3. Turn the heat down to low and pour the egg mixture into the broth. Cook for 5 minutes, whisking the whole time. Taste and adjust seasoning. The egg mixture will curdle and form soft flakes. Ladle the soup into individual bowls and add the marjoram.

PREPARATION

The soup takes only 2 or 3 minutes to make once the broth has come to the boil. You can mix the eggs, semolina, and parmesan up to 1 hour in advance.

SERVES 8

Vitello al limone
Veal with Lemon and Cream

1 boneless veal leg roast, tied into a neat roll (3½ pounds)
2 large lemons
salt and freshly ground black pepper
sprig fresh rosemary
6 fresh sage leaves
2 sprigs fresh thyme

2 tablespoons celery leaves
½ cup flat-leaf parsley leaves
1 garlic clove, peeled
6 tablespoons unsalted butter
1¼ cups heavy cream

1. Put the veal in a bowl and squeeze the juice of 1 lemon over it. Season with salt and pepper and marinate for about 2 hours.

2. Chop the rosemary, sage, thyme, celery, parsley, and garlic and put in an oval casserole which will hold the piece of meat rather snugly. Add the butter and sauté herbs for 1 minute.

3. Dry the meat thoroughly and add to the casserole. Sauté gently on all sides until the meat loses its raw color.

4. While the veal is sautéing, peel the other lemon to the quick and slice it very thin. Tuck the slices under the meat. Heat the cream and pour over the meat. Sprinkle with salt and pepper. Cover the casserole, leaving the lid slightly askew. This will intensify the flavor of the sauce by letting the vapors evaporate. Cook for 1½ to 2 hours, turning the veal over from time to time.

5. When the veal is cooked, tender all the way through when pricked with a fork, transfer the veal to a carving board and cover loosely with foil. Let rest for 5 minutes. Taste and check the seasonings of the sauce. If it seems a little watery, reduce by boiling fast until it is rich and full flavored.

6. Carve the meat into ½-inch slices and lay them, slightly overlapping, on a heated dish. Spoon some of the sauce over the meat and serve the rest separately in a sauceboat.

continued

PREPARATION

The dish can be prepared up to 2 days in advance and refrigerated. It can also be frozen in which case it must be thawed before reheating. Carve before you reheat it in the casserole.

SERVES 8

Coppette di frutta al caramello

Fruit Salad in a Caramel Sauce

———

4 bananas	*seedless green grapes, about 1 pound*
6 tablespoons strained lemon juice	*5 tablespoons sugar*
7 to 9 clementines or tangerines, according to size	*6 tablespoons orange juice, strained*

1. Peel the bananas and cut into ½-inch-thick rounds. Put in a bowl and sprinkle with a little lemon juice. Mix, cover the bowl with plastic wrap, and chill for half an hour.

2. Peel the clementines and remove as much of the stringy white pith as time and your patience allow. Put in a bowl, sprinkle with a little lemon juice, cover with plastic wrap and chill.

3. Wash and dry the grapes. Set aside.

4. Put the sugar and 3 tablespoons cold water in a small aluminum or unlined copper saucepan. Put the pan over medium heat and heat until the mixture becomes golden. Do not stir, in spite of the temptation to do so. It will take a good 5 to 7 minutes to begin to become golden, then it will quickly darken in color. At that moment remove from the heat immediately. While the sugar is melting, slowly heat the orange juice and the remaining lemon juice. Add to the caramel, stirring hard, as soon as you remove the caramel from the heat. I heat the juice to keep the caramel from turning hard, but if this should happen, put the pan back on the heat and stir hard until all lumps of caramelized sugar have melted. Leave aside to cool.

5. About 1 hour before serving, divide the fruit into 8 glass bowls. Spoon the sauce over and return to the refrigerator.

PREPARATION

The dessert can, if necessary, be prepared up to 1 day in advance, but the bananas will darken. Prepare everything except the bananas the day before and add the bananas 1 hour before serving.

SERVES 8

A BASIL-FLAVORED DINNER FOR EIGHT

Patate e fagiolini al pesto
Potatoes and Green Beans with Pesto

———

Dentice al forno
Baked Porgies with Tomatoes and Basil

———

Spinaci all'agro
Lemon Spinach (page 331)

———

Sorbetto di limone al basilico
Basil-Lemon Sorbet (page 109)

*B*asil has been known in Mediterranean countries since antiquity, when it was considered a sacred plant. In one of Boccaccio's stories, the heroine, Isabella, buries her murdered lover's head in a pot of basil. The story inspired Keats to write: "And so she ever fed it with thin tears,/ Whence thick and green and beautiful it grew." A seventeenth-century visitor to Italy wrote, "Amongst their Medicinall Plants scarce known amongst us, I took notice of one Odiferous Hearbe called Basilico."

Basil is still very much associated with Italy, and especially with the cooking of Liguria. Pesto was created there because that is where the best basil is to be found. The climate is ideal, combining moist sea breezes with warm, dry sunshine. Basil is now all the rage in northern Europe and the United States, where people have discovered it at long last. In early summer, when the basil is particularly sweet, I make and freeze pesto but without the garlic or cheese. I add them later when I use it.

The warm potato and bean salad in this menu is based on the Genoese dish *trenette al pesto,* in which trenette, a kind of homemade tagliatelle is cooked with potatoes and green beans. Here omit the pasta, which always needs to be cooked at the last minute, and serve the vegetables on their own. For this dish the pesto is made without cheese.

The fish course is very simple, but it must be cooked shortly before serving. The fish used in Italy for this dish is *dentice,* an excellent Mediterranean fish. As *dentice* is not available away from the Mediterranean, I use porgies, which are almost as good. You can get small porgies about ¾ pound each or larger ones weighing 2 to 3 pounds. I prefer to buy two large fish rather than eight little ones; it is simpler to cook them and they look grander when brought to the table. The basil in this course is part of the overall Mediterranean flavor. Lemon spinach is a perfect accompaniment to the fish.

The finale is the very original basil-lemon sorbet (page 109), as delicious as it is attractive.

Patate e fagiolini al pesto
Potatoes and Green Beans with Pesto

2 pounds new potatoes
1½ pounds green beans
5 tablespoons extra-virgin olive oil

5 tablespoons pesto (recipe follows)
salt and freshly ground black pepper

1. Boil the potatoes in their skins. When ready, drain and peel them while still hot. Set aside.

2. Tip and tail the beans and wash them. Cook them in plenty of salted water until cooked but not overcooked or undercooked. When green beans are nearly ready, they give off a characteristic aroma. They usually need a few more minutes, then drain them and transfer them to paper towels to dry. Cut the beans into 1-inch pieces.

3. While the beans are cooking, cut the potatoes into ¾-inch cubes, put them in a bowl, and dress with the olive oil.

4. Add the beans and toss. Add the pesto and toss thoroughly but gently. Serve warm.

PREPARATION

You can cook the vegetables up to 2 hours in advance and dress them with the olive oil. Reheat them by placing the salad bowl, covered with a lid, over a saucepan of simmering water. It will take 10 minutes to reheat. Mix thoroughly, then add the pesto.

SERVES 8

Pesto for Potatoes and Green Beans

1½ cups fresh basil leaves
2 garlic cloves, peeled
3 tablespoons pine nuts

2 tablespoons extra-virgin olive oil
salt and freshly ground black pepper

Put all the basil, garlic, nuts, and oil in the food processor and process at high speed until blended. Taste and check the seasonings.

PREPARATION

Pesto can be made in advance and refrigerated or frozen. For potatoes and green beans with pesto, I omit the cheese. To make pesto with cheese, stir in 6 tablespoons grated parmesan and/or pecorino at the end, before seasoning with salt.

MAKES 1 CUP

Dentice al forno
Baked Porgies with Tomatoes and Basil

———

2 large porgies with heads and tails (about 3 pounds each)

salt and freshly ground black pepper

6 garlic cloves, peeled and bruised

½ cup chopped flat-leaf parsley

6 tablespoons olive oil

⅔ cup dry white wine

8 ripe tomatoes, peeled, seeded, and cubed

1 dried chili

24 fresh basil leaves, torn into small pieces

2 tablespoons anchovy paste

1. Preheat the oven to 400° F.

2. Wash the fish and check that all the scales and the gills have been removed. Dry the fish thoroughly and season with salt and pepper inside and out. Place 1 garlic clove and ½ tablespoon parsley into each cavity.

3. Brush an ovenproof dish with 1 tablespoon of the oil and place the fish in it. Pour over the wine and 3 tablespoons of the remaining oil and place the dish in the oven. Bake for 25 minutes, basting occasionally. The fish is ready when the eye bulges out and the flesh parts easily from the bone. Keep warm while you prepare the sauce.

4. Put the rest of the oil, the tomato cubes, chili, basil, anchovy paste, and the remaining garlic cloves in a frying pan and cook for 5 minutes. Spoon a few tablespoons of the cooking juices into the sauce and add salt to taste. Remove the garlic and the chili and pour the sauce into a heated bowl. When you serve the fish, sprinkle with the remaining parsley, spoon a little of the cooking juices over each portion, and pass around the sauce separately.

PREPARATION

This is a dish that must be cooked shortly before eating. You can keep the fish warm, covered with foil, in the oven with the heat turned off, while you serve the first course. The sauce can also be kept warm or it can be reheated.

SERVES 8

A MILANESE DINNER FOR EIGHT

Minestra mariconda
Parmesan and Parsley Dumplings in Broth

~~~

Manzo alla California
Beef Braised in Vinegar and Cream

~~~

Il panettone col mascarpone
Panettone with Mascarpone

*L*ombardy offers quite a number of delicate and attractive looking soups. These are based on good broth made with the right proportion of meat to bone (see the recipe on page 338), then richly yet delicately flavored. Minestra mariconda, one of these soups, contains little cheese-flavored dumplings. I have adapted the recipe from a book, *Il cuoco senza pretese* (The Unpretentious Cook), a collection of recipes from Lombardy published in 1834. The original recipe suggests using fish broth for days of abstinence. What fascinates me in this book is that at the end of each recipe there is a list of the cost for each ingredient and the total. This soup, with quantities for at least twelve people, cost 53 lire, equal, today, to about a dime.

The California in the name of the meat course is, unexpectedly, a locality north of Milan. It is tempting to think that the other one was named by emigrants from Lombardy, but this seems unlikely since it was originally a Spanish colony. The cooking of northern Italy boasts many braised meat dishes, which are traditional for dinner parties and Sunday lunch. They are ideal for a large dinner party because the meat, which is cooked in a single piece, needs little attention and can even be cooked in advance. The best accompaniments are mashed potatoes and a bowl of spinach sautéed in butter and flavored with freshly grated nutmeg.

For dessert I thought nothing could be more suitable than panettone, the Milanese cake par excellence. In the past it was eaten only in Lombardy at Christmastime, but now it is eaten in most parts of Italy all year round. It has also conquered the world with its light texture and buttery taste. The tall, cylindrical shape created by Angelo Motta in 1921 has given way in the last decade to the original shape of a squat dome.

This was the sweet bread which became a big seller in the fifteenth century and made Toni, the poor baker, wealthy, and his beautiful daughter happy. A local nobleman wanted to marry the daughter and so he gave Toni money to buy the best eggs, flour, and butter, as well as golden raisins and candied orange and citron. The delicious sweet bread the baker was able to make became known as *Pan di Toni* and the prosperous Milanese flocked to Toni's bakery to buy it.

This is just one of the many stories surrounding the origin of panettone. It certainly is an ancient bread, possibly dating from the Middle Ages. A less romantic, and perhaps more plausible, explanation of the odd name lies in the Milanese penchant for diminutives. Thus *pane* became *panetto,* and, being bigger than most small breads, it became *panettone.*

As a native Milanese, I love my panettone. I like it plain for breakfast or for tea, with sweet white wine or vinsanto, but I like it best for dinner with another notable Lombard product, mascarpone. So when I want to serve it at the end of the meal, I buy a good panettone, one with chocolate bits in it, put a few slices in a moderate oven for 10 minutes, and serve it hot with mascarpone, which melts into the hot panettone. You will need a pound of mascarpone, about two cups, for eight. Put it into a bowl and pass it around.

Minestra mariconda
Parmesan and Parsley Dumplings in Broth

---

*3 cups fresh white breadcrumbs,
crusts removed*

1 cup whole milk

8 tablespoons (1 stick) unsalted butter

2 eggs

1 cup freshly grated parmesan

4 tablespoons chopped flat-leaf parsley

¼ nutmeg, grated

salt and freshly ground black pepper

8 cups Italian broth (page 338)

1. Soak the breadcrumbs in the milk for 10 minutes, then squeeze the milk out very thoroughly. Heat the butter in a small frying pan, add the breadcrumbs and sauté for 10 minutes, until the mixture is very dry, like dry paste. Transfer to a bowl.

2. Add the eggs to the bowl and then add ½ cup of the parmesan, the parsley, nutmeg, salt, and pepper. Mix thoroughly with a fork, cover the bowl with plastic wrap, and refrigerate for at least 2 hours.

3. Bring the broth slowly to a boil in a large saucepan. Taste and adjust the seasoning.

4. Pick up ½ teaspoon of the egg mixture and with the back of another teaspoon, push it down into the broth. If the mixture is hard enough, you can make little pellets, the size of hazelnuts, with your hands. To keep the dumplings from breaking, keep the heat low so that the broth barely simmers. Cook gently for 5 minutes, then ladle the soup into heated soup bowls. Serve with the rest of the Parmesan passed separately.

PREPARATION

You can prepare the dumpling mixture up to 1 day in advance and keep it, covered, in the refrigerator. Ideally the dumplings should be cooked shortly before serving, but I have cooked them about 1 hour before, left them in the soup, and reheated the soup very slowly.

SERVES 8

Manzo alla California
Beef Braised in Vinegar and Cream

---

8 tablespoons (1 stick) unsalted butter
2 onions, very finely chopped
2 celery stalks, very finely chopped
2 carrots, very finely chopped
1 tablespoon vegetable oil

1 chuck or rump roast, neatly tied (4 pounds)
½ cup red wine vinegar
salt and freshly ground black pepper
2 cups heavy cream

1. Melt the butter in a deep casserole. Add the vegetables and sauté gently for 10 minutes, stirring frequently.

2. Heat the vegetable oil in a nonstick pan and sear the meat on all sides. Transfer the meat to the bed of vegetables.

3. Pour the vinegar into the nonstick pan and deglaze rapidly. Pour over the meat and season with salt and pepper.

4. Heat the cream and when it begins to show bubbles at the edge, pour into the casserole. Bring slowly to a boil and simmer over very low heat for 2½ to 3 hours, or until the meat is very tender when pricked with a fork. Turn the meat 3 or 4 times during the cooking. When the meat is ready, remove to a plate and keep warm, covered with foil. Skim off as much fat as you can from the surface of the sauce. Puree the sauce and vegetables in a food processor. Transfer to a clean saucepan and heat slowly. Taste and adjust the seasoning. If the sauce is not tasty enough, boil briskly to reduce.

5. Slice the meat across the grain into ½-inch-thick slices and lay them, slightly overlapping, in a heated dish. Cover with some of the sauce and serve the rest in a heated bowl.

PREPARATION

The dish can be prepared up to 3 days in advance and refrigerated. Skim the fat off the sauce when the sauce is cold; it is much easier to do this then. Slice the meat and reheat very gently in the sauce. The dish can also be frozen.

SERVES 8

Minestra di cavolfiore

Cauliflower Soup

Brasato cotto a crudo

Braised Beef

Polenta

Polenta (page 332)

Funghi al funghetto

Sautéed Mushrooms (page 328)

Bônet

Amaretti Pudding

*L*ast year I was given a small cookery book from sixty years ago, a book totally unknown to me, which I read the same day, taking notes and marking useful tips, while savoring the wonderful dishes conjured up for me. The book is called *La cucina elegante* and was written by E. V. Quattrova. That is not, as I thought, a nom-de-plume, even though it means four eggs! It is in fact the name of a society lady of the 1930s. She gives excellent, elegant recipes as well as advice on how to entertain. This recipe for cauliflower soup, like many in the book, is easy to prepare.

The main course is braised beef with a difference. *Brasato,* a very popular dish in Italy, consists of a piece of meat that is usually sautéed or seared, then cooked slowly in wine and/or stock and/or tomato sauce. This recipe, which comes from my mother's recipe book, is the only one I know where the meat, after being marinated overnight, is cooked *a crudo,* i.e., without being seared, in a covered pan. Nor are the other ingredients, including the onions, sautéed first. I find the flavor of the meat lighter cooked this way.

I serve polenta (page 332) to mop up the juices and the sautéed mushrooms with oregano and garlic on page 328 with the meat.

The dessert is a soft dark pudding. It is a specialty of Piedmont. *Bônet* means bonnet, and the pudding is so named because the copper mold in which it is cooked is shaped like a bonnet. You can use any sort of shape, though the bonnet is prettier. I have also made *bônet* in a ring mold, filling the hole with whipped cream. The cream is my addition; I find it lightens the pudding and combines perfectly with the almond-caramel flavor.

Minestra di cavolfiore
Cauliflower Soup

---

1 medium white cauliflower (about 1¼ pounds)	4 egg yolks
8 cups Italian broth (page 338)	3 tablespoons unsalted butter, cut into small pieces
⅔ cup heavy cream	salt and freshly ground white pepper
2 tablespoons rice flour	croutons for serving

1. Cut the cauliflower into florets, discarding the leaves and core, and wash the florets.

2. Bring the broth to a boil and add the florets. Cook until al dente but tender, then lift out of the stock.

3. Push the florets through a food mill fitted with the large-hole disk directly back into the broth, or chop the florets by hand. A food processor would give the wrong texture. The cauliflower should be grainy, not pureed.

4. Heat the cream but do not bring it to a boil.

5. Put the rice flour in a small saucepan and add 2 ladlefuls of hot broth. Cook for 10 minutes. Remove from the heat and mix in the egg yolks, one at a time. Stir this mixture into the soup and remove the soup from the heat. Mix in the cream and the butter. As soon as the butter has melted, pour the soup into individual soup bowls and serve with croutons.

PREPARATION

The soup can be prepared 2 days in advance, but the egg liaison and the cream and butter must be added shortly before serving. The croutons can be prepared days or weeks in advance and frozen in plastic bags.

SERVES 8

Brasato cotto a crudo
Braised Beef

—

1 chuck roast, neatly tied (4 pounds)	*2 sprigs fresh rosemary*
3 garlic cloves	*4 sprigs fresh thyme*
salt and freshly ground black pepper	*4 sprigs flat-leaf parsley*
1 bay leaf	*1 large onion*
3 tablespoons olive oil	*5 tablespoons unsalted butter*
1 slice pancetta or unsmoked streaky bacon, blanched (1 ounce)	*1¼ cups red wine*
4 fresh sage leaves	

1. Rub the meat with 2 of the garlic cloves, salt, and pepper. Place it in a bowl with all the garlic and the bay leaf, then pour over the oil. Cover and let stand overnight in the refrigerator.

2. Chop the pancetta or bacon and the herbs. Add salt and pepper and lard the meat by making small incisions with a sharp-pointed knife along the grain of the meat and pushing small lumps of the mixture into the meat.

3. Cut the onion into thick slices and put them into a casserole, preferably oval, with 4 tablespoons of the butter. Season with a little salt and pepper. Lay the meat on top of the onion and cover the casserole.

4. Put the casserole over medium heat and cook for 5 minutes. Turn the meat over and continue cooking for 30 minutes, keeping the lid on. If the onion begins to brown lower the heat slightly.

5. Heat the wine and add to the casserole. Cover and cook over very low heat for about 2½ hours, by which time the meat should be done. Remove the meat to a plate and cover with foil while you prepare the sauce.

Taste the cooking juices. You may need to reduce them over high heat. Puree the juices through a sieve or in a food processor and return to the pan. Gradually add the remaining butter cut into small pieces and cook until the last piece has melted.

Carve the meat into ¼-inch slices. Lay the slices, slightly overlapping, on a hot serving dish and spoon over a little of the sauce. Serve the rest of the sauce separately in a heated sauceboat. *continued*

PREPARATION

You can carve the meat and prepare the sauce up to 30 minutes in advance. Put the slices back into the casserole and cover with sauce. Keep warm in a cool oven. You can cook the meat the day before and reheat it whole in a hot oven, well covered, for 20 minutes.

SERVES 8

Bônet
Amaretti Pudding

CARAMEL
4 tablespoons sugar
1 teaspoon lemon juice
PUDDING
1½ cups heavy cream
1¼ cups whole milk
5 eggs
½ cup sugar

1⅓ cups crushed amaretti biscuits (5 ounces)
3 tablespoons unsweetened cocoa powder
1 tablespoon dark rum
1 tablespoon Amaretto
1½ cups heavy cream

1. Preheat the oven to 325° F. and place a 4-cup mold in it to heat for 5 minutes.

2. Put the sugar, lemon juice, and 2 tablespoons water in a small saucepan and bring to a boil over medium heat. Do not be tempted to stir; the sugar will dissolve and the lemon juice will keep crystals from forming. When the syrup begins to turn dark brown, remove from the heat and pour into the heated mold. Tip the mold in all directions to coat the sides and bottom evenly. It is necessary to heat the mold because if it is cold, the caramel may set before you can cover the whole surface of the mold with it. Set aside while you make the pudding.

3. Combine the cream and milk and bring to a simmer. Beat the eggs with the ½ cup sugar until frothy and light. Pour the milk mixture over the eggs in a slow stream from a height so as to cool the milk mixture, beating constantly.

4. Mix the amaretti biscuits into the egg mixture together with the cocoa, rum, and Amaretto. Beat thoroughly, using a balloon whisk rather than an electric beater, which would spatter the mixture all over your kitchen.

5. Pour into the prepared mold. Place the mold in a roasting pan and add enough very hot (but not actually boiling) water to come halfway up the side of the roasting pan. Place the pan in the preheated oven to cook for about 1 hour, or until the pudding is set. To test, insert the blade of a knife into the middle of the pudding. It should come out dry.

6. Remove from the oven and let cool in the mold. When cold, place the mold in the fridge and leave for at least 3 hours. To unmold, loosen the pudding all around with a spatula. Place a round dish over the mold and turn the mold over onto the dish. Give a few sharp jerks to the dish and then lift the mold away. Put the mold back over the pudding to protect it and refrigerate until ready to serve.

7. Whip the cream and pipe it around the pudding or if you are using a ring mold, fill the center with it.

PREPARATION

Bônet is better made 1 or 2 days in advance, for the flavors to blend, and refrigerated. It can also be frozen, but do not leave too long in the freezer or the flavor will evaporate.

SERVES 8

A BOLOGNESE FEAST
FOR THIRTY

Maccheroni gratinati con la luganega e l'aglio

Baked Ziti with Sausage and Garlic

Lasagne verdi al forno

Baked Green Lasagne

Penne ai quattro formaggi

Penne with Four Cheeses

Tagliatelle gratinate al prosciutto cotto e piselli

Baked Tagliatelle with Ham and Peas

Insalata verde

Green Salad (page 325)

Insalata di fagiolini e pomodori

Green Bean and Tomato Salad

Finocchio al parmigiano

Fennel Salad with Parmesan

Crostata di conserva di amarena

Sour Cherry Jam Tart

La bonissima

Walnut and Honey Pie (page 229)

Pasta is my favorite food. It so happens that it is also fashionable, nourishing, and easy. To any Italian living abroad, pasta is also the food that, more than any other, brings back nostalgic memories. A charming anecdote about Rossini, "the greatest composer among gourmets and the greatest gourmet among composers," illustrates how pasta can linger in the memory. A man sat next to Rossini at a dinner party one day and said, "You remember me, I'm sure, Maestro. I met you at that dinner given in your honor when there was a splendid dish of baked macaroni. Rossini thought for some time, then slowly shook his head. "I certainly remember the macaroni," he said, "but I'm afraid I don't remember you."

Bologna is the home of many of the best pasta dishes in Italy and pasta is the ideal food for a large party. Thus this Bolognese pasta feast. The dishes I have chosen are all baked ones, which means they can be prepared in advance. You can even taste and correct them in advance and thus be sure of bringing to the table just what you had in mind. You only need to heat them in the oven before serving them. By the time people begin to help themselves, the dishes will have been out of the oven long enough for the flavors to blend. And as these four pasta dishes go well together, four small portions can happily share the same plate. Put a few bowls of freshly grated parmesan here and there for your guests to help themselves.

After that you need a few different salads. Serve them after, not with, the pasta.

The green salad should be a mixture of Boston or romaine lettuce, mâche, Belgian endive, curly endive, and radicchio. On page 325 you will find the recipe for my kind of green salad. Make two large bowls of green salad because everybody will take some.

In addition to the green salad I suggest you serve two or three other salads. Green bean and tomato salad is classic. Another classic is the zucchini and tomato salad on page 119, which you might prefer if the zucchini in the shops looks better than the beans. The other salads I would recommend are the celery root, Belgian endive, and radicchio salad on page 235 and the tomato, cucumber, and peppers on page 115.

The fennel with parmesan is the perfect transition between the salads and the cheese. Serve at least four different cheeses, with plenty of good bread.

For dessert I would choose two sweets based on fruit and two traditional sweets from Emilia-Romagna: a sour cherry jam tart and a rich walnut and honey pie, for which you will find the recipe on page 229. Instead of sour cherry jam, I have sometimes used damson jam, which is particularly delicious when homemade. Whatever you use, the jam must be tart and fruity.

Prepare a cleansing, refreshing sweet based only on fruit, such as your favorite fruit salad, any seasonal fruits, and one or two of my fruit desserts. Choose the persimmons with lime juice (page 177), the oranges and kiwis (page 64), or the poached plums (page 127), according to the season.

Maccheroni gratinati con la luganega e l'aglio

Baked Ziti with Sausage and Garlic

———

2 heads garlic, peeled

2 pounds luganega or sweet Italian sausage

2 tablespoons vegetable, corn, or olive oil

12 fresh sage leaves

1 sprig fresh rosemary

BÉCHAMEL

9 cups whole milk

10 ²⁄₃ tablespoons unsalted butter

1 cup flour

salt

³⁄₄ cup grated parmesan

³⁄₄ cup grated gruyère

freshly ground black pepper

2 pounds ziti or any other large tubular pasta

3 tablespoons unsalted butter

1. Put the peeled garlic cloves in a small saucepan and cover with about 1 cup water. Bring to a boil, cover the pan tightly, and cook very gently for about 1 hour. Check that there is always water in the pan and add some boiling water if necessary. At the end there should be no more than 3 or 4 tablespoons of water left.

2. Puree the contents of the pan through a sieve or a food mill or in the food processor. It is also quite easy to mash the garlic with a fork.

3. While the garlic is boiling, skin the sausage, crumble it, and put in a nonstick frying pan with the oil. Chop the sage and rosemary and add to the sausage. Fry over low heat until the fat runs out, then turn the heat up to medium and fry until the meat is brown, about 20 minutes. Remove the sausage from the pan with a slotted spoon, leaving the fat behind.

4. Heat the milk until it just begins to bubble at the edge. Meanwhile, melt the butter in a heavy-bottomed saucepan over low heat. Blend in the flour, stirring vigorously. Remove the pan from the heat and add the hot milk, a few table-spoons at a time, letting the flour mixture absorb each addition thoroughly before going on to the next stage. When all the milk has been absorbed, return

continued

the pan to the heat. Add salt to taste and bring to a boil. Cook the sauce for at least 20 minutes, either setting the pan in a bain-marie or over a flame tamer or using a double boiler. Mix in the garlic puree and the grated cheeses. Season with a lot of pepper. Taste and add salt, bearing in mind that the sausage may be on the salty side.

5. Generously butter a large baking dish or lasagne pan.

6. Cook the pasta in plenty of salted boiling water. If you do not have a large enough saucepan, cook it in 2 batches. Drain when slightly undercooked and dress immediately with about three-quarters of the béchamel and add the sausage meat. Turn into the prepared dish. Spread the remaining béchamel all over the top and dot with butter.

7. About 45 minutes before you want to serve the dish, preheat the oven to 400° F. When the oven is hot, put the pasta dish in and bake until done, about 15 to 20 minutes. To test if it is hot enough, insert a knife into the middle of the dish and feel the bits that stick to the blade. Let the dish stand for a few minutes at room temperature outside the oven before bringing it to the table.

PREPARATION

The whole dish can be prepared up to 1 day in advance, covered with plastic wrap and refrigerated. It can also be frozen.

SERVES 8 TO 10

Lasagne verdi al forno
Baked Green Lasagne

4 tablespoons unsalted butter

½ cup olive oil

½ cup finely chopped (¼ pound) pancetta or blanched bacon

2 small onions, finely chopped

1 carrot, finely chopped

2 celery stalks, finely chopped

2 garlic cloves, finely chopped

2 bay leaves

2½ tablespoons tomato paste

1 pound lean ground beef

1¼ cups dry white wine

1¼ cups meat stock

salt and freshly ground black pepper

green lasagne made with 2⅓ cups unbleached white flour, 3 eggs, and ½ pound cooked or frozen spinach, or 1½ pounds fresh green lasagne, or 1 pound dried green lasagne

1 tablespoon vegetable oil

1¼ cups freshly grated parmesan

2 tablespoons butter, melted

BÉCHAMEL

6 cups whole milk

10 tablespoons unsalted butter

¾ cup flour

salt

¼ teaspoon grated nutmeg

1. Heat the butter and olive oil in a saucepan and cook the pancetta for 2 minutes. Add the onions, and when they begin to soften, add the carrot, celery, garlic, and bay leaf. Cook for a couple of minutes, stirring constantly. Add the tomato paste and cook over low heat for 30 seconds. Put in the ground beef and cook briskly for 3 to 4 minutes, or until the meat loses its raw color, stirring with a fork to break up the lumps. Splash with the wine and boil for 2 minutes or so, until the liquid has almost evaporated. Fish out and discard the bay leaf and pour in stock. Mix well, season and simmer, uncovered, for about 2 hours, adding a little warm water if the sauce gets too dry. The heat should be as low as possible, so that just a few bubbles break the surface of the sauce.

2. For the béchamel, heat the milk until it just begins to bubble at the edge. Meanwhile, melt the butter in a heavy-bottomed saucepan over low heat. Blend in the flour, stirring vigorously. Remove the pan from the heat and add the hot milk, a few tablespoons at a time, to let the flour mixture absorb each addition thoroughly before going on to the next stage. When all the milk has been

continued

absorbed, return the pan to the heat. Add salt to taste and bring to a boil. Cook over very gentle heat for 20 minutes, stirring frequently. You can put the pan over a flame tamer or in a bain-marie or use a double boiler. Add the nutmeg and check the seasoning. The sauce should have the consistency of heavy cream.

3. If you are making your own lasagne, follow the directions on pages 333–335.

4. Preheat the oven to 400° F.

5. If your lasagne is homemade, bring a large saucepan of salted water to a boil. Add the vegetable oil. Place a large bowl of cold water near the stove and lay some clean and dry dish towels nearby. When the water boils, drop in 5 or 6 pieces of pasta and stir with a wooden spoon. Cook for about 1 minute after the water returns to a boil, then lift each sheet of pasta out with a pancake turner and plunge it into the bowl of cold water. Lift it out and lay it on the towels. Continue until all the pasta is cooked. Pat the top of the cooked lasagne dry. Storebought fresh lasagne will take a little longer to cook. If you are using commercial lasagne, cook according to the directions on the package.

6. Generously butter a large baking dish or lasagne pan. Spread 2 tablespoons of the meat sauce over the bottom, cover with a layer of lasagne, and spread over a little more sauce and some béchamel. Sprinkle with grated cheese. Cover with another layer of lasagne and continue, finishing with a layer of béchamel. Sprinkle with the remaining cheese and drizzle the melted butter all over the top.

7. Bake in the oven for 15 to 20 minutes, until the top has formed a golden crust. Let the dish settle for at least 5 minutes before serving.

PREPARATION

The dish can be prepared totally up to 1 day in advance and refrigerated, covered with plastic wrap. The meat sauce can be made up to 3 days in advance and refrigerated. It also freezes well.

SERVES 8 TO 10

Penne ai quattro formaggi
Penne with Four Cheeses

1½ pounds penne or other tubular pasta

salt

¼ pound gruyère

¼ pound bel paese

¼ pound mozzarella

8 tablespoons (1 stick) unsalted butter, melted

⅔ cup freshly grated parmesan

cayenne

1. Drop the pasta into salted boiling water.

2. While the pasta is cooking, cut the gruyère, bel paese, and mozzarella into small pieces.

3. Preheat the oven to 400° F.

4. Drain the pasta when it is still slightly undercooked and return it immediately to the saucepan. Add half the butter, the parmesan, all the other cheese and 2 or 3 pinches of cayenne. Mix thoroughly.

5. Smear a large baking dish or lasagne pan with a little of the melted butter and transfer the pasta to it. Drizzle the remaining butter all over the top and bake for about 15 minutes.

PREPARATION

The dish can be prepared up to 1 day in advance. Drizzle the butter on the top just before you put the dish in the oven and bake for a little longer to heat the pasta through.

SERVES 8

Tagliatelle gratinate al prosciutto cotto e piselli

Baked Tagliatelle with Ham and Peas

tagliatelle made with 3 cups unbleached flour and 4 eggs or 2 pounds fresh store-bought tagliatelle or 1½ pounds dried egg tagliatelle

4 tablespoons unsalted butter

2 shallots, very finely chopped

salt

¾ pound ham

1 pound cooked fresh peas or thawed frozen peas (about 2 cups)

2⅔ cups heavy cream

freshly ground black pepper

½ cup freshly grated parmesan

½ cup whole milk

1. If you are making your own tagliatelle, do this first, following the directions on pages 333–335.

2. Melt 1 tablespoon of the butter in a frying pan. Add the shallots and a pinch of salt and sauté until soft. The salt helps release the moisture from the shallots, thus keeping them from browning.

3. Meanwhile cut the ham into thin short strips and add to the shallots. Cook for a minute or so, then stir in the peas. Let them *insaporire* (take up the flavor) for 1 or 2 minutes, then pour in the cream. Bring slowly to a boil and simmer for 5 minutes. Add salt and pepper to taste. Set aside.

4. Cook the pasta in plenty of salted boiling water. Drain when al dente, return the pasta immediately to the cooking pot, and dress with the remaining butter and the cheese. Spoon over the sauce and toss thoroughly.

5. Preheat the oven to 400° F.
   Choose a baking dish large enough for the tagliatelle to spread out loosely and not pile up. Generously butter the dish and fill it with the pasta. Just before you want to put the dish in the oven, heat the milk and dribble a few tablespoons all over the dish. This is to keep the tagliatelle moist while baking. Bake for about 15 to 20 minutes, until hot all through.

PREPARATION

The dish can be prepared totally up to 1 day in advance and refrigerated, covered with foil. Add the milk before baking and bake for a little longer to heat the pasta properly. This dish does not freeze well.

SERVES 8

Insalata di fagiolini e pomodori
Green Bean and Tomato Salad

7 tablespoons olive oil	*2 pounds green beans*
6 garlic cloves, bruised	*salt*
2 tablespoons lemon juice	*1 pound firm ripe tomatoes*
freshly ground black pepper	*12 fresh basil leaves*

1. Put 3½ tablespoons of the oil, the garlic, lemon juice, and plenty of pepper in a bowl and let stand for at least 1 hour.

2. Tip and tail the beans. Wash well and cook, uncovered, in plenty of boiling salted water until al dente. The beans give off a characteristic odor when they are nearly cooked. Be sure to add plenty of salt to the water, as green beans can be insipid. Drain and refresh quickly under cold water. Blot with paper towels, heap them in the middle of a dish, and dress with the remaining oil while still warm.

3. While the beans are cooking, drop the tomatoes into the saucepan with the beans. Count to 8, then remove them with a slotted spoon and plunge them immediately into a bowl of cold water. Peel them and cut into wedges or slices, discarding the seeds.

4. Lay the tomatoes all around the beans and season them with salt and pepper. Remove and discard the garlic from the dressing and spoon it over the beans and tomatoes. Scatter the basil leaves over the salad.

continued

PREPARATION

The beans can be cooked up to 2 days in advance and refrigerated in a closed container. The tomatoes can be peeled and cut a few hours in advance. Put them in an airtight container. Dress the salad at the last minute.

SERVES 8

Finocchio al parmigiano
Fennel Salad with Parmesan

6 fennel bulbs, preferably round
½ cup extra-virgin olive oil
4 tablespoons lemon juice
salt and freshly ground black pepper

¼ pound parmesan, preferably Parmigiano-Reggiano or grana padano

1. Remove the stalks and any outside brown leaves from the fennel. Cut vertically into quarters, then cut across into very thin strips. Wash in plenty of water, drain, and dry well.

2. Put the fennel in a salad bowl and dress with the oil, lemon juice, salt, and pepper. Do not put on too much salt, since the cheese is salty. Toss thoroughly and taste. Leave for about 30 minutes.

3. Cut the parmesan into slivers and lay on top of the fennel.

PREPARATION

The fennel can be sliced and washed the day before and kept in the refrigerator. It should be wrapped in a clean dish towel.

SERVES 8

Crostata di conserva di amarena
Sour Cherry Jam Tart

PASTRY	2 egg yolks
½ teaspoon salt	*1 egg yolk and 1 tablespoon of milk for glazing*
½ cup sugar	
1 teaspoon grated lemon peel	FILLING
1½ cups flour	*4 tablespoons ground almonds*
8 tablespoons (1 stick) unsalted butter, cold	*12 ounces sour cherry or damson jam*
	2 tablespoons lemon juice

1. For the pastry, mix the salt, sugar, and lemon peel into the flour. Cut in the butter. Add the egg yolks and work quickly to form a ball. If you prefer, make the pastry in a food processor. Wrap in foil and chill for at least 30 minutes.

2. Preheat the oven to 400° F.

3. Butter an 8- or 9-inch tart pan with a removable bottom and sprinkle with 1 tablespoon flour. Shake off the excess.

4. Remove the dough from the refrigerator. Put aside about one-third and roll the rest into a circle. Line the prepared pan with the circle of dough and press it down firmly into the angle between the base and the side.

5. Sprinkle the ground almonds over the bottom.

6. Put the jam in a bowl and mix in the lemon juice. Spread the jam on top of the almonds. Roll out the reserved dough and cut several strips a little less than ½ inch wide. Place these strips over the tart to form a lattice that goes right across the tart. Patch the strips if needed; once the tart is baked it won't show. Brush the lattice with the egg yolk and milk glaze.

7. Bake for about 10 minutes. Turn the heat down to 350° F. and bake for 20 minutes more, until the pastry turns light golden brown. Leave to cool in the pan and then transfer to a wire rack.

PREPARATION

Make the tart on the day you want to eat it. The pastry can be made up to 2 days in advance and refrigerated, wrapped in foil. It also freezes well.

SERVES 8

BASIC RECIPES

Insalata verde
Green Salad
3 2 5

Patate arrosto
Roast Potatoes
3 2 6

Patate trifolate
Braised Potatoes with Parsley
3 2 7

Funghi al funghetto
Sautéed Mushrooms
3 2 8

Le carote di Ada Boni
Italian-style Carrots
3 2 9

Pomodori in teglia
Baked Tomatoes
3 3 0

Spinaci all'agro
Lemon Spinach
3 3 1

Polenta
Polenta
3 3 2

Pasta
Pasta
3 3 3

Il sugo di Guy
Guy's Tomato Sauce
3 3 6

Il sugo di Julia
Julia's Tomato Sauce
3 3 7

Il brodo
Italian Broth
3 3 8

Brodo di pesce
Fish Broth
3 4 0

Cornetti alle mandorle di Vera
Almond Crescents
3 4 1

Meringhine al limone
Lemon Meringues
3 4 2

Pan di spagna
Sponge Cake
3 4 3

Insalata verde
Green Salad

Buy a selection of greens, such as romaine and Boston lettuce, Belgian endive, mâche, Bibb lettuce, curly endive, and radicchio for color. I am not very keen on lollo rosso, but if you like it, use a few leaves. I would never add iceberg as it has the wrong texture, one that does not go with the others. To this basic selection, add a few leaves of arugula, shredded so that its peppery flavor can be detected in every mouthful. Pick over, wash, and thoroughly dry the greens, then cut or tear the leaves into small pieces; only mâche should be left whole. Allow about 1½ cups mixed greens per person.

For the dressing, I start with herbs from the garden: sorrel, spring borage, basil, chives, lovage leaf, and a little fresh oregano or marjoram, all chopped, then put in the salad bowl. The red-wine vinegar I use for the salad dressing is garlic-flavored. For this what you have to do is peel and bruise a few garlic cloves, about 6 to 2 cups of vinegar, and let them steep. The garlic aroma permeates the vinegar in a subtle manner. Add about 2 tablespoons of this garlic-flavored red wine vinegar, 2 teaspoons sea salt, and a generous amount of black pepper to the herbs. Next gradually add about 8 tablespoons extra-virgin olive oil, while beating with a fork. The proportion of vinegar to oil depends on personal taste, on the fruitiness of the oil, and on the acidity of the vinegar; my quantities are a rough guide. I sometimes like to add 1 to 1½ teaspoons Dijon mustard, not an Italian habit but one I am delighted to borrow from France.

Put about half the greens in the bowl, toss thoroughly, then add the rest. The secret of a good salad is to be patient and mix very well (in Italy it is said that 36 times is the magic number!), otherwise the first people to help themselves will have dry rabbit food, while the last will have a soup.

PREPARATION

Salad greens can be prepared up to 1 day in advance and kept in the refrigerator wrapped in a clean cloth. The herb dressing should be prepared up to 1 hour in advance to allow the flavors to blend, but the salad must be tossed at the last minute.

SERVES 6 TO 8

Patate arrosto

Roast Potatoes

⌒⌒⌒⌒

I find this unorthodox method of roasting potatoes ideal when I have friends to dinner. The potatoes cook, covered, in the oven so that you can forget about them, and they are very good. You can flavor them with rosemary, bay leaves, or fennel seeds.

24 to 30 small new potatoes	*salt and freshly ground black pepper*
3 tablespoons olive oil	*1 sprig fresh rosemary or 2 bay leaves*
4 garlic cloves, peeled	*or 1 teaspoon fennel seeds*

1. Scrape the potatoes. Wash and dry thoroughly.

2. Preheat the oven to 400° F. and place an oven dish in it to heat up.

3. Pour the olive oil into a large frying or sauté pan large enough to hold the potatoes in a single layer and add the garlic. Place the pan on medium high heat and when the garlic becomes pale gold, remove it. Slip in the potatoes and fry them for 7 to 8 minutes, shaking the pan frequently, so that they turn golden all over.

4. Transfer the potatoes and the oil left at the bottom of the pan to the oven dish. Season the potatoes with salt and pepper and add the herb of your choice. Tightly cover the dish with a lid or with foil. Bake until the potatoes are done, about 30 to 40 minutes.

PREPARATION

Potatoes cooked this way keep warm in the turned-off oven for a good half hour.

SERVES 6

Patate trifolate
Braised Potatoes with Parsley

3 pounds new potatoes
2 tablespoons olive oil
4 tablespoons unsalted butter

4 tablespoons chopped flat-leaf parsley
3 garlic cloves, bruised
salt and freshly ground black pepper

1. Peel the potatoes and rinse them. Cut them into ¾-inch cubes and dry thoroughly.

2. Heat the oil and the butter with the parsley and the garlic in a large frying pan. When the butter foam begins to subside, remove the garlic and add the potatoes. Cook over medium heat for about 8 minutes, turning them over and over until they are well coated with the oil and just beginning to brown at the edges.

3. Turn the heat down to very low and add ½ cup hot water. Mix well, cover the pan tightly with a lid and cook for about 30 minutes, or until done. Shake the pan and stir occasionally during the cooking. Use a fork to stir, as it is less likely to break the potatoes. If the potatoes get too dry, add a little more hot water.

4. When the potatoes are tender, add salt and pepper to taste. It is better to add the salt at the end of the cooking, because salt tends to make potatoes disintegrate. Mix well, taste, and check seasoning.

PREPARATION

Potatoes really should not be reheated. But if necessary you can cook them up to 1 hour in advance and keep them in the tightly covered pan. They will keep warm for quite a long time. Before serving, reheat them over high heat for 5 minutes, stirring very frequently.

SERVES 8

Funghi al funghetto
Sautéed Mushrooms

This is my adaptation of a recipe that appears in the classic book *La cuciniera genovese* by G. B. and Giovanni Ratto, which is now, after a century, in its eighteenth edition. The mushrooms used in the original recipe are, of course, fresh porcini. As these can be difficult to find, I suggest you use a selection of what you can buy. Wild mushrooms will give your dish a better flavor.

1½ pounds mixed mushrooms	*salt*
4 garlic cloves	*1 tablespoon dried oregano*
5 tablespoons olive oil	*freshly ground black pepper*

1. Clean the mushrooms by wiping them with paper towels. Thinly slice them.

2. Chop 2 of the garlic cloves very fine. Thread a wooden toothpick through the other 2 so that you can find them easily and remove them at the end of the cooking.

3. Put all the garlic and the oil in a large sauté pan. Add the mushrooms and the salt and cook over high heat, stirring frequently, until all the liquid that came out at the beginning has evaporated. Season with the oregano and with pepper.

4. Continue cooking for 15 minutes, taking care that the mushrooms do not stick to the bottom of the pan. If they do, add a couple of tablespoons of water and stir well. Fish out the garlic cloves and serve immediately.

PREPARATION

The dish should not be refrigerated, because mushrooms lose their flavor. You can cook them up to 1 day in advance and reheat them, uncovered, over low heat before serving.

SERVES 6

Le carote di Ada Boni
Italian-style Carrots

———

This is a recipe from the great classic, *Il talismano della felicità,* by Ada Boni.

2 pounds carrots	*1 teaspoon sugar*
4 tablespoons unsalted butter	*2 teaspoons flour*
salt and freshly ground black pepper	*1½ cups meat or vegetable broth*

1. Peel and wash the carrots and cut them into 2-inch pieces. Cut each piece into quarters lengthwise and remove, if necessary, the hard inner core. Cut each quarter into matchsticks.

2. Melt the butter in a large sauté pan, add the carrots, and sauté gently for 5 minutes. Season with salt, pepper, and sugar and sprinkle with the flour. Stir well and cook for 1 minute. Add just enough broth to cover the carrots. Bring to a boil and cover with a tight-fitting lid.

3. Turn down the heat and cook very gently for about 30 minutes, stirring every now and then. By the end the carrots should be soft. Taste and adjust seasonings. If there is still too much liquid when the carrots are ready, transfer them to the serving dish with a slotted spoon and reduce the cooking juices rapidly. Pour the juices over the carrots.

PREPARATION

The carrots can be cooked up to 1 day in advance. Keep them in the same sauté pan. They do not need to be refrigerated. Reheat very gently before serving.

SERVES 8

Pomodori in teglia
Baked Tomatoes

10 ripe tomatoes	*4 tablespoons chopped flat-leaf parsley*
salt	*2 tablespoons dried breadcrumbs*
5 tablespoons extra-virgin olive oil	*freshly ground black pepper*

1. Wash and dry the tomatoes and cut them in half crosswise. Gently squeeze out some of the seeds or fish them out with the tip of a teaspoon. If you have time, sprinkle them with salt and lay them on a dish, cut side down, then leave them in the refrigerator for 1 hour or so.

2. Preheat the oven to 375° F.

3. Grease a baking pan with some of the oil. Dry the inside of the tomatoes with paper towels and put them in the pan, cut side up. Mix the parsley and breadcrumbs together, season with salt and pepper, and spoon a little of the mixture over each tomato half. Drizzle with the rest of the oil and bake for 20 minutes, until just soft.

PREPARATION

You can bake the tomatoes up to 1 day in advance and reheat them in a low oven. Or you can serve them at room temperature; they are just as good, if not better.

SERVES 6 TO 8

Spinaci all'agro
Lemon Spinach

‿‿‿

3 pounds spinach	*2 garlic cloves, peeled and bruised*
salt	*4 tablespoons lemon juice*
7 tablespoons extra-virgin olive oil	

1. Pick over the spinach, cutting off the roots and/or longer stems. Put it in a basin of cold water or the sink, shake it around, and leave it for a few minutes for the dirt to fall to the bottom of the sink. Scoop out the spinach and change the water at least 2 more times, or until no more soil settles on the bottom of the basin or sink.

2. Transfer the spinach to a saucepan, with only the water that clings to the leaves. Add 1 teaspoon salt, cover the pan, and cook over high heat until the spinach is cooked, turning it over frequently. When the spinach is cooked—test by eating a leaf with a stem—drain it and rinse under cold water. Drain it again and squeeze out all the liquid with your hands. Cut it into chunks.

3. Put the oil and garlic in a frying pan, add the spinach, and sauté over low heat for 10 minutes, stirring frequently. Remove the garlic, pour over half the lemon juice, and toss thoroughly. Taste and adjust seasoning, adding more lemon juice to your liking.

PREPARATION

The dish can be made up to 1 day in advance and refrigerated. The spinach can be reheated in the oven. Or the spinach can be cooked in advance, then sautéed before serving. Don't worry if it is not hot; it is also perfect warm.

SERVES 6

Polenta
Polenta

2 teaspoons salt | *1½ cups coarse-ground cornmeal*

1. Choose a large, deep, and heavy saucepan and fill it with 7 cups of water. When the water comes to a boil, add the salt. Turn the heat down and add the cornmeal in a very thin stream, letting it fall through your nearly closed fist while you stir constantly with a long-handled wooden spoon with your other hand. Cook the polenta for at least 40 minutes, stirring constantly for the first 10 minutes and then every minute or so.

2. Moisten a bowl with cold water. When the polenta is ready, transfer it to the bowl. Let stand for a few minutes, then turn the bowl upside down onto a large round platter or a wooden board covered with a white napkin. The polenta will fall onto it and look like a golden mound. (If some of the polenta sticks to the bottom of the pan, cover with water and leave for a few hours. The polenta will then be easily washed away.)

3. To make polenta in the oven, increase the amount of cornmeal to 1¾ cups. Bring the salted water to a simmer, add the cornmeal in a thin stream, bring slowly to a boil, and boil for 5 minutes, stirring constantly. Pour the mixture into a buttered baking dish, cover with buttered foil, and bake for 1 hour at 375° F.

SERVES 6

Polenta alla griglia
Grilled Polenta

───⌇───

Prepare the polenta either on top of the stove or in the oven. Pour it out on a dish or board and spread it out to a thickness of about 2 inches. When the polenta is cool, cut it into ½-inch slices. Brush the slices with olive oil and grill on both sides until a crust forms. Sliced polenta is also excellent fried in butter or olive oil until a light crust forms on each side.

Pasta
Pasta

───⌇───

Here is my recipe for making the traditional pasta from Emilia-Romagna. This is the pasta Italians like best to make because it is the best pasta. It is a pasta you can bite into and one that cooks well. Use free-range eggs for a stronger flavor.

about 1⅓ cups unbleached flour ⎮ *2 large eggs*

1. *Making the dough.* Put the flour on the work surface and make a well in the center. Break the eggs into the well. Beat them lightly with a fork and gradually work in the flour from the inner wall of the well. When the eggs are no longer runny, work in enough flour to enable you to knead the dough with your hands. You may not need all the flour; if so, push some to the side and add only what is needed. On the other hand, you might need a little more, so keep the bag at hand. Work until the flour and eggs are thoroughly amalgamated, then put the dough to one side and scrape the work surface clean. Wash and dry your hands. Proceed to knead the dough by pressing and pushing with the heel of your palm, folding it back, and giving it a half turn. Repeat these movements for about 7 to 8 minutes if you are going to make your pasta by hand, 3 to 4 minutes if you

continued

are going to use a machine. Wrap the dough in plastic wrap and let it rest for at least 30 minutes (you can leave it for up to 3 hours).

2. *Rolling out pasta by hand.* Dust the work surface and the rolling pin with flour. Roll out the dough with a long rolling pin, working away from you, while turning the widening circle of dough so that it keeps a circular shape. The dough must be rolled out until it is no thicker than 1/16 inch. In theory it should be transparent. This thinning process must be done very quickly, in 8 to 10 minutes, or the sheet of dough will dry out, lose its elasticity, and become impossible to roll thin.

3. *Rolling out pasta by machine.* Follow the manufacturer's instructions, but remember to knead the dough by hand first for at least a few minutes, even if the instructions say that the machine can do that for you.

Divide the dough into 3 or 4 parts and thin out one part at a time, keeping the rest covered by a bowl or wrapped in plastic wrap. Knead by hand for a minute or so and then proceed to knead with the machine for 5 or 6 times. Roll out the dough through the rollers; I usually stop at the next-to-the-last notch, when the sheet is about 1/20-inch thick.

4. *Cutting pasta.* Tagliatelle and tagliolini can be cut by hand or in the machine. There is also an attachment for ravioli which is quite good, although I prefer to make ravioli by hand. Other shapes must be made by hand and I have explained how to make them in the relevant recipes. For tagliatelle and tagliolini, the sheets of dough must be allowed to hang to dry until dry to the touch and just beginning to become leathery, or the strands will stick to each other. Lasagne stuffed pasta must not be left to dry. For lasagne, cut the pasta into rectangles about 5 x 3 inches.

5. *Cooking pasta.* We say in Italy, *Gli spaghetti amano la compagnia* (spaghetti loves company). You should never leave the kitchen while pasta is in the pot. Timing is crucial. Bring a large pot of water to a boil, then add about 1½ tablespoons of coarse salt. Slide all the pasta into the boiling water, stir with a wooden fork or spoon to separate the pasta, and cover the pan, so that the water returns to a boil as soon as possible. Remove the lid and adjust the heat so that the water boils briskly but does not boil over. Cook until al dente, then drain and dress immediately with the sauce. If the sauce is not ready, toss the pasta with a little butter or olive oil.

Cook lasagne in a large shallow pan of salted boiling water with 1 tablespoon of oil added, no more than 6 or 7 pieces at a time. As soon as the noodles are cooked, lift them out of the water and plunge them into a bowl of cold water. Fish them out of the bowl and lay them on clean dish towels. Pat dry with paper towels.

6. *The Agnesi method.* When I went to Imperia many years ago to see the Agnesi pasta factory, the late Vincenzo Agnesi told me how he liked to cook pasta. His method is only suitable for dried pasta. Bring a large pot of water to a boil, add salt to taste, then add the pasta and stir. When the water has come back to a boil, cook for 2 minutes, stirring frequently. Turn off the heat, put a Turkish towel over the pan and close with a tight-fitting lid. Leave for the same length of time that the pasta would take to cook if it were still boiling. When the time is up, drain the pasta.

7. *Draining pasta.* Never overdrain pasta, particularly such long pasta as spaghetti and tagliatelle; the other shapes have holes and hollows in which they retain a few drops of water. In Naples, the motherland of spaghetti, long pasta is lifted from the water with a long fork instead of being drained through a colander. You might also keep aside a cupful of the pasta water, to add a few tablespoons to the sauce if needed to achieve the right consistency.

SERVES 2 TO 3

Il sugo di Guy
Guy's Tomato Sauce

2½ cups canned plum tomatoes
2 teaspoons tomato paste
1 teaspoon sugar
2 onions, chopped
2 celery stalks, chopped

5 tablespoons extra-virgin olive oil
salt and freshly ground black pepper
4 tablespoons red wine
2 tablespoons unsalted butter

1. Coarsely chop the tomatoes. This is best done by pouring a little of the liquid into a heavy-based saucepan, then cutting the tomatoes with kitchen scissors while still in the can. Add the chopped tomatoes to the saucepan, together with the tomato paste, sugar, onions, celery, olive oil, salt, and pepper. Cook for 15 minutes or so, then puree the sauce through a food mill.

2. Return the sauce to the pan and add the wine. Continue cooking for another 30 minutes. Mix in the butter, taste, and check seasoning.

PREPARATION

The sauce can be made up to 4 days in advance and kept in the refrigerator. It can also be frozen.

MAKES 2 CUPS

Il sugo di Julia

Julia's Tomato Sauce

2 white onions, thickly sliced

6 tablespoons extra-virgin olive oil

3 garlic cloves, peeled

2 tablespoons fresh oregano or 12 fresh basil leaves

2½ cups canned plum tomatoes, coarsely chopped

1 scant teaspoon sugar

salt and freshly ground black pepper

1. Put the onions into a saucepan with a very heavy bottom, preferably a shallow round earthenware pot with a long handle, the kind that can be put directly on the heat. Add the oil, the garlic, and the herb. Add the tomatoes to the pan with their juice. Season with the sugar, salt, and pepper and bring to a boil. Cook very gently for 1 hour.

2. Puree the sauce through a food mill. Taste and check seasonings.

PREPARATION

The sauce keeps very well in the refrigerator for up to 4 days, and it freezes very well. If you plan to refrigerate it, put less oil in the pan, reserving 2 tablespoons to cover the sauce in its container in the refrigerator. Mix it in when you heat the sauce.

MAKES 2 CUPS

Il brodo
Italian Broth

Italian broth, which is needed for making a good risotto or a delicate clear soup, is much more delicate than English or French meat stock. *Brodo* is made from beef and veal, with some chicken and a few bones, in the proportion of two-thirds meat and one-third bones. Lamb and pork are never used. I include two pieces of osso bucco, a piece of beef shank with bone, a few chicken wings, or a small carcass, if I have one.

3½ pounds assorted meat

1 onion, cut in half and stuck with 3 cloves

1 or 2 carrots, cut in pieces

2 celery stalks, cut in pieces

1 fennel stalk or a few fennel tops, if available

1 leek, thoroughly washed and cut in pieces

mushroom peelings or stalks, if available

6 parsley stalks

1 bay leaf

1 garlic clove, peeled

1 ripe tomato, quartered

6 peppercorns

1 teaspoon salt

1. Put all the ingredients in a stockpot. Add about 3 quarts of cold water, or enough to cover, and bring to a boil. The water must be cold to start with, so that the meat and the vegetables can slowly release their juices. Set the lid very slightly askew so that the steam can escape. Turn the heat down to the minimum for the stock to simmer. The best stock is made from liquid that cooks at a temperature of 175° F., rather than 200° F., the boiling point. Using a slotted spoon, skim off the foam that comes to the surface at the beginning. Cook for about 3 hours. Strain the broth through a large strainer lined with cheese cloth. Leave to cool and then put in the refrigerator.

2. Remove the fat that solidifies on the surface. When it is hard to remove the last remaining specks of fat, heat the broth, then lay a piece of paper towel on the top of the broth and drag it gently across the surface. All the bits will stick to the paper.

3. Taste and if you think it is a bit too mild, reduce over high heat, remembering, however, that the broth may taste mild because it contains a minimal amount of salt. Cover with plastic wrap and keep in the refrigerator for up to 3 days or in the freezer for up to 3 months.

4. Clarify the broth before you use it to make the clear soups in this book. Put 2 egg whites and 4 tablespoons of sherry in a pan. Beat in the cold broth while the pan is on the heat. Bring to a simmer while beating constantly. Now let the broth simmer very gently for 15 minutes without touching it. Strain the broth through a large sieve lined with a piece of cheesecloth folded double. The broth is now ready for the soup.

MAKES 6 TO 8 CUPS

Brodo di pesce
Fish Broth

For a good fish broth you must use only white fish. With any luck your fish-monger will give you some sole bones and heads, haddock, hake, and so on. Make up the rest with an inexpensive fish, such as whiting.

3 pounds white fish bones and heads	1 dozen peppercorns
3 tablespoons olive oil	1 teaspoon salt
1 large onion, quartered	4 sprigs flat-leaf parsley
2 carrots, thickly sliced	2 bay leaves
a few fennel tops	6 garlic cloves, unpeeled
2 celery stalks, thickly sliced	1⅓ cups dry white wine
2 tomatoes, quartered	

1. Cut off and discard the gills as they would give the stock a bitter taste. Rinse the fish carcasses.

2. Heat the oil and the vegetables in a stockpot and sauté for 7 to 8 minutes. Rinse the fish, add to the pan, and sauté for 5 minutes. Add 3 quarts of cold water, the peppercorns, salt, parsley, bay leaves, and garlic. Bring to a boil and skim well. Simmer for 15 minutes, then pour in the wine and simmer for 15 minutes more. Strain through a large sieve lined with a piece of cheesecloth. Cool, skim again if necessary, and blot off any surface fat, using paper towels.

3. Transfer the broth to a clean pan and reduce over high heat until you have only 6 cups left.

MAKES 6 CUPS

Cornetti alle mandorle di Vera
Almond Crescents

This is an excellent recipe from my Italian friend Vera Collingwood. The biscuits are good served with fruit desserts or ice cream.

10 tablespoons unsalted butter	*1 cup cake flour*
½ cup ground almonds	*6 drops vanilla extract*
3 tablespoons sugar	*confectioners' sugar, sifted*

1. Cream the butter, almonds, and sugar until pale and fluffy. Stir in the flour with a wooden spoon and add the vanilla extract. (The dough can also be made in the food processor.) Roll into sausage shapes, 6 x ½ to ⅔ inch, on a board sprinkled with flour. Flour your hands, too. Wrap the "sausages" in foil and chill for 30 to 45 minutes.

2. Preheat the oven to 300° F. Butter and flour a large baking sheet.

3. Cut the "sausages" into 2½-inch-long pieces with a sharp knife. Roll lightly in the floured palms of your hands or on the floured board, and shape into small crescents.

Lay the crescents on the baking sheet about 1 inch apart. Bake until very lightly colored, about 25 minutes. Allow to cool slightly, then transfer to a rack. Do this very carefully because the cookies are very fragile. When the cookies are cold, dredge them in sifted confectioners' sugar. Store in an airtight tin between layers of wax paper.

MAKES 35 COOKIES

Meringhine al limone
Lemon Meringues

2 egg whites, at room temperature | 2 teaspoons grated lemon rind
½ cup sugar |

1. Preheat the oven to 325° F.

2. Put the egg whites in a very clean copper, ceramic, or stainless-steel bowl. Do not use a plastic bowl. Beat the egg whites until stiff. Add half the sugar and continue beating until glossy, then fold in the remaining sugar and the lemon rind.

3. Line 2 baking sheets with parchment paper. Butter the paper, and using a pastry bag or a spoon, lay small blobs of the mixture on the sheet, 2 inches apart. Bake until dry and just golden, about 30 minutes. Cool on a wire rack. When cold, store in an airtight tin.

MAKES ABOUT 25 MERINGUES

Pan di spagna
Sponge Cake

---

4 eggs, separated	*1 cup cake flour*
½ cup sugar	*½ teaspoon salt*

1. Preheat the oven to 350° F. Generously butter a 6-cup loaf pan, dust with flour, and shake off the excess.

2. Beat the egg yolks with the sugar until pale yellow and forming soft peaks. You can use a hand electric mixer but not a food processor.

3. Sift the flour with ¼ teaspoon of the salt at least twice, letting the flour drop from a height to aerate it.

4. Put the egg whites and the rest of the salt in a very clean bowl and beat until stiff but not dry. Scoop out a couple of tablespoons of the egg whites and drop them over the yolk mixture. Sprinkle with 2 tablespoons of the flour and delicately fold into the yolk mixture with a metal spoon. Repeat, adding more egg white and flour and folding them in until you have incorporated all the egg white and the flour. Do this with a light movement, raising the spoon high so as to aerate the mixture. Stop folding as soon as the mixture becomes homogeneous.

5. Pour the mixture into the prepared pan and bake for about 40 minutes, until the cake is spongy to the touch and has shrunk from the sides of the pan. Loosen the cake from the sides with a knife and turn onto a wire rack. Leave to cool completely, then wrap with foil or store in a cake tin.

PREPARATION

This cake is best used within 1 day of making, although it can be made well in advance and frozen, wrapped in foil. Allow to defrost completely before using.

MAKES ONE ¾-POUND CAKE

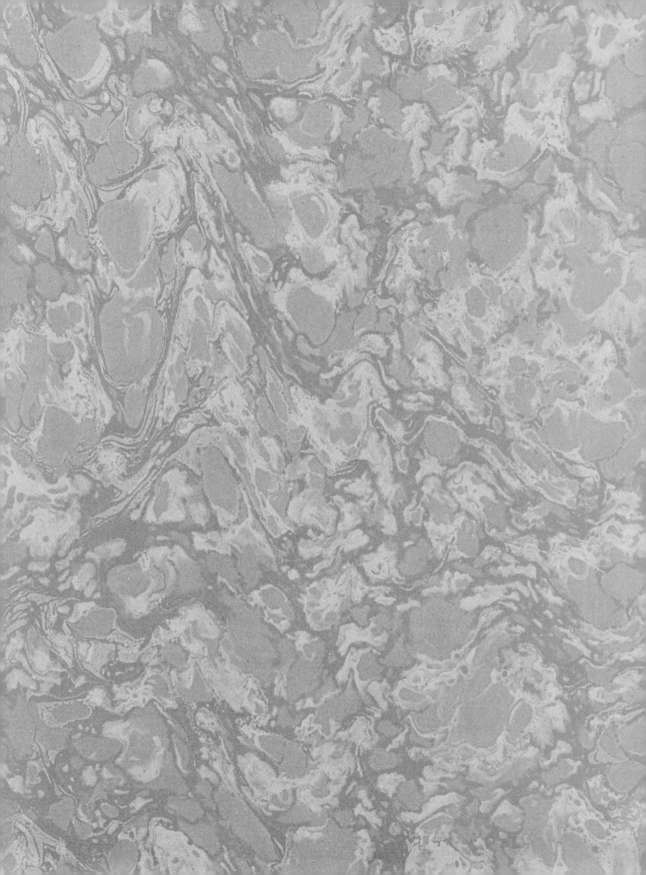

INDEX OF RECIPES

Aceto
  balsamico
    gelato di fragola all', 287
    insalata di zucchine e pomodori alla
      menta e all', 119
    petti di anatra all', 285
  peperoni all', 73
Aglio
  linguine, olio, peperoncino, e, 86
  maccheroni gratinati con la luganega
    e l', 313
Agnello
  arrosto alla moda del rinascimentale, 62
  arrosto con le cipolline, cosciotto
    di, 22
Albicocca(-che)
  e arancie, e banane al vino, 207
  gelato di, 116
Almond(s)
  crescents, 341
  and potato cake, 49
  and ricotta cake with orange sauce, 188
Amarena, crostata di conserva di, 321
Amaretti pudding, 308
Ananas e arancie, 161
Anatra, petti di, all'aceto balsamico, 285
Anchovy(-ies)
  cauliflower salad with pine nuts and, 239
  and onion sauce, whole-wheat spaghetti
    with, 210
  rice salad with mozzarella and, 72
Angel hair soufflé, 93
Apple(s)
  salad of celery, carrot, and, with a wine
    and cilantro dressing, 195
  snow in a ring, 279
Apricot(s)
  dried, with oranges and bananas in
    wine syrup, 207
  ice cream, 116
Apulian fish pie, 193
Aragosta, soffiato di riso all', 271

Arancia(-e)
  albicocche, banane, e, al vino, 207
  ananas e, 161
  caramellate, 246
  e kiwi, 64
  insalata di finocchio, cicoria belga, ed, 169
  torta di ricotta e mandorle con le
    salsina di, 188
Arista alla toscana, 215
Arrosto morto, 29
Artichoke(s)
  chicken breasts stuffed with, 272
  tagliatelle with, 60
Arugula
  bresaola with, 45
  salad of mâche, fennel, and, 24
Asparagi alla milanese, 14
Asparagus Milanese, 14
Autumn fruit compote, 198

Baked green lasagne, 315
Baked hake, 211
Baked penne with chicken and prosciutto,
  277
Baked porgies with tomatoes and basil, 298
Baked rhubarb with orange, 50
Baked tagliatelle with ham and peas, 318
Baked tagliatelle with tomato sauce and
  mozzarella, 225
Baked tomatoes, 330
Baked ziti with eggplant, 106
Baked ziti with sausage and garlic, 313
Balsamic vinegar
  roasted Belgian endive with, 283
  sauce, duck breasts with, 285
  strawberry ice cream flavored with, 287
  zucchini and tomato salad with mint
    and, 119
Bananas, dried apricots, and oranges in
  wine syrup, 207
Banane, albicocche, e arancie, al vino, 207
Barbabietola, insalata agra di, 152

Basil
  baked porgies with tomatoes and, 298
  -lemon sorbet, 109
  pesto, 297
    potatoes and green beans with, 296
  tomatoes with, 90
Basilico
  pomodori al, 90
  sorbetto di limone al, 109
Bavarese lombarda, 57
Bean(s)
  cannellini and tomatoes, sautéed, 216
  fava, 33
  fava, raw, pecorino, 33
  and pasta soup with radicchio, 39
  and shrimp salad, 100
Beef
  in boiled dinner, Italian, 240
  braised, 307
    in vinegar and cream, 303
Beet, watercress, and grapefruit salad, 152
Belgian endive
  broiled radicchio and, 147
  roasted, with balsamic vinegar, 283
  salad
    celery root, radicchio, and, 235
    fennel, orange, and, 169
Bell peppers with vinegar, 73
Bigoli in salsa, 210
*Bocconcini di coda di rospo alla pure
    di lenticchie,* 120
Boiled dinner, Italian, 240
Bollito misto, 240
Bomba di panna e marrons glacés, 263
Bônet, 308
Bonissima, la, 229
Braised beef, 307
Braised chicken with rice, 55
Braised new potatoes, 222
Braised potatoes with parsley, 327
Braised quail in a nest of straw and hay, 34
Braised rabbit, 187
Brasato cotto a crudo, 307
Bread, grilled, with olive oil, garlic,
    and tomato, 71
Bresaola
  about, 44
  with arugula, 45
Bresaola con la rucola, 45
Broccoli, filetti di San Pietro in salsa di,
    108
Broccoli sauce, fillet of flounder in, 108

Brodo, il, 338
  di pesce, 340
Broiled eggplant with lemon-mustard
    dressing, 186
Broiled radicchio and Belgian endive, 147
Broth
  fish, 340
  Italian, 338
  Parmesan and parsley dumplings in, 302
Bruschetta toscana, 71
Budino alla pesca, 96
Butter, spinach and pasta roll with
    Parmesan and, 46

Cachi al sugo di lime, 177
Caffè, granita al, 103
Cake
  chocolate and nut, 244
  potato and almond, 49
  rice, 196
  ricotta and almond, with orange sauce, 188
  Sicilian cassata, 170
  sponge, 343
  Easter *(colomba pasquale),* 20
Canapés, chicken liver, 214
Cannellini beans and tomatoes, sautéed, 216
Cannelloni, eggplant, with tomato sauce,
    101
Cannelloni di melanzane in salsa, 101
Capelli d'angelo, soffiato di, 93
Caponata with chocolate, 164
Caponatina di melanzane, 164
Cappelletti alle erbe, 12
Cappelletti filled with ricotta and herbs, 12
Cappellini and braised quail, 34
Cappone, petti di, alla stefani, 126
Caramel
  sauce, fruit salad in a, 293
  syrup, oranges in, 246
Caramello, copette di frutta al, 293
*Caramellone natalizie con crema alla
    zenzero, le,* 254
Carciofi
  petti di pollo farciti di, 272
  tagliatelle coi, 60
Carote
  di Ada Boni, le, 329
  *insalata di sedano, mela, e, al sapor di
    coriandolo,* 195
  sformato di patate e, 227
Carrot(s)
  Italian-style, 329

Carrot(s) *(cont.)*
 and potato mold, 227
 salad of celery, apple, and, with a wine
  and cilantro dressing, 195
Cassata, Sicilian, 170
Cassata siciliana, 170
Casserole, vegetable, 206
Castagne, ripieno di, 252
Cauliflower
 salad with anchovies and pine nuts, 239
 soup, 306
Cavolfiore
 insalata di, alla salsa bianca, 239
 minestra di, 306
Ceci, pasta asciutta e, 205
Celery
 pasta salad with fontina, walnuts, and, 136
 puree, 286
 salad of carrot, apple, and, with a wine
  and cilantro dressing, 195
 soup, cream of, 174
Celery root, salad of Belgian endive,
  radicchio, and, 235
Cervo alla casalinga, 182
Cetrioli, insalata di pomodori, peperoni, e,
  115
Cheese(s)
 fontina
  and cream sauce, 48
  pasta salad with walnuts, celery, and,
   136
 Gorgonzola, risotto with, 219
 mascarpone
  cream, raspberries with, 15
  ice cream, 128
 mozzarella
  baked tagliatelle with tomato sauce and,
   225
  rice salad with anchovies and, 72
 Parmesan
  with fennel salad, 320
  and lemon and egg soup, 290
  and parsley dumplings in broth, 302
  and pecorino wedges with green
   olives, 77
  spinach and pasta roll with butter and, 46
  walnuts, grapes, and, 153
 pecorino
  and Parmesan wedges with green
   olives, 77
  and raw fava beans, 33
 penne with four, 317

Cheese(s) *(cont.)*
 ricotta
  and almond cake with orange sauce,
   188
  cappelletti filled with herbs and, 12
  ice cream, 138
Cherries, poached, 50
Chestnut and sausage stuffing, 252
Chicken, 214
 in boiled dinner, Italian, 240
 braised, with rice, 55
 breasts
  seventeenth-century style, 126
  stuffed with artichokes, 272
 liver canapés, 214
 penne with chicken and prosciutto,
  baked, 277
Chick peas, pasta with, 205
Chilies. *See* Pepper(s), hot
Chocolate
 caponata with, 164
 nougat, soft, 236
 and nut cake, 244
Christmas "crackers" with ginger custard,
  254
Cicoria belga
 insalata di finocchi, arancie, e, 169
 sul letto d'indivia, 283
Cilantro and wine dressing, salad of celery,
  carrot, and apple with a, 195
Ciliegie cotte al vino, 50
Cioccolato, torta di, di Julia, 244
Cipolle
 coniglio con le, 187
 frittata di, 79
Cipolline, cosciotto di agnello arrosto
 con le, 22
Coda di rospo, bocconcini di, alla pure
 di lenticchie, 120
Coffee granita, 103
Conchiglie rosse ripiene di spaghettini
 in insalata, 137
Coniglio
 al rosmarino, 220
 con le cipolle, 187
Copette di frutta al caramello, 293
Coppetti di pompelmo e uva, 183
Coriandolo, insalata di sedano, carote,
 e mela al sapor di, 195
Cornetti alle mandorle di Vera, 341
Cosciotto di agnello arrosto con le cipolline,
  22

Cozze
  all'Italiana, 276
  tagliatelle con porri e, 233
Cream
  beef braised in vinegar and, 303
  of celery soup, 174
  dessert, molded, 36
  mascarpone, raspberries with, 15
  sauce
    for cappelletti filled with ricotta and
      herbs, 12
    fontina and, 48
  veal with lemon and, 291
Crema
  alla zenzero, le caramellone natalizie con,
    254
  di frutti della passione, 74
Crescents, almond, 341
Crostata di conserva di amarena, 321
Crostini alla toscana, 214
Croutons, peppers stuffed with eggplant
  and, 156
Cucumber, salad of tomato, pepper, and,
  115
Custard, ginger, Christmas "crackers" with,
  254

Dentice al forno, 298
Desserts
  amaretti pudding, 308
  apple snow in a ring, 279
  apricot ice cream, 116
  basil-lemon sorbet, 109
  chocolate and nut cake, 244
  chocolate nougat, soft, 236
  Christmas "crackers" with ginger custard,
    254
  coffee granita, 103
  dried apricots, oranges, and bananas in
    wine syrup, 207
  Easter cake, 20
  fruit salad in a caramel sauce, 293
  grapefruit cups with grapes, 183
  Lombardy marquise, 57
  marron glacé bombe, 263
  mascarpone ice cream, 128
  molded cream, 36
  oranges in caramel syrup, 246
  passion fruit fool, 74
  persimmons with lime juice, 177
  plums stewed in wine, 127
  poached cherries, 50

Desserts *(cont.)*
  poached pears with pear liqueur cream,
    139
  raspberries with mascarpone cream, 15
  rice cake, 196
  ricotta and almond cake with orange sauce,
    188
  Sicilian cassata, 170
  sour cherry jam tart, 321
  walnut and honey pie, 229
  zampone with zabaglione, 261
Dolci
  albicocche, arancie, e banane al vino, 207
  ananas e arancie, 161
  arance caramellate, 246
  bavarese lombarda, 57
  bomba di panna e marrons glacés, 263
  bônet, 308
  la bonissima, 229
  cachi al sugo di lime, 177
  le caramellone natalizie con crema alla
    zenzero, 254
  cassata siciliana, 170
  ciliegie cotte al vino, 50
  copette di frutta al caramello, 293
  coppetti di pompelmo e uva, 183
  cornetti alle mandorle di Vera, 341
  crema di frutti della passione, 74
  crostata di conserva di amarena, 321
  gelato di albicocca, 116
  gelato di mascarpone, 128
  granita al caffè, 103
  lamponi con crema di mascarpone, 15
  macedonia di frutta con la neve al
    limone, 122
  mela in tortiglié, 279
  panna cotta, 36
  pere alla crema del lario, 139
  prugne al vino, 127
  sorbetto di limone al basilico, 109
  torrone molle, 236
  torta di cioccolato di Julia, 244
  torta di ricotta e mandorle con le salsina
    di arancia, 188
  torta di riso, 196
  zampone allo zabalione, 261
Dressing, wine and cilantro, salad of celery,
  carrot, and apple with a, 195
Dried apricots, oranges, and bananas in
  wine syrup, 207
Duck breasts, with balsamic vinegar sauce,
  285

Dumplings, Parmesan and parsley, in broth, 302

Easter lunch, 17–24
Easter torta, 20
Eggplant
  baked ziti with, 106
  cannelloni with tomato sauce, 101
  grilled, 82
  grilled, with lemon-mustard sauce, 186
  peppers stuffed with croutons and, 156
Egg(s)
  frittata
    onion, 79
    pepper and tuna, 80
    zucchini, 81
  and lemon and Parmesan soup, 290
  and lemon sauce, 89
  salami and, 17
Endive. *See* Belgian endive

Fagioli
  all'uccelletto, 216
  pasta e, alla contadina, 39
Fagiolini
  e patate al pesto, 296
  insalata di pomodori e, 319
Fava beans, pecorino and raw, 33
Fave, pecorino con le, 33
Fennel
  with Parmesan salad, 320
  roast pork with rosemary and, 215
  salad of Belgian endive, orange, and, 169
  salad of mâche, arugula, and, 24
Fillet of flounder with broccoli sauce, 108
Filetti
  di pesce con le scaglie di patate, 95
  di San Pietro in salsa di broccoli, 108
Finocchio(o)
  al Parmigiano, 320
  insalata di cicoria belga, arancie, e, 169
Fiore di melanzane alla senape, il, 186
Fish
  broth, 340
  fillets with potato scales, 95
  flounder, fillet of, with broccoli sauce, 108
  hake, baked, 211
  lasagne, 158
  monkfish morsels with lentil puree, 120
  pie, Apulian, 193
  porgies baked with tomatoes and basil, 298
  ravioli, 112

Fish *(cont.)*
  tuna
    and pepper frittata, 80
    roll, 87
    sauce, veal in, 132
Flounder, fillet of, with broccoli sauce, 108
Fontina
  and cream sauce, 48
  pasta salad with walnuts, celery, and, 136
Fontina
  insalata di pasta, noci, sedano, e, 136
  salsa alla panna e, 48
Fool, passion fruit, 74
Formaggi, penne ai quattro, 317
Formaggio, rotolo di spinaci al burro e, 46
Fragola(-e)
  gelato di, all'aceto balsamico, 287
  zabaione con la purè di, 30
Frittata
  onion, 79
  pepper and tuna, 80
  zucchini, 81
Frittata
  di cipolle, 79
  di peperoni e tonno, 80
  di zucchine, 81
Fruit
  salad
    in a caramel sauce, 293
    with lemon granita, 122
  stuffing, 251
Frutta(-i)
  copette di, al caramello, 293
  della passione, crema di, 74
  macedonia di, con la neve al limone, 122
  ripieno di, 251
Funghi al funghetto, 328

Gamberi in salsa all'Abruzzese, 114
Garlic
  baked ziti with sausage and, 313
  grilled bread with olive oil, tomato, and, 71
  linguine with oil, hot peppers, and, 86
Gelato
  di albicocca, 116
  di fragola all'aceto balsamico, 287
  di mascarpone, 128
  di ricotta, 138
Ginger custard, Christmas "crackers" with, 254
Gorgonzola, risotto with, 219
Gorgonzola, risotto al, 219

Granita
  coffee, 103
  lemon, fruit salad with, 122
Granita al caffè, 103
Gran raviolo, il, 259
Grapefruit
  cups with grapes, 183
  salad of beets, watercress, and, 152
  salad of vegetables, shrimp, and, 192
Grapes
  grapefruit cups with, 183
  walnuts, Parmesan, and, 153
Green bean(s)
  and potatoes with pesto, 296
  and tomato salad, 319
Green lentils with sage, 262
Green salad, 325
Green sauce, 242
Grilled bread with olive oil, garlic,
    and tomato, 71
Grilled vegetables, 82
Guy's tomato sauce, 336

Hake, baked, 211
Ham
  baked tagliatelle with peas and, 318
  mousse, truffle-flavored, 134
Herb(s). *See also specific herbs*
  cappelletti filled with ricotta and, 12
Honey and walnut pie, 229

Ice cream
  apricot, 116
  mascarpone, 128
  ricotta, 138
  strawberry, flavored with balsamic
    vinegar, 287
Insalata
  agra di barbabietola, 152
  bianca e verde, 24
  conchiglie rosse ripiene di spaghettini in,
    137
  di cavolfiore alla salsa bianca, 239
  di fagiolini e pomodori, 319
  di finocchi, cicoria belga, ed arancie, 169
  di Luisetta, l', 188
  di pasta, fontina, noci, e sedano, 136
  di pomodori, cetrioli, e peperoni, 115
  *di sedano, carote, e mela al sapor di
    coriandolo,* 195
  *di zucchine e pomodori all'aceto balsamico
    e alla menta,* 119

Insalata (cont.)
  riso all', 72
  verde, 325
  veronese, 235
Italian boiled dinner, 240
Italian broth, 338
Italian roast veal, 29
Italian-style carrots, 329

Julia's tomato sauce, 337

Kiwi, arancie e, 64
Kiwis, oranges and, 64

Lamb
  about, 17–18
  leg of, Renaissance style, 62
  roast leg of, with small onions, 22
Lamponi con crema di mascarpone, 15
Lasagne
  baked green, 315
  fish, 158
Lasagne verdi al forno, 315
Leek(s)
  and rice torta, 150
  tagliatelle with mussels and, 233
Leg of lamb Renaissance style, 62
Lemon
  -basil sorbet, 109
  and egg and Parmesan soup, 290
  and egg sauce, 89
  granita
    fruit salad with, 122
  meringues, 342
  -mustard sauce, grilled eggplant with, 186
  spinach, 331
  veal with cream and, 291
Lenticchie
  bocconcini di coda di rospo alla pure di,
    120
  in umido, 262
Lentil(s)
  green, with sage, 262
  puree, monkfish morsels with, 120
Lime, cachi al sugo di, 177
Lime juice, persimmons with, 177
Limone
  macedonia di frutta con la neve al, 122
  meringhine al, 342
  sorbetto di, al basilico, 109
  stracciatella al sapor di, 290
  vitello al, 291

Linguine with garlic, oil, and hot peppers, 86
Linguine aglio, olio, e peperoncino, 86
Lobster and rice soufflé, 271
Loin of pork braised in milk, 175
Lombardy marquise, 57
Luganega, maccheroni gratinati con l'aglio e la, 313
Lunch
  Easter, 17–24
  vegetarian, 11–15

Maccheroni
  gratinati con la luganega e l'aglio, 313
  timballo di, alla Pampadur, 277
Macedonia di frutta con la neve al limone, 122
Mâche, salad of arugula, fennel, and, 24
Maiale al latte, 175
Mandorle
  cornetti alle, di Vera, 341
  torta di mandorle e, 49
  torta di ricotta e, con le salsina di arancia, 188
Manzo alla California, 303
Marquise, Lombardy, 57
Marron glacé bombe, 263
Marrons glacés, bomba di panna e, 263
Mascarpone
  cream, raspberries with, 15
  ice cream, 128
Mascarpone
  gelato di, 128
  lamponi con crema di, 15
Mela
  insalata di sedano, carote, e, al sapor di coriandolo, 195
  in tortiglié, 279
Melanzane
  cannelloni di, in salsa, 101
  caponatina di, 164
  pasticcio di pasta e, in bianco, 106
Menta, insalata di zucchine e pomodori all'aceto balsamico e alla, 119
Meringhine al limone, 342
Meringues, lemon, 342
Minestra
  cavolfiore, 306
  mariconda, 302
Mint, zucchini and tomato salad with balsamic vinegar and, 119
Molded cream dessert, 36

Monkfish morsels with lentil puree, 120
Mousse
  ham, truffle-flavored, 134
  peach, 96
Mousse di prosciutto cotto, 134
Mozzarella
  baked tagliatelle with tomato sauce and, 225
  rice salad with anchovies and, 72
Mozzarella, pasticcio di tagliatelle, pomodori, e, 225
Mushroom(s)
  grilled, 82
  sautéed, 328
Mussels
  Italian-style, 276
  risotto with, 146
  tagliatelle with leeks and, 233
Mustard-lemon sauce, grilled eggplant with, 186

Nasello, trance di, al forno, 211
Noci
  insalata di pasta, fontina, sedano, e, 136
  uva, grana, e, 153
Nougat, soft chocolate, 236
Nut(s)
  and chocolate cake, 244
  pine, cauliflower salad with anchovies and, 239

Olio, linguine aglio, peperoncino, e, 86
Olive oil
  grilled bread with garlic, tomato, and, 71
  linguine with garlic, hot peppers, and, 86
Olive(s)
  green, pecorino and Parmesan wedges with, 77
  spaghettini with sundried tomatoes, hot peppers, and, 78
Olive verdi, schegge di pecorino e Parmigiano con le, 77
One egg ravioli in clear broth, 259
Onion(s)
  and anchovy sauce, whole-wheat spaghetti with, 210
  frittata, 79
  rabbit braised with, 187
  roast leg of lamb with small, 22
  venison stew with, 182
Orange(s)
  in caramel syrup, 246

Orange(s) *(cont.)*
  dried apricots, bananas, and, in wine
      syrup, 207
  and kiwis, 64
  pineapple and, 161
  salad of fennel, Belgian endive, and, 169
  sauce, ricotta and almond cake with, 188
Osso bucco, in Italian boiled dinner, 240

Pan di Spagna, 343
Panna
  bomba di marrons glacés e, 263
  cotta, 36
  salsa alla fontina e, 48
Parmesan cheese
  with fennel salad, 320
  and lemon and egg soup, 290
  and parsley dumplings in broth, 302
  and pecorino wedges with green olives,
      77
  spinach and pasta roll with butter and, 46
  walnuts, grapes, and, 153
Parmigiano
  finocchio al, 320
  *schegge di pecorino e, con le
      olive verdi*, 77
Parsley
  braised potatoes with, 327
  and Parmesan dumplings in broth, 302
Passato
  di pomodoro, 125
  di sedano, 174
Passion fruit fool, 74
Pasta, 333
  and bean soup with radicchio, 39
  braised quail in a nest of straw and hay, 34
  with chick peas, 205
  eggplant cannelloni with tomato sauce, 101
  fish lasagne, 158
  fish ravioli, 112
  lasagne, baked green, 315
  linguine with garlic, oil, and hot peppers,
      86
  penne with chicken and prosciutto,
      baked, 277
  ravioli, one egg, in clear broth, 259
  salad, with fontina, walnuts, and celery,
      136
  spaghetti, whole-wheat, with onion and
      anchovy sauce, 210
  spaghettini, radicchio leaves filled with,
      137

Pasta *(cont.)*
  and spinach roll with butter and
      Parmesan, 46
  tagliatelle
    and artichokes, 60
    baked, with ham and peas, 318
    baked, with tomato sauce and
        mozzarella, 225
  ziti
    baked, with eggplant, 106
    baked, with sausage and garlic, 313
Pasta, 333
  asciutta e ceci, 205
  cannelloni di melanzane in salsa, 101
  *conchiglie rosse ripiene di spaghettini in
      insalata*, 137
  e fagioli alla contadina, 39
  il gran raviolo, 259
  insalata di fontina, noci, sedano, e, 136
  lasagne verdi al forno, 315
  linguine aglio, olio, e peperoncino, 86
  *maccheroni gratinati con la luganega
      e l'aglio*, 313
  pasticcio di melanzane e, in bianco, 106
  pasticcio di pesce, 158
  *pasticcio di tagliatelle, pomodori,
      e mozzarella*, 225
  penne ai quattro formaggi, 317
  ravioli di pesce, 112
  tagliatelle coi carciofi, 60
  tagliatelle con cozze e porri, 233
  *tagliatelle gratinate al prosciutto cotto
      e piselli*, 318
  timballo di maccheroni alla Pampadur, 277
Pasticcio
  di pasta e melanzane in bianco, 106
  di pesce, 158
  di tagliatelle, pomodori, e mozzarella, 225
Patate
  arrosto, 326
  e fagiolini al pesto, 296
  filetti di pesce con le scaglie di, 95
  sformato di carote e, 227
  torta di mandorle e, 49
  trifolate, 327
  in umido, 222
Peach(es)
  mousse, 96
Pears, poached, with pear liqueur cream,
      139
Peas, baked tagliatelle with prosciutto
      and, 318

Pecorino
  and Parmesan wedges with green olives, 77
  and raw fava beans, 33
Pecorino
  con le fave, 33
  schegge di Parmigiano e, con le olive verdi, 77
Penne ai quattro formaggi, 317
Penne
  baked, with chicken and prosciutto, 277
  with four cheeses, 317
Peoci, risotto coi, 146
Peperoncino, linguine aglio, olio, e, 86
Peperoni
  all'aceto, 73
  frittata di tonno e, 80
  insalata di pomodori, cetrioli, e, 115
  ripieni della zia Renata, 156
Pepper(s), hot
  linguine with garlic, oil, and, 86
  spaghettini with sundried tomatoes, olives, and, 78
Pepper(s), sweet bell
  salad of tomato, cucumber, and, 115
  stuffed with eggplant and croutons, 156
  and tuna frittata, 80
  with vinegar, 73
Pere alla crema del lario, 139
Persimmons with lime juice, 177
Pesca(-e)
  brodo di, 340
  budino alla, 96
  filetti di, con le scaglie di patate, 95
  pasticcio di, 158
  ravioli di, 112
  tiella di, 193
Pesto
  for potatoes and green beans, 297
  potatoes and green beans with, 296
Pesto, 297
  patate e fagiolini al, 296
Petti di anatra all'aceto balsamico, 285
Petti di cappone alla stefani, 126
Petti di pollo farciti di carciofi, 272
Piatto rustico, 206
Pie. *See also* Torta
  fish, Apulian, 193
  from *The Leopard,* 166
  walnut and honey, 229
Pineapple and oranges, 161

Pine nuts, cauliflower salad with anchovies and, 239
Piselli, tagliatelle gratinate al prosciutto cotto e, 318
Plums stewed in wine, 127
Poached pears with pear liqueur cream, 139
Polenta, 332
  grilled, 333
Polenta, 332
  alla griglia, 333
Pollastri al riso, 55
Pollo, petti di, farciti di carciofi, 272
Polpettone di tonno della Mamma, il, 87
Pomodoro(i)
  al basilico, 90
  insalata di cetrioli, peperoni, e, 115
  insalata di fagiolini e, 319
  insalata di zucchine e, all'aceto balsamico e alla menta, 119
  passato di, 125
  pasticcio di tagliatelle, mozzarella, e, 225
  in teglia, 330
Pompelmo, coppetti di uva e, 183
Porgies baked with tomatoes and basil, 298
Pork
  loin of, braised in milk, 175
  roast, with rosemary and fennel, 215
Porri
  tagliatelle con cozze e, 233
  torta di, 150
Potato(es)
  and almond cake, 49
  in Apulian fish pie, 193
  braised, with parsley, 327
  and carrot mold, 227
  and green beans with pesto, 296
  new, braised, 222
  roast, 326
  scales, fish fillets with, 95
Prosciutto, baked penne with chicken and, 277
Prosciutto cotto
  tagliatelle gratinate al piselli e, 318
  cotto, mousse di, 134
Prugne al vino, 127
Pudding, amaretti, 308
Pumpkin risotto, 180
Puré di sedano, 286

Quaglie nel nido di paglia e fieno, 34
Quail, braised, in a nest of straw and hay, 34

Rabarbaro all'arancia, 50
Rabbit
  braised, 187
  with tomato and rosemary sauce, 220
Radicchio
  bean and pasta soup with, 39
  broiled Belgian endive and, 147
  leaves filled with spaghettini, 137
  salad
    Belgian endive, celery root, and, 235
Radicchio alla trevisana, 147
Raspberries with mascarpone cream, 15
Ravioli
  fish, 112
  one egg, in clear broth, 259
Raviolo, il gran, 259
Ravioli di pesce, 112
Red sauce, 241
Ricchi e i poveri, i, 100
Rice. *See also* Risotto
  braised chicken with, 55
  cake, 196
  and leek torta, 150
  and lobster soufflé, 271
  salad with anchovies and mozzarella, 72
Ricotta
  and almond cake with orange sauce, 188
  cappelletti filled with herbs and, 12
  ice cream, 138
Ricotta
  gelato di, 138
  torta di mandorle e, con le salsina
    di arancia, 188
Ripieno
  di castagne, 252
  di frutta, 251
Riso
  all'insalata, 72
  pollastri al, 55
  soffiato di, all'aragosta, 271
  torta di, 196
Risotto
  with Gorgonzola, 219
  molded with vegetables, 27
  with mussels, 146
  pumpkin, 180
Risotto
  al Gorgonzola, 219
  coi peoci, 146
  con la zucca, 180
  con le verdure in forma, 27
Roast leg of lamb with small onions, 22

Roast pork with rosemary and fennel, 215
Roast potatoes, 326
Roasted Belgian endive with balsamic
    vinegar, 283
Roll, tuna, 87
Rosemary
  roast pork with fennel and, 215
  and tomato sauce, rabbit with, 220
Rosmarino, coniglio al, 220
Rotolo de spinaci al burro e formaggio, 46
Rucola, bresaola con la, 45

Sage, green lentils with, 262
Salad
  cauliflower, with anchovies and pine
      nuts, 239
  celery, carrot, and apple, with a wine and
      cilantro dressing, 195
  celery root, Belgian endive, and radicchio,
      235
  fennel
    Belgian endive, orange and, 169
    with Parmesan, 320
  fruit
    in a caramel sauce, 293
    with lemon granita, 122
  green, 325
  pasta, with fontina, walnuts, and celery,
      136
  rice, with anchovies and mozzarella, 72
  shrimp and bean, 100
  tomato
    cucumber, pepper, and, 115
    green beans and, 319
    zucchini and, with balsamic vinegar
        and mint, 119
  vegetable, grapefruit, shrimp, and, 192
Salami and hard-boiled eggs, 17
Salsa
  all'Abruzzese, gamberi in, 114
  alla fontina e panna, 48
  bianca, insalata di cavolfiore alla, 239
  bigoli in, 210
  cannelloni di melanzane in, 101
  d'api, 243
  di broccoli, filetti di San Pietro in, 108
  rossa, 241
  verde, 242
Salsina
  all'uovo, 89
  di arancia, torta di ricotta e mandorle
    con le, 188

Sauce
  balsamic vinegar, duck breasts with, 285
  broccoli, fillet of flounder in, 108
  caramel, fruit salad in a, 293
  cream
    for cappelletti filled with ricotta and
      herbs, 12
    fontina and, 48
  egg and lemon, 89
  green, 242
  lemon-mustard, grilled eggplant with, 186
  onion and anchovy, whole-wheat
    spaghetti with, 210
  orange, ricotta and almond cake with, 188
  red, 241
  tomato
    baked tagliatelle with mozzarella and, 225
    eggplant cannelloni with, 101
    Guy's, 336
    Julia's, 337
    piquant, shrimp in, 114
    rabbit with rosemary and, 220
  walnut, 243
Sausage
  baked ziti with garlic and, 313
  and chestnut stuffing, 252
Sautéed cannellini beans and tomatoes, 216
Sautéed mushrooms, 328
Scarpazzone lombardo, 41
*Schegge di pecorino e Parmigiano con
    olive verdi,* 77
Sedano
  *insalata di carote, mela, e, al sapor di
      coriandolo,* 195
  insalata di pasta, fontina, noci, e, 136
  passato di, 174
  purè di, 286
Sformato di patate e carote, 227
Shellfish
  lobster and rice soufflé, 271
  mussels
    Italian style, 276
    tagliatelle with leeks and, 233
  shrimp. *See* Shrimp
Shrimp
  and bean salad, 100
  in a piquant tomato sauce, 114
  salad of vegetables, grapefruit, and, 192
Sicilian cassata, 170
Soffiato
  di capelli d'angelo, 93
  di riso all'aragosta, 271

Soft chocolate nougat, 236
Sorbet, basil-lemon, 109
Sorbetto di limone al basilico, 109
Soufflé
  angel hair, 93
  rice and lobster, 271
Soup
  bean and pasta, with radicchio, 39
  cauliflower, 306
  cream of celery, 174
  lemon, egg, and Parmesan, 290
  Parmesan and parsley dumplings in
    broth, 302
  tomato, 125
  vegetable, 54
Sour cherry jam tart, 321
Spaghetti, whole-wheat, with onion and
    anchovy sauce, 210
Spaghettini
  radicchio leaves filled with, 137
  with sundried tomatoes, hot peppers,
    and olives, 78
Spaghettini
  conchiglie rosse ripiene di, in insalata, 137
  eccitanti, 78
Spinach
  lemon, 331
  and pasta roll with butter and Parmesan,
    46
  torta, 41
Spinaci
  all'agro, 331
  rotolo di, al burro e formaggio,
    46
Sponge cake, 343
Stew, venison, with onions, 182
Stracciatella al sapor di limone,
    290
Strawberry(-ies)
  ice cream, flavored with balsamic
    vinegar, 287
  zabaglione with puree of, 30
Stuffed roast turkey, 249
Stuffing
  chestnut and sausage, 252
  fruit, 251
Sugo
  di Guy, il, 336
  di Julia, il, 337
Sundried tomatoes, spaghettini with hot
    peppers, olives, and, 78
Syrup, caramel, oranges in, 246

Tacchino arrosto ripieno, 249
Tagliatelle
  with artichokes, 60
  baked, with ham and peas, 318
  baked, with tomato sauce and
    mozzarella, 225
  with mussels and leeks, 233
Tagliatelle
  coi carciofi, 60
  con cozze e porri, 233
  gratinate al prosciutto cotto e piselli, 318
  pasticcio di pomodori, mozzarella, e,
    225
Tart, sour cherry jam, 321
Tiella di pesce, 193
Timballo
  del Gattopardo, *il,* 166
  di maccheroni alla Pampadur, 277
Tomato(es)
  baked, 330
  with basil, 90
  cannellini beans and, 216
  grilled bread with olive oil, garlic, and, 71
  porgies baked with basil and, 298
  salad
    cucumber, pepper, and, 115
    green beans and, 319
    zucchini and, with balsamic vinegar
      and mint, 119
  sauce
    baked tagliatelle with mozzarella and, 225
    eggplant cannelloni with, 101
    Guy's, 336
    Julia's, 337
    piquant, shrimp in, 114
    rabbit with rosemary and, 220
  soup, 125
  sundried, spaghettini with hot peppers,
    olives, and, 78
Tonno
  frittata di peperoni e, 80
  polpettone di, della Mamma, 87
  vitello tonnato alla milanese, 132
Torrone molle, 236
Torta
  Easter, 20
  leeks and rice, 150
  spinach, 41
Torta
  di cioccolato di Julia, 244
  di patate e mandorle, 49
  di porri, 150

Torta (cont.)
  di ricotta e mandorle con le salsina di
    arancia, 188
  di riso, 196
  pasqualina, la, 20
Trance di nasello al forno, 211
Truffle-flavored ham mousse, 134
Tuna
  and pepper frittata, 80
  roll, 87
  sauce, veal in, 132
Turkey, stuffed roast, 249

Uove, salsina all', 89
Uva
  coppetti di pompelmo e, 183
  noci, grana, e, 153

Veal
  with lemon and cream, 291
  roast, Italian, 29
  in tuna sauce, 132
Vegetable(s)
  casserole, 206
  grilled, 82
  risotto molded with, 27
  salad, grapefruit, shrimp, and, 192
  soup, 54
Vegetarian lunch, 11–15
Venison stew with onions, 182
Verdure
  alla griglia, 82
  risotto con le, in forma, 27
Vinegar
  balsamic
    roasted Belgian endive with, 283
    sauce, duck breasts with, 285
    strawberry ice cream flavored with, 287
    zucchini and tomato salad with mint
      and, 119
    beef braised in cream and, 303
    bell peppers with, 73
Vino
  albicocche, arancie, e banane al, 207
  prugne al, 127
Vitello
  al limone, 291
  tonnato alla milanese, 132

Walnut(s)
  grapes, Parmesan, and, 153
  and honey pie, 229

Walnut(s) *(cont.)*
    pasta salad with fontina, celery, and,
        136
    sauce, 243
Watercress, salad of beets, grapefruit,
    and, 152
Whole-wheat spaghetti with onion and
    anchovy sauce, 210
Wine
    and cilantro dressing, salad of celery,
        carrot, and apple with, 195
    plums stewed in, 127
    syrup, dried apricots, oranges, and
        bananas in, 207

Zabaglione
    with strawberry puree, 30
    zampone with, 261
Zabaione, zampone allo, 261

Zabaione con la purè di fragole, 30
Zampone allo zabaglione, 261
Zampone with zabaglione, 261
*Zenzero, crema alla, le caramellone
    natalizie con,* 254
Ziti
    baked, with eggplant, 106
    baked, with sausage and garlic, 313
Zucca, risotto con la, 180
Zucchine
    frittata di, 81
    *insalata di pomodori e, all'aceto balsamico
        e alla menta,* 119
Zucchini
    frittata, 81
    grilled, 82
    and tomato salad with balsamic vinegar
        and mint, 119
Zuppa alla santé, 54